India Studies in Business and Economics

The Indian economy is one of the fastest growing economies of the world with India being an important G-20 member. Ever since the Indian economy made its presence felt on the global platform, the research community is now even more interested in studying and analyzing what India has to offer. This series aims to bring forth the latest studies and research about India from the areas of economics, business, and management science, with strong social science linkages. The titles featured in this series present rigorous empirical research, often accompanied by policy recommendations, evoke and evaluate various aspects of the economy and the business and management landscape in India, with a special focus on India's relationship with the world in terms of business and trade. The series also tracks research on India's position on social issues, on health, on politics, on agriculture, on rights, and many such topics which directly or indirectly affect sustainable growth of the country.

Review Process

The proposal for each volume undergoes at least two double blind peer review where a detailed concept note along with extended chapter abstracts and a sample chapter is peer reviewed by experienced academics. The reviews can be more detailed if recommended by reviewers.

Ethical Compliance

The series follows the Ethics Statement found in the Springer standard guidelines here. https://www.springer.com/us/authors-editors/journal-author/journal-author-helpdesk/before-you-start/before-you-start/1330#c14214

Subhas Ranjan Chakraborty · Paula Banerjee ·
Kaustubh Mani Sengupta
Editors

The Long 2020

Reflections of Epidemiological Times

Springer

Editors
Subhas Ranjan Chakraborty
Presidency College
Kolkata, India

Paula Banerjee
Asian Institute of Technology
Pathum Thani, Thailand

Kaustubh Mani Sengupta
Department of History and Archaeology
Shiv Nadar Institution of Eminence
Greater Noida, India

ISSN 2198-0012 ISSN 2198-0020 (electronic)
India Studies in Business and Economics
ISBN 978-981-99-4814-7 ISBN 978-981-99-4815-4 (eBook)
https://doi.org/10.1007/978-981-99-4815-4

This Springer imprint is published by the registered company Springer Nature Singapore Pte Ltd.
The registered company address is: 152 Beach Road, #21-01/04 Gateway East, Singapore 189721, Singapore

Paper in this product is recyclable.

Acknowledgement

The volume is the outcome of the project *The Long 2020* conducted at the Mahanirban Calcutta Research Group during 2020–2021, funded by The Institute for Human Sciences (IWM), Vienna, Austria, under its project 'Migration and Forced Migration Studies with Particular Focus on South Asia and its European-Asian Dimension (2019–2021)', in collaboration with the Calcutta Research Group (CRG). A Planning Meeting was held on 26 March 2021, and a workshop was held on 7 October 2021. We are grateful to all the participants in the workshop for their valuable comments and suggestions that went into the making of the volume.

The general idea behind the entire research project came from Professor Ranabir Samaddar. He conceptualized the theme, pushed us to think beyond the immediate, and prodded us to make connections with the past that would shed new light on the present. His constant guidance and encouragement shaped the individual chapters as well as the overall presentation of the volume. Though his name does not appear on the cover or the content page, needless to say, its presence can be felt in every chapter.

We received particular encouragement from Professor Sabyasachi Basu Ray Chaudhury in carrying out the project. We thank the members, researchers and staff of CRG for their generous support and help during the preparation of the volume. We gratefully acknowledge the assistance of the editorial team at Springer Nature for their guidance, support, and patience in publishing the volume.

We hope that the chapters in the volume will make us think of long-term connections and patterns in human history that would help in a better understanding of the present crises of life and livelihood across the world.

Subhas Ranjan Chakraborty
Paula Banerjee
Kaustubh Mani Sengupta

Contents

1 **Introduction: The Long 2020: Reflections of Epidemiological Times from India** 1
Subhas Ranjan Chakraborty, Paula Banerjee, and Kaustubh Mani Sengupta

Part I Of Past and Futures of Studying Epidemics

2 ***'Longue Durée', 'Conjoncture', 'Event'*: Notion of Plural Time in History** 17
Subhas Ranjan Chakraborty

3 **Locating the Diseased Body** 31
Paula Banerjee

4 **Structure, Agency, Temporality: Revisiting Historical Analyses to Study the Contemporary** 49
Kaustubh Mani Sengupta

5 **The Island of the Day After: Digital Epidemiology, Artificial Intelligence and a Biopolitics of Future** 65
Iman Mitra

Part II Global and Local Response to 2020

6 **Global Capitalism and Corona Pandemic—In Search for Radical Solution** 81
Byasdeb Dasgupta

7 **The Long 2020/21 in India: Models of Pandemic Management and Logistics of Governance** 97
Amit Prakash

Part III Refugees and Labouring Lives

8 Politics of Health in Post-partition Calcutta: The Refugees, the Left Movements and the Question of Life in the City 125
Priyankar Dey

9 Guest Workers in Kerala: Is Welfarism Enough? 143
Jyothi Krishnan, R. Prasad, and Abey George

10 Long 2020 and the Informal Care Economy: Case Studies of Select Careworkers 163
Sabir Ahamed and Madhurilata Basu

Part IV Literature and the Literary World

11 Coronavirus and Other Epidemics in Bengal: A Reckoning Through Literature 183
Samata Biswas

12 Books—And the Time-Warp of Long-COVID 199
Ritu Menon

References 211

Editors and Contributors

About the Editors

Subhas Ranjan Chakraborty was a member of the West Bengal Education Service from 1968 to 2005 and taught at Darjeeling Government College, Maulana Azad College, Hooghly Mohsin College, Jhargram Raj College and Presidency College. He has edited a few volumes of essays in English and Bengali and contributed several essays to edited volumes and academic journals.

Paula Banerjee is currently IDRC Endowed Research Chair, Asian Institute of Technology Thailand. She is a professor (on lien) at the University of Calcutta and a member of the Calcutta Research Group. She is best known for her work on women in borderlands and women and forced migration. She served as the vice-chancellor of the Sanskrit College and University. Winner of many awards and accolades, in 2013, she was awarded the Distinguished Fulbright SIR Award and a Visiting Professorship to SUNY, Oswego. Acknowledged as a radical and prolific speaker, she has delivered lectures on all five continents.

Kaustubh Mani Sengupta teaches at Shiv Nadar Institution of Eminence, India. His research focuses on urban history of South Asia, early colonial state in India, history of infrastructure and space. He has co-edited *Rethinking the Local in Indian History: Perspectives from Southern Bengal* and *Itihaser Bitarka, Bitarker Itihas: Ateeter Bharat O Ajker Gabeshona* [in Bengali]. His research articles have appeared in journals like *The Indian Economic and Social History Review, Studies in History, Economic and Political Weekly, South Asia Research,* and *History Compass.*

Contributors

Sabir Ahamed Pratichi (India) Trust and MCRG, Kolkata, India

Paula Banerjee Asian Institute of Technology, Bangkok, Thailand;
MCRG, Kolkata, India

Madhurilata Basu Department of Political Science, Sarojini Naidu College and MCRG, Kolkata, India

Samata Biswas Department of English, The Sanskrit College and University & MCRG, Kolkata, India

Subhas Ranjan Chakraborty Department of History, Presidency College, and MCRG, Kolkata, India

Byasdeb Dasgupta Department of Economics, University of Kalyani, and MCRG, Kolkata, India

Priyankar Dey Anandabazar Online, Kolkata, India

Abey George KILA-CHRD, Kerala, India

Jyothi Krishnan Department of MSW Disaster Management, Loyola College of Social Sciences, Trivandrum, India

Ritu Menon Women Unlimited, New Delhi, India;
MCRG, Kolkata, India

Iman Mitra Department of History and Archaeology, Shiv Nadar Institution of Eminence, Delhi NCR & MCRG, Kolkata, India

Amit Prakash Centre for the Study of Law and Governance, Jawaharlal Nehru University, New Delhi & MCRG, Kolkata, India

R. Prasad Department of MSW Disaster Management, Loyola College of Social Sciences, Trivandrum, India;
Department of Sociology, University of Calicut, Calicut, India

Kaustubh Mani Sengupta Department of History and Archaeology, Shiv Nadar Institution of Eminence, Delhi NCR, India

Chapter 1
Introduction: The Long 2020: Reflections of Epidemiological Times from India

Looking Beyond the Immediate

Subhas Ranjan Chakraborty, Paula Banerjee, and Kaustubh Mani Sengupta

Keywords COVID 19 · *longue duree* · contemporary history · epidemic · public health · Anthropocene

1.1 Introduction

This book brings together scholars from different fields to think of our *present* during the time of COVID-19 pandemic in a longer temporal frame. It looks at the current crises of life and livelihood following the global epidemiological crisis and various

The book is a product of the project on the Long 2020 conducted at the Mahanirban Calcutta Research Group during 2020–2021, funded by The Institute for Human Sciences (IWM), Vienna, Austria, under its project "Migration and Forced Migration Studies with Particular Focus on South Asia and its European-Asian Dimension (2019–2021)," in collaboration with the Calcutta Research Group. A Planning Meeting was held on 26 March 2021 and a workshop was held on 7 October 2021. The reports of these meetings contain some parts of the earlier drafts of the chapters of this book. The reports can be accessed at the following links: http://www.mcrg.ac.in/IWM_Migration_2021/Report_long_2020.pdf, http://www.mcrg.ac.in/IWM_Migration_2021/Final_Report_of_Long%202020.pdf

S. R. Chakraborty (✉)
Department of History, Presidency College, and MCRG, Kolkata, India
e-mail: srchakraborty@gmail.com

P. Banerjee
Asian Institute of Technology, Bangkok, Thailand

MCRG, Kolkata, India

K. M. Sengupta
Department of History and Archaeology, Shiv Nadar Institution of Eminence, Delhi NCR, India

S. R. Chakraborty et al. (eds.), *The Long 2020*, India Studies in Business and Economics, https://doi.org/10.1007/978-981-99-4815-4_1

strategies to manage them as a long unfolding of past trends and future possibilities of epidemiological governance, restructuring of economy and public health policies, systems of protection and care, and the role of state in that. With this agenda, this book brings together eleven essays which deal with a variety of themes like histories and politics of epidemic controls and public health, care economy, the question of labour, migrants and refugees, as well as methodological issues concerning the 'time' of the present. The articles compiled here range from historical narratives, ethnographic accounts, socio-economic analyses to more conceptual and theoretical pieces. The experiences of last 2 years have inspired some very important academic and scholarly interventions. Social scientists, mainly historians, have sought to contextualise the present in a *longue durée* framework and arrive at a more complex understanding of it. Following that route and covering a variety of sub-themes from different, often contrasting perspectives, this book will provide crucial insights for future studies on the pandemic.

The use of the word 'Long' in the title and the basic premise behind the collection of essays stem from the historiographical notion of the 'long', used previously, among others, to describe the 'long nineteenth century' (Eric Hobsbawm) or 'the long twentieth century' (Giovanni Arrighi). The basic argument states that the features of a particular century are not confined to the 100 calendar years only; rather, as historians and historical sociologists, we need to peek beyond the rigid time-frame to understand the structural elements of society and economy as well as the processes of change. Similarly, for our volume, we have chosen to explain the events of the single year 2020 in a longer time-frame and look at various moments of the past to understand the present scenario. The notion of the 'long 2020' helps us to think of our present as an unfolding of historical trends and past experiences of epidemiological management, environmental and ecological concerns, a combination of several crises in the form of a pandemic, public health policies, and practices, migration realities in the wake of an epidemic, and issues of life and death raising their heads through the time of an epidemic. Yet, even though an epidemic such as this is preceded in history by other epidemics, each repetition of history is also a new beginning. The 'long' can also be thus understood in reference to the projection of a current crisis and the responses into the future by looking back into the past.

Along with this notion of the 'long', the chapters collected in this volume have variously deployed the Braudelian idea of the *longue durée*, insights from medical and environmental histories, and the debates and discussion around the concept of the Anthropocene to understand the structural components of epidemiological crises at different moments of early modern and modern history. We will discuss these theoretical moorings of our volume in subsequent sections of this Introduction.

1.2 Year 2020: The Setting

Andy Horowitz (Horowitz, 2022: 18) makes a pertinent observation when he writes: "For historians, who write stories in order to account for change over time, the problem of assigning...causes and consequences arrives as a problem of narrative. Therefore, often the most important analytical decision a historian has to make is where to begin. Consider the stakes of this seemingly simple question: When did the history of the COVID-19 pandemic start?" This innocuous query, however, makes us pause, pushes us to think beyond the immediate, and to look back at the pre-existing conditions that have shaped human existence in this planet before the pandemic (Sugrue, 2022). Social, economic, political, medical, and ecological factors have combined to create a situation of rapid dissemination of zoonotic diseases during the last couple of decades. In their volume on the plights of the migrant workers in India during the lockdown of 2020, Bandyopadhyay et al., (2021: 5) have noted that

> The current crisis needs to be understood as a conjuncture and cannot be reduced to a question of tackling a menace from the outside. Externalizing the virus and the migrant as an 'outsider' will not help us address the crisis. The book is a plea to treat both the spread of the virus and the migrant as intimate to the capitalist mode of production. The book goes on describing the current crisis as a combination of an epidemiological (the breakdown of the public health infrastructure), an economic (recession and the collapse of the global supply chains) and a political (authoritarianism and centralization of power) crisis.

The plea to treat the COVID-19 crisis 'as intimate to the capitalist mode of production' also forces us to recapitulate the transformation of world politics from the time of 'age of discovery' and 'scientific revolution', and re-evaluate the 'industrial age' of human civilisation from the point of view of exploitation of natural resources on an unprecedented scale. The discovery of the 'new world' inaugurated the 'Columbian Exchange' which led to 'ecological imperialism' and rapid transmission of diseases across vast geography (Crosby, 1986, 2003). Scholars have forcefully argued that present-day pandemics are "the outcome of the frictionless circulation of bodies and things under supply-chain capitalism. As commodities transcend the boundaries of ecological zones, they destroy local ecological specificities that could otherwise have checked the proliferation of virulent pathogen population. The growing travel of humans and global livestock trade networks 'deliver' the pathogens from one socio-ecological context to another in 'record time'." (Bandyopadhyay et al., 2021: 19) Against this backdrop of unbridled circulation we need to situate the year 2020.

1.3 Environment, Ecology, and the Question of Human Agency

In terms of historical inquiry, though, these issues often found little or no mention in standard textbooks. Environment—and its links with political and economic structures of the world—as a category of historical investigation did not enthuse historians for a long time. For example, as Davis (2002: 8) has noted, "Almost without exception, modern historians writing about nineteenth-century world history from a metropolitan vantage-point have ignored the late Victorian mega-droughts and famines that engulfed what we now call the "third world." Eric Hobsbawm, for example, makes no allusion in his famous trilogy on nineteenth-century history to the worst famines in perhaps 500 years in India and China.... The great famines are the missing pages...in virtually every overview of the Victorian era." Davis turns his attention to the "political ecology of famine", combining environmental history and Marxist political economy, to write a searing critique of the imperial rule in the colonies during the late nineteenth century. (Davis, 2002: 15) This remains a crucial framework to reflect on state policies, plights of migrants and labourers, issues of hunger and deprivation, questions of health and economy in large parts of the modern world. As Samaddar (2020) mentions, "even today the combined force of environmental change, resource crisis, and migration act as the locomotive of accumulation and development. Colonial history is crucial, because an understanding of the colonial times helps us to see how the postcolonial destiny awaits the entire world."

In geological terms, climate scientists have for long now termed the industrial age as the Anthropocene, when human exploits of fossil fuel have made them a geological agent, having the capacity to alter the basic nature of life on this planet.[1] However, scholars like Jason W. Moore argues that often the idea of the 'Anthropocene' as propounded by climate scientists overlooks the inequities among the people of the world and their role in shaping the political and economic order. He writes, "The Anthropocene makes for an easy story. Easy, because it does not challenge the naturalized inequalities, alienation, and violence inscribed in modernity's strategic relations of power and production.... It reduces the mosaic of human activity in the web of life to an abstract, homogenous humanity." (Moore, 2016: 82) Instead, he terms the changes in human history and the environment with the rise of capitalist production relations as 'Capitalocene'. Pushing back the transformation of environment and ecology associated with the industrial age, Moore argues that, "The Capitalocene argument posits capitalism as a situated and multispecies world-ecology of capital, power, and re/production. As such it pushes back—strongly—against the Anthropocene's love affair with Two Century model of modernity: industrial society, industrial civilization, industrial capitalism. The model has obscured something hidden in plain sight: the remarkable remaking of land and labor beginning in the long sixteenth century, ca. 1450–1640..." (Moore, 2016: 94).

[1] There is now a vast literature on the notion of the Anthropocene. For an accessible introduction, see Chakrabarty (2021b).

This narrative puts much of the onus on the advanced capitalist countries (and the erstwhile imperial powers) for most of world's carbon emission and environmental degradation, leading to the rise in average global temperature. In November 2022, COP27 (the United Nations Climate Change Conference, held from November 6–18, 2022 at Sharm El-Sheikh, Egypt) adopted the "Loss and Damage" Fund for Vulnerable Countries. The UN news reported, "Set against a difficult geopolitical backdrop, COP27 resulted in countries delivering a package of decisions that reaffirmed their commitment to limit global temperature rise to 1.5 °C above pre-industrial levels. The package also strengthened action by countries to cut greenhouse gas emissions and adapt to the inevitable impacts of climate change, as well as boosting the support of finance, technology and capacity building needed by developing countries. Creating a specific fund for loss and damage marked an important point of progress, with the issue added to the official agenda and adopted for the first time at COP27."[2] However, this is only the beginning. There was no agreement reached on how the fund would be raised and who would actually pay.

Recognising the role of some historical actors and social systems in destabilising the ecology of the planet and others having to bear the brunt of it, the philosopher Thomas Nail nevertheless cautions us that these ecological problems "will not be solved using our old paradigm of humans *as separate from* nature. New epochal problems require new philosophical and historical orientations…" (Nail, 2021: 2, emphasis in original) During the last couple of years, climate crisis and issues regarding the environment suddenly became a part of the everyday for the general public across the globe. Both natural and social scientists have pointed towards the connections between the pandemic and the larger crisis of the climate as well as the undeniable links between the human and the nonhuman worlds. The consensus runs that we have entered the 'era of pandemics'—H1N1 'swine' influenza in 2009, chikungunya in 2014, Zika in 2015, etc., are all zoonotic in origin—infections resulting from viruses and bacteria passing from animals to humans as hosts. Sivasundaram (2020: 301) notes that "the transference of zoonotic diseases now occurs more rapidly because of the way humans have altered nature over centuries." For him, historicizing COVID-19 does not necessarily mean to compare and contrast the present situation with past epidemics. Rather, he proposes to study it as part of long-term environmental crisis and decentre the human subject. But that does not mean minimising "the salient challenges to human subjectivity posed by the current dilemma or to forget the structural inequalities in human society…" (Sivasundaram, 2020: 296) To get into the prehistory of COVID-19, he turns to the human-animal relationship and the role of climate. He further elaborates,

> zoonotic transfer occurs where relations between humans and animals have been unstable or where they are entering a new phase of contact. Such transfer is linked with the climate emergency because life on the planet is being radically changed by accelerating extinctions caused partly by humans entering biodiverse areas and using land in new ways. This is altering the interspecies frontier. In turn, what is needed from historians—instead of a simple 'compare and contrast' exercise between COVID-19 and past diseases—is an explanation

[2] https://unfccc.int/news/cop27-reaches-breakthrough-agreement-on-new-loss-and-damage-fund-for-vulnerable-countries.

> that tracks the environmental past of the virus and the relation between the planet's illness and human illness. Such a history might include the intensifying structures of colonization, capitalism and settlement as they alter interspecies relations. (Sivasundaram, 2020: 296–297)

Studying interspecies relations to understand the past of the planet is fast becoming an important arena for the historians and the social scientists. New works on medical history, animal studies, genetics, crops and food, to name a few, have alerted us to the intertwined nature of humans and nonhumans in shaping our environment. Agreeing with the fact that "intra-human injustice" is important to acknowledge, historian Chakrabarty nevertheless wants to point towards the connected nature of the crises that speaks of the larger chasm between the humans as a whole and the nonhumans. For him, "a larger question from the history of life stares us in the face through this pandemic. Homo sapiens are a minority form of life while they, the microbes, comprise the majority forms of life. They have also been the architects of life on this planet and are central to its maintenance. Their presence inside our bodies makes us what we individually are." (Chakrabarty, 2021a: 342) While this is a novel of way of understanding the crisis on a planetary scale, still, immediate questions of social inequities and social justice prick our conscience when, in the wake of the pandemic, we witnessed events of mass migration or loss of jobs and became aware of the basic lack of health infrastructure in large parts of the world. These old questions keep coming back to interrogate state actions and human empathy.

1.4 Epidemics, State Action, and Ethics of Care: Past, Present, and the Future in India

Like scholars working on different geographical regions of the world, for historians working on the subcontinent, the crises of 2020 brought back episodes from South Asian past in conversations and writings. Much ink has been spilt on the comparison, similarities, as well as divergences from past occurrences, with particular focus especially on the nature of state action during the plague epidemic at the turn of the twentieth century. Historian Pratik Chakrabarti mentions, "Colonialism provided the first model of using scientific means of pandemic control for the large scale and often coercive regulation of people's lives and livelihoods." (Chakrabarti, 2021: 46) The invocation of the Epidemic Diseases Act, 1897 (originally devised by the British colonial state during the plague outbreaks) point towards similar mode of thinking of the state authorities across a period of 120 years. Prashant Kidambi (2020) draws our attention to the knee-jerk reaction of the state and the middle-class who generally quickly assume a direct correlation between the poor and the diseased body. This was true in case of the bubonic plague in Bombay in 1896–97. The initial days of the pandemic in 2020 witnessed this tendency. Thus, from the beginning, Dharavi became a central focus of the administration. But, for Kidambi, there are differences in the two contexts as well, especially with regard to the issue of the working population of the urban poor. He notes that.

> the bubonic plague in *fin-de-siecle* Bombay made visible the urban poor and their abysmal conditions of life in the city. It was not only the colonial government but also Indian social reformers and intellectuals who now began to take an interest in what one might loosely call the "labor question."…
>
> the current pandemic has also revived the question of how the urban poor work and live in contemporary India. The impact of the lockdown on migrants fleeing cities was a prominent theme in public debate during the early months of the pandemic. However, as that crisis diminished in significance, the public interest in it also waned. So the visibility of the "labor question" appears to have been a temporary phenomenon; the issue receded from public consciousness as swiftly as it arose. (Kidambi, 2020)

The current pandemic also forcefully brought forth the conditions of workers in various Indian cities. The Great Trudge across India's highways and railway tracks were rude reminders of the abysmal working conditions for people employed in the vast informal sector of the Indian economy. These moments bring forth larger structural issues which are otherwise much more endemic and entrenched in our socio-economic conditions and everyday lives. Sheetal Chhabria argues, "In both nineteenth century and in the present, the eventfulness of the chosen crisis displaces attention away from longstanding structural vectors of inequality and mortality. The force of the market, ideologically and materially, determines which events can be narrated as a crisis and which cannot, just as it determined the government's priorities in managing it." (Chhabria, 2021: 55) Chhabria asserts that state's neglect in creating a good public health system provides the perfect condition for pathogens to thrive. Structural inequities in the society aid the spread of endemic and epidemic diseases. She connects the spread of disease to the economic and political structures when she argues that

> pathogens are not outside of the world of commerce we have created. They are its effects. It takes human effort to make pathogens work. Cholera and malaria thrive where public water works are neglected. Influenza thrives under conditions of starvation. Malnourishment is the perfect breeding ground for a whole host of illnesses. To produce malnourishment, one has to neglect or mystify decades-long agricultural crises, farmers' demands, and the basic right to food and health. To be so vulnerable to viral illness like COVID-19, one has to tether pharmaceutical industries to endless profit rather than public welfare. (Chhabria, 2021: 61)

The structural fault lines within Indian society have been exposed severely by the present pandemic. The poor state of the public health infrastructure has been laid bare. The scenario urges for a new politics of life and importance of care in such politics, asserts Ranabir Samaddar. For him, the COVID-19 crisis "calls for a new type of public power which values care as the guiding principle of organising society, which will be treated as commons." (Samaddar, 2021: 135) He hopes for a 'bio-politics from below', "which may be understood as a congealed form of the response of the lower classes in society to the crisis of life.... Bio-politics from below is fundamentally horizontal in nature. The solidarity it evokes and the trust it bases itself on in order to protect life run along a horizontal line." (Samaddar, 2021: 206–07) In the exemplary courage shown by the care-givers, nurses and doctors, the workers in essential sectors, the neighbourhood associations, and the many relief organisations providing food, Samaddar views this emergence of a new form of public power which "derives its legitimacy from the capacity to protect lives, its ability to foster care, and to accord recognition and dignity to the non-market values of compassion and solidarity…" (Samaddar, 2021: 207) Perhaps, these are the takeaways from this period of uncertainty.

1.5 Chapters in the Volume

There are four sections in the volume. The first section, 'Of Past and Futures of Studying Epidemics' looks at the theoretical underpinnings of studying epidemiological crises. Looking mainly at historical understanding of past events, the essays in this section delineate the ways in which historians and social scientists have sought to comprehend various moments of medical crises, where notions of time, structure, and events are evaluated and discussed.

In the second chapter, Subhas Ranjan Chakraborty discusses the notion of plural temporal scales in historical narratives. He says that the method of using a longer time-frame to understand the long-term processes of evolution in societies was not unknown to earlier historians. In the nineteenth-century historians of law, authors of medical treatises on chronic disease, sociologists studying unemployment or economists tracing long-term movements were familiar with the notion of what Fernand Braudel would later conceptualise as 'longue durée'. The practice of traditional history was concerned with the short time span- the individual, the event. Economic and social history put 'cyclical movement' in the forefront. Thus along with the old narrative history, there was an account of 'conjuncture' which lays open larger sections of the past-10, 20, 50 years at a stretch for examination. The different temporal conceptions may provide relational keys to interpretation and analysis. Time for historians is in constant motion and their task is to account for both its 'plurality' and its different 'rhythms'. Chakraborty suggests that we may also look at a different kind of historical construction, as a counterpoint to the long-term view. Historians like Carlo Ginzburg, Giovanni Levi and others practised what came to be known as microhistory. They did not represent a system, but rather constituted a community. It came as a reaction/response to the *longue durée* tradition and they pursued what some have called 'eclectic' historical practices. They reduced the scale and looked at a village community, a family, an individual, or a particular event. When one looks contemporaneously at a huge phenomenon like the pandemic of 2020, both these approaches may provide useful tools to explore the complex, multi-layered phenomenon, with its local and global ramifications. A very relevant context for studying the pandemic is provided by the history of plague from the very ancient period. The second section of the chapter reflects on the various ways historians have dealt with that epidemic.

In the third chapter, Paula Banerjee looks at the blame game that accompanies any epidemic outbreak. The twentieth century closed with the AIDS epidemic and the twenty-first began with the SARS virus that was identified in 2003. People spent days debating on the uncertain animal reservoir that ultimately infected humans.

The AIDS, the northern world decided began in Africa and the first known infections of SARS, it was speculated appeared in Guangdong Province of China in 2002 so the world heaved a sigh of relief because it could now be logged as the Chinese pandemic. The SARS was followed by the swine-origin H1N1 in 2009 and this time it was Mexico. The world was caught up in H5N1 from Asia and then came H1N1. Now the blame game was centred on another poor, impoverished exotic culture and the global North could easily blame another underdeveloped country albeit with a rich history but an impoverished economy. The trope that pandemics only affect poor countries lived on and the global North again remained under-prepared but happy that such diseases did not touch them. The world remained unconscious because if Europe and USA were not affected then everyone could sleep peacefully. The diseased body was happily located elsewhere. It will not be remiss to say that this hunt for "Patient Zero," which today is more a metaphor than a real person, has been a recurring phenomenon in the last few hunts for the pandemic. Locating the diseased body has now become an industry with fancy surveillance systems all in the name of science. In this chapter, Banerjee seeks to address a few questions: (1) In any pandemic in the long 2020 why has finding the diseased body become such a crucial aspect of disease management? Is it more to do with ordering of society or rather fear of social disorder? (2) How did the idea of locating the diseased body come to exert such a strong influence in popular imagination? (3) What are the essential elements in this hunt for a diseased body? And why pandemics always lead to this hunt? (4) Is this a recent phenomenon? If not, then why has it acquired such significance in this present times?

In the next chapter, Kaustubh Mani Sengupta discusses a few methodological issues that can help us understand the year 2020, the sufferings of the working population, the crisis in the economy, and the varied social, political, economic, and epidemiological responses that we encountered. These are methods that historians have used to analyse various moments of the past—be it collective action, everyday situation, common mentality at times of war, famine, or epidemic. He suggests that an understanding of these methodological issues may help us with grapple the complexities of the ongoing crises and situate them in a historical context. Similar to Chakraborty's chapter, Sengupta proposes certain ways through which we can try and make meaning of the events that unfolded during 2020–21. To situate 2020 in a historical frame, he focuses on three crucial elements that historians and social scientists have dealt with in great detail regarding their craft. These are: (a) the question of structure, event, and agency; (b) the question of time and temporality; and (c) the question of everyday life in history and relating it to the concerns of state, politics, and bio-power in the context of 2020.

As some commentators have observed, one of the major differences between the influenza pandemic of 1918 and the COVID-19 outbreak can be sought in the relatively faster response time in the latter case. For any other epidemic or pandemic in the past, the response from the medical professionals, researchers, pharmaceutical companies and the governments came only after the spread of the disease entered a critical stage. Even though the response time is quicker this time, it is certainly not because we know more about the virus or viruses that have caused the pandemic.

Rather, as Iman Mitra suggests in the last chapter of this section, we must note that the knowledge of the disease in the case of a global pandemic such as this assumes a seemingly loose, flexible form, which is different from other forms of knowledge that can afford meticulous reflection and offer conjectures. Once the speed of the circulation of knowledge becomes more important than the accuracy of its content, we enter the domain of logistics. In this chapter, Mitra explores the logistics of knowledge production during the pandemic, which, he argues, springs from an intersection of economic rationality and epidemiological reason under the rubric of neoliberalism. He studies this logistical imagination at the moments of the convergence between economics and epidemiology, both as epistemic constellations as well as technologies of intervention. Moreover, it inaugurates an era of digital epidemiology based on artificial intelligence and machine learning that reshapes some of the earlier notions and practices of governmentality.

The second section, 'Global and Local Response to 2020' studies the various ramifications of the events of the first pandemic year in India as well as globally in terms of crisis of capitalist production process and logistics of governance. In fact, COVID-19 pandemic triggered the third capitalist crash in the global economy in the present century. As Byasdeb Dasgupta suggests in his chapter, may be the crash was anyway inevitable; but the pandemic has aggravated the dimensions of the crash hitherto unknown. The problems that are associated with the current global capitalism in this age of neoliberal globalisation remain unresolved. The crash, even though aggravated by the pandemic, is systemic in nature. The inherent tendency of capitalism as an economic system is to produce recurring crashes and the radical solutions to that sickness of the system are beyond the imagination of the politics as it is practised today in various parts of the world—mainly in the garb of liberal democracy. Dasgupta argues that three basic problems can be attributed to global capitalism as an economic system. First, the economic space of capitalism as it is ruled by several capitalist enterprises is undemocratic. And this undemocratic nature of capitalism in the economic sphere keeps it away from the general well-being of the majority. The second problem associated with global capitalism is its inherent tendency of generating crash or crisis every 4–7 years which damage the enterprises and the economy—rather, the majority of the enterprises, and the current pandemic is no exception. Thirdly, capitalism in general and global capitalism in particular generates inequalities of wealth and income which widen further at the time of crash or crisis. Dasgupta's chapter on global capitalism and COVID-19 pandemic attempts to decipher these three basic problems of capitalism as an economic system and would try to see if any radical solution is plausible in terms of reforming the system as Keynes advocated at the time of Great Depression during the 1930s.

In the next chapter of this section, Amit Prakash looks at the logistics of governance that unfolded in the wake of the pandemic in early 2020 and suggests that they were far more expansive than that dictated by the medical emergency. Mainly, two legal mechanisms were deployed by the state: first was the invocation of the colonial era Epidemic Diseases Act, 1897 (popularly called the Plague Act), swiftly amended by an ordinance on April 22, 2020, to ostensibly offer protections for healthcare personnel combatting epidemic diseases; and, second was the invocation of the National Disaster Management Act, 2005 under which the National Disaster Management Authority, headed by the Union Home Secretary, can (and did) arrogate to itself powers to issue any direction to anybody, including State governments. Prakash examines these processes across two axes: (a) the logic, mechanisms and implication of the National Disaster Management Act/ Authority and the Epidemic Diseases Act, 1897; and (b) political economy of testing and vaccine delivery in terms of its conversion of the process of governance from that of political to mere management. He argues that this process which started unfolding during the Long 2020 will have a much longer and multidimensional impact on the fundamentals of governance processes in the country. The chapter seeks to identify, document, and analyse this complex process in terms of the étatisation of the polity and implications thereof for liberal democracy in India, as well as the impact of such logistics of governance on the right to life and livelihood, especially that of the poor and marginalised.

The third section, 'Refugees and Labouring Lives' looks at various vulnerable groups during moments of crises, and how the state responded to both their demands and plights. The group of chapters in this section opens with an essay on the refugees who came to Calcutta during the tumultuous post-Partition decades. Priyankar Dey investigates how the presence of these refugees from East Bengal within the city of Calcutta shaped the discourses and the practices of public health of the city in the post-partition decades. The refugees in the city laid bare the fault lines in the 'social' discourse of public health of the time which is reflected in the peculiar pathological figuration of the displaced population in the contemporary municipal debates. Further, focusing on the struggles of the refugee squatters in ensuring healthcare facilities, Dey shows how the question of public health could produce different forms of alliances and solidarity networks within the refugee colony and beyond its confines. Public health practices in the refugee colonies assembled many different actors, not all of them were residents of these colonies. A close investigation of these networks then problematizes the standard historiographical tradition of casting the history of refugee rehabilitation into a neat binary between charity and self-reliance. Finally, linking the above discussion with the healthcare movement organised by the Left in the decades under consideration, the chapter argues that all of these point towards alternative ideals of protection and care. They hinted towards a newly emerging *politics of life* in the city, which would be reflected in the populist rhetoric of the Left in the years to follow.

Moving ahead to the present context, we found that the spread of the COVID-19 pandemic and subsequent lockdown measures revealed the scale of internal migration in India. While the Long March of 2020 brought to light the arduous and painstaking journey back home, it also revealed the precarious livelihood scenario of the migrants and their families. Migrant workers were therefore compelled to return to the towns and cities once the lockdown restrictions began to be lifted. Jyothi Krishnan and Prasad R. discuss the case of Kerala which has witnessed a steep increase in the migrant worker population over the past decade. The increasing shortage of manual labourers in the state has created a situation wherein migrant workers have become an inevitable component of the state's economy. While it is acknowledged that Kerala provides better working and living conditions to the large migrant workforce in the state, a preliminary review of legislations and policies reveals that all is not well. The ambiguity surrounding the terms and conditions under which migrant workers are hired by contractors enhances the possibility of them being hired against advances, leaving much room for exploitation. While the Kerala government was one of the first to formulate welfare programmes for the migrant workers, the overall approach towards the migrant population in the state has been couched in the language of welfare. The presence of such schemes and programmes is viewed as an end in themselves, providing demonstrable evidence of the state's welfare objectives. However, the articulation of rights and accountability mechanisms to define and enforce the responsibilities of the employers/contractors appears to be weak, which leads to a compromise of labour rights vis a vis the accumulation of capital in a state that relies heavily on the availability of migrant labour. While the state administration referred to migrant workers as 'guest workers' during the roll out of the lockdown, it is important to assess the overall well-being and degree of inclusion that the migrants themselves experienced during this period. The authors contextualise the examination of issues related to migrant workers within the existing paradox of combining welfarism with a neoliberal development paradigm in the state.

The next chapter looks at the healthcare crises during the pandemic. The health system in India consists of a public sector, a private sector and an informal network of care providers. Though for the formal sectors there have been policies, schemes operative for long, in case of the informal network, due to various reasons (limited access, further worsened by the poor functioning of public health system is one among many), the act of 'caring' takes place mostly in an unregulated environment. Sabir Ahamed and Madhurilata Basu argue in their chapter that the health care crisis in 2020 was a result of collective economic strategies adopted by various governments which gave primacy to big capital, infrastructure and financial services and comparatively, less importance was attached to social sectors like health and education. The sudden visibility that careworkers (including the ones from formal as well as informal sectors) have gained during the pandemic should not be easily forgotten, and for that, discussions on public health, contagion, health security, etc., should keep focus on areas beyond medical, virological and epidemiological concerns. Based on personal interviews, articles, reports published during the pandemic along with other relevant documents, this chapter shows how three categories of informal careworkers, namely ASHA workers, *ayahs* and *safaikarmacharis*, negotiated with the pandemic on the one hand, and societal expectations on the other.

The last section of the book, 'Literature and the Literary World' discusses the ways in which epidemics have been represented in fictions, their impacts on the novelists' imagination, and the wider ramifications of pandemic on the literary world. Samata Biswas gives an overview of the contemporary literary productions in Bengali, in the wake of the COVID-19 pandemic and the ensuing lockdown. She also describes late nineteenth and early twentieth century Bengali literature's engagement with multiple epidemics like cholera and smallpox that had devastated the Bengal countryside. The repeated waves of pandemics and their representation in Bengali literature were integral in the construction of the Bengali realist novel, creating a space of ferment which allowed for the reconstruction of society, reconsideration of social divisions and consolidation of social work as an extension of nationalist activities. Biswas enquires in some detail about these texts, ranging from Bankim Chandra Chattopadhyay's *Anandamath* to Sarat Chandra Chatopadhyay's *Srikanta*, from Bibhuti Bhushan Bandyopadhyay's *Aranyak* to Banaphul's *Jangam*. The last part of the chapter analyses the construction of an alternate society through Tarasankar Bandyopadhyay's social realist novels, written and set in the 1920s and 30 s, in rural Bengal and in Calcutta. Most of his novels (like *Ganadebata*, *Dhatridebata*) reckon with a society in flux, dealing on one hand with colonialism, and on the other, with the gradual transformation in traditional societies, the destabilisation of existing hierarchies, and creation of new ones. In each of these moments of epidemiological crisis, the novels also recognise extraordinary characters, individuals who had been pushed to the margins of traditional society. In moments of crisis, they transcend their marginalities through agentive action and empathy. Their action in the course of the novels, Biswas argues, become crucial in framing the post-pandemic social relations.

The last chapter by Ritu Menon focuses on her experience as a book publisher during the period of lockdown, quarantine, and 'social distancing'. She describes how the usual meaning of 'time' itself got altered during these times. Any future plan of publishing comes with a set of basic questions: Who will buy? Will people rush out to buy books just because they have been confined, or will they have had their fill of reading already, because they could do so little else? Maybe the last thing they will want to do is pick up another book. But at another level, she is beset by the thought that whether she would be around to see those books published if they are not published soon. She asks, "Shouldn't I be accelerating instead of slowing down? What if I run out of time? And so, I manoeuvre myself into that tiny space, that sliver of time between lockdown and post-lockdown, whenever that might be, to think and plan for a week at a time, which seems to me a good compromise between the everyday and the existential."

In a sense, all of us have been making this compromise between the everyday and the existential to navigate the precarious nature of life that this planet seems to offer us now.

References

Bandyopadhyay, R., Banerjee, P., & Samaddar, R. (2021). *India's migrant workers and the pandemic*. Routledge.

Chakrabarti, P. (2021). COVID-19 and the Spectres of Colonialism. In *India and the pandemic: The first year, essays from The India Forum*. Orient Blackswan.

Chakrabarty, D. (2021a). The chronopolitics of the anthropocene: The Pandemic and Our Sense of Time. *Contributions to Indian Sociology, 55*(3), 324–348.

Chakrabarty, D. (2021b). *The climate of history in a planetary age*. Primus Books.

Chhabria, S. (2021). Manufacturing epidemics: Pathogens, poverty and public health crises in India. In *India and the pandemic: The first year, essays from The India Forum*. Orient Blackswan.

Crosby, A. W. (1986). *Ecological imperialism: The biological expansion of Europe, 900–1900*. Cambridge University Press.
Crosby, A. W. (2003). *The Columbian exchange. Biological and cultural consequences of 1492*. Praeger.
Davis, M. (2002). *Late Victorian holocausts: El Nino famines and the making of the third world*. Verso.
Horowitz, A. (2022). Pandemics as history. In T. J. Sugrue & C. Zaloom (Eds.), *The long year: A 2020 reader*. Columbia University Press.
Kidambi, P. (2020). A tale of two epidemics: Mumbai, bubonic plague and COVID-19. https://www.indiachinainstitute.org/2020/10/22/a-tale-of-two-epidemics-mumbai-bubonic-plague-and-covid-19/
Moore, J. W. (2016). The rise of cheap nature. In J. W. Moore (Ed.), *Anthropocene or Capitalocene: Nature, history, and the crisis of capitalism*. PM Press.
Nail, T. (2021). *Theory of the earth*. Stanford University Press.
Samaddar, R. (2020). *The postcolonial age of migration*. Routledge.
Samaddar, R. (2021). *A pandemic and the politics of life*. Women Unlimited.
Sivasundaram, S. (2020). The human, the animal, and the prehistory of COVID-19. *Past and Present, 249*, 295–316.
Sugrue, T. J. (2022). Introduction: Preexisting conditions. In T. J. Sugrue & C. Zaloom (Eds.), *The long year: A 2020 reader*. Columbia University Press.

Part I
Of Past and Futures of Studying Epidemics

Chapter 2
'*Longue Durée*', '*Conjoncture*', '*Event*': Notion of Plural Time in History

Subhas Ranjan Chakraborty

> *Time present and time past*
> *Are both perhaps present in time future*
> *And time future contained in time past.* (Eliot, 2004: 171)

Abstract The historian can never get away from the question of time in history. In the nineteenth century historians of law, authors of medical treatises on chronic disease, sociologists studying unemployment or economists tracing long-term movements were familiar with the notion of what Braudel would later conceptualize as '*longue durée*'. He writes that all historical work is concerned with breaking down time past, choosing among its chronological realities according to more or less conscious preferences and exclusions. The practice of traditional history was concerned with the short time span—the individual, the event. Economic and social history put 'cyclical movement' in the forefront. Thus along with the old narrative history, there was an account of 'conjuncture' which lays open larger sections of the past 10, 20, 50 years or centuries at a stretch for examination. The different temporal conceptions may provide relational keys to interpretation and analysis. We may also look at a different kind of historical construction, as a counterpoint to the long-term view. Historians like Carlo Ginzburg, Giovanni Levi, and others practised what came to be known as microhistory. They reduced the scale and looked at a village community, a family, an individual, or a particular event. When one looks contemporaneously at a huge phenomenon like the pandemic of 2020, both these approaches may provide useful tools to explore the complex, multi-layered phenomenon, with its local and global ramifications. A very relevant context for studying the pandemic is provided by the history of plague from the very ancient period. The second section of the paper reflects on the various ways historians have dealt with that epidemic.

Keywords Temporal scale · Fernand Braudel · *Longue duree* · Microhistory · Plague

---

S. R. Chakraborty (✉)
Department of History, Presidency College, and MCRG, Kolkata, India
e-mail: srchakraborty@gmail.com

S. R. Chakraborty et al. (eds.), *The Long 2020*, India Studies in Business and Economics, https://doi.org/10.1007/978-981-99-4815-4_2

2.1 Braudel and *Longue Durée*

The historian can never get away from the question of time in history. How does the present connect to the past and to the future is a kind of conundrum that intrigues the historian. Churchill once said that the 'longer you look back, the further you can look forward'. The method of using a longer time frame to understand the long-term processes of evolution in societies was deployed by historians even in the nineteenth century, when historians of law, authors of medical treatises on chronic disease, sociologists studying unemployment or economists tracing long-term movements were apparently familiar with the notion of what Braudel would later conceptualize as '*longue durée*'. In *History and the Social Sciences: The Longue Durée*', Braudel examined the concept of historical time in the various social sciences and sought to emphasize the importance of 'plural temporalities and the *longue durée* as methodological ground for a unified historical social science' (Tomich, 2011: 54). He writes that all historical work is concerned with breaking down time past, with historians choosing among its chronological realities according to more or less conscious preferences and exclusions. The practice of traditional history was concerned with the short span—the individual, the event. Economic and social history put 'cyclical movement' in the forefront. Thus, along with the old narrative history, there was an account of 'conjuncture' which addressed relatively longer periods spanning a few decades at a stretch. Beyond this there is a history capable of traversing even greater distances, a history to be measured in centuries—the history of the long, even of the very long time span, of the *longue durée*. 'This is a phrase I have become accustomed to in order to distinguish the opposite of what François Simiand called "*l'histoire événmentielle*"', wrote Braudel, and added, 'The phrases matter little; what matters is the fact that our discussion will move between these two poles of time, the instant and the *longue durée*' (Braudel, 1988: 72). Lucien Febvre once described events as 'visible crusts of history' implying that it was the 'most visible', but also the 'the most superficial' (Carrard, 1995: 31).

Braudel applied his idea of *longue durée* in his *Mediterranean and the Mediterranean World in the Age of Philip II* by using three time frames—the very long term ('The Role of the Environment', 'geographical time' of man's relations to the environment), the long term ('Collective Destinies and General Trends', or 'social time' of institutions and attitudes) and the short term ('Events, Politics, People', 'individual time' of events). His approach was both experimental and empirically oriented. He conceived *longue durée* as a 'real historical structure formed at the interface of human activity with geography and nature' (Carrard, 1995: 31; Tomich, 2011: 54). 'Events are the ephemera of history; they pass across its stage like fireflies, hardly glimpsed before they settle back into darkness and as often as not into oblivion', wrote Braudel, 'Every event, however brief, has to be sure, a contribution to make, lights up some dark corner or even some wide vista of history…every historical landscape …is illuminated by the intermittent flare of the event…I am by no means the sworn enemy of the event' (Braudel, 1995: 901; Tomich, 2011: 57). The different temporal conceptions may provide meaningful tools for use in interpretation and analysis. Unlike sociologists and anthropologists, who conduct direct investigations in 'short term', which they reduce to the present, or they search for the unchanging in a 'long term' which is so long as to become still, time for historians is in 'constant motion' and their task is to account for both its 'plurality' and its different 'rhythms'. Historians strongly privilege correlations of this plural time. It is interesting to note that Marshall Sahlins in *Islands of History* has used Braudel's categories of *longue durée*, conjuncture and event in his anthropology, but has looked afresh at them and has reinterpreted his meanings of 'structure' and 'conjuncture'. He would privilege the 'event' and the historical agent at the core of historical transformations.

> Sahlins's text neatly performs his analytical principles in relation to Braudel's text: using old names, the agent (Sahlins) changes the meaning of cultural schema (conjuncture). This takes place in the "event" of the text, the practice of intellectual life, the collision of different agents and structures of thought (Braudel, Bloch, Sahlins and their texts). (Champion, 2019: 265)

Le Roy Ladurie explained that the term *'l'histoire immobile'* in the context of 'long' may indicate a paradox, but it does not mean a total stability. He claimed to have described the eco-demography of France from the fourteenth to the eighteenth century. It had its 'oscillations' and 'fluctuations' (Carrard, 1995: 32, 46).

2.2 Variations of Long-Term Perspectives

Quite a few other books had been influential, without necessarily theorizing, in propagating the long-term view of historical evolution. Mahan's book *Influence of Sea Power in History (1660–1783)* was not only an influential book, but provided both the rationale and the blueprint for the expansion of naval power among the European powers in the late nineteenth century (the Anglo-German Naval rivalry, for example, was thought to have been a potential cause of the World War I). I. Wallerstein's *'The Modern World System'* would also fall within this category of a long-term view spanning the period from 1450 to 1815 in the first two volumes. He, moreover, was looking at global history and noted

> …there seems to be widespread consensus that some great structural changes did occur in the world in the last seven hundred years, changes that make the world of today qualitatively different from the world of yesterday. (Wallerstein, 1974: 3)

Ernest Labrousse's classic on the movement of prices and wages in France under the *ancien régime* is an appropriate example of the use of 'cyclical time'. He used the reconstruction of statistical data on economy and society to understand the origins of the French Revolution by establishing causal relations between the price movements and their effects on various social groups. Using these he finds a specific 'conjuncture of long-term and intermediate economic cycles together with short-term agricultural cycles' in France prior to the beginning of the Revolution. His normal time span is about 100 years; the shortest period he considers is the 'intercycle'—a decade and a half. Labrousse, it may be important to remember, was using these statistics to establish the causal relations behind the French Revolution of 1789. Pierre Goubert's book on the Beauvaisis brought back to life the demographic *ancien regime* of the seventeenth- and eighteenth-century France (Ladurie, 1979: 111–112). Hobsbawm took a long view of historical evolution as is evidenced by his construction of the 'Long Nineteenth Century' in contrast to the 'Short Twentieth Century'. He, however, did not offer any methodological novelty. On the other hand, Giovanni Arrighi in *The Long Twentieth Century* traces the relationship between the development of capitalism and state formation over a few centuries. Arrighi argues that capitalism developed over successive centuries, each of which produced a new power that secured control over an expanding world-economic space. He examined, inter alia, the changing fortunes of Florentine, Venetian, Genoese, Dutch, English and finally American capitalism. Arrighi concludes with an examination of the forces that have shaped and are now poised to undermine America's world dominance (Arrighi, 1994).

It may not be irrelevant to have a brief look at the ideas of presentism in history as elaborated by François Hartog. Time, he asserts, has recently become something of an obsession.

> As a historian who tries to be attentive to his time, I have observed how the category of the present has taken hold to such an extent that one can really talk of an omnipresent present. This is what I call presentism… A presentist approach considers the past with an eye on the present, whereas a historicist approach focuses on the past for itself alone. (Hartog, 2015: 9)

Hartog also cites Hannah Arendt to introduce the concept of a gap between past and future. This gap is an 'odd in-between period…in historical time which is entirely determined by things that are no longer and by things that are not yet' (Arendt, 1993: 3 and 9; Hartog, 2015, 5). Hartog defines 'regime of historicity' in two ways—in a narrow sense, it is 'the way in which a given society approaches its past and reflects upon it'. But, in a broader view, it refers to the 'modalities of self-consciousness that each society adopts in its constructions of time' (Hartog, 2015: 9–10). This in a way echoes the idea of Benedetto Croce that all history is contemporary history. There is reason behind such construction as often recourse to history is occasioned by a sudden crisis in the present. The present pandemic may be a case in point. When Hartog was writing his book, he was influenced by the world recession of 2008.

2.3 Historians and Plurality of Time

The concept of the different time frames used by historians has been subjected to a thorough scrutiny by historians as well as social scientists. We propose to look at some of these observations presented in a recent issue of the Past and Present. Fryxell argues in his study of current trends in the history of modern temporalities that these provide a chance to understand what he calls the 'intersubjective' experience of the past. What emerges is that 'pluritemporalities of modernity are as subjective as they are scientific' (Fryxell, 2019, 291). He cites the fascist experience as an example of what he calls 'historical time' that produced 'temporalities encompassing radical renewal as well as nostalgia for a mythical and timeless past' (Fryxell, 2019, 293).

Vanessa Ogle would understand time as indicated by clock, calendar and natural phenomena (Ogle, 2019). Temporality is taken to describe how past, present and future relate to each other. It can be a form of experience of historical actors and can be used as a category of analysis through which the historian in the present seeks to understand certain developments/processes in the past (Ogle, 2019: 314). There is a fascinating example of 2020 when work from home (familiar in some regions of the world from the 1990s) raises its relation to the notion of time. What Jonathan Crary calls 'the 24 × 7 society' no longer measures time for sleep and rest (Crary, 2013; Ogle, 2019: 318). New normal or exceptional normal? Is this unique to 2020? Koselleck had suggested that one moment might encapsulate 'multiple temporalities' and put forward the idea of 'layers of time' (Koselleck, 2004; Ogle, 2019: 319). Koselleck worked on the semantics of 'historical time' and examined the experiences of history by posing a question, 'how, in a given present, are the temporal dimensions of past and future related' (Hartog, 2015; Koselleck, 2004). Koselleck once considered 'progress as the first genuinely historical category of time.' Time and temporality, argues Ogle, can occupy a central position in new histories of capitalism, but it must include issues of 'gender, culture and globality in historicizing economic life'.

Priya Satia, in a recent book, talks of the Enlightenment changing the notion of cyclical time to a linear vision of history which, it was now believed, moved irresistibly forward (Satia, 2020). This idea of 'the flow of time' or 'progress' (privileged by Koselleck as we have noted earlier) is found to be 'irrational'. The flawed notion is predicated on the assumption that humans make history rather than simply being made by history. The result was that history came to be seen as something that automatically progresses. This is, in her opinion, a view of history that allows certain peoples and nations to be damned as backward or obsolete. This can be seen as providing 'moral justification for colonialism'. It also rationalizes present sufferings as being necessary for a better future. The discipline of history took shape among a tiny group of elite Europeans. Satia's book is about the discipline of history and how it helped make empires. Satia's point is that the notion that history is progress has been radically altered by experiences of climate disruptions. Reviewing the book, Amitav Ghosh writes, 'Let us make no mistake…: it is climate change above all that has upended our expectations of the future, thereby exposing the fundamental fallacies that underlie the idea that history is linear chronicle of progress' (Ghosh, 2021).

2.4 Microhistory vis-à-vis *Longue Durée*

We may now turn to a different kind of historical construction, as a counterpoint to the long-term view. Historians like Carlo Ginzburg, Giovanni Levi and others practised what came to be known as microhistory. They did not represent a system, but rather constituted a community. It came as a reaction/response to the *longue durée* tradition and they pursued what some have called 'eclectic' historical practices. They reduced the scale and looked at a village community, a family, an individual, or a particular event. Levi argued that the approaches adopted by these historians exercised freedom 'beyond, though not outside, the constraints of the normative system'. Levi makes convincing arguments about the need for comprehensive studies of particular aspects of history. Microhistory seeks to overcome the limitations of deterministic social history or the anthropological approach which relies so heavily on relativistic notions that they miss the generalizations. Hobsbawm, however, did consider microhistory as a particularly clear expression of the cultural turn. Ginzburg, on the other hand, wanted *The Cheese and the Worm,* for example, to be explicitly understood in terms of a 'concept of class structure' in the tradition of Marx and Gramsci. The political undertones of Ginzburg's work were understood by his reviewers. As has been said by Gribaudi (Levi's friend), in the 1970s microhistory was less of an academic project and more of a political intervention in the debates of the Marxist Left (Bernet, 2020: 41–43).

The idea of microhistory vis-à-vis macrohistory or more recently global history has attracted a very lively debate among practitioners of different genres of history. Some of these, the product of a conference, were compiled in a special supplement of the seminal journal the *Past & Present.*[1] We may begin with the ideas put forward by Giovanni Levi in his essay, 'Frail Frontiers?' (Levi, 2019: 37–49). He suggests that it is not the 'microness' of a phenomenon that constitutes the core of microhistory, but rather putting under the microscope issues and facts to highlight their relevance (Levi, 2019, 38). 'It seems to me to be less characterized by spatial dimensions than by the network of meanings and interrelations set up by the practical phenomenon being studied'. As far as time is concerned global history tends to regard it as homogeneous in historical perspective, without 'allowing relevance for different temporalities that might come together in a single moment' Microhistory finds more relevance in the disjunctions of time and 'models of historicity' and it adopts a vision of time in which remote or recent causes intermingle in unpredictable ways (Levi, 2019, 40). Microhistory uses archives and all kinds of records. Practitioners read beyond the 'edge of the page' to elicit the clues hidden in a language. He mentions the concept of 'exceptional normal' which may be a useful tool to read a pandemic (Levi, 2019, 41).

As far as microhistory is concerned, history is a discipline of general questions and "local" answers (Levi, 2019, 45). 'Even the apparently minutest action of, say,

---

[1] I am indebted to Dr. Debarati Bagchi for not only drawing my attention to this collection, but also for kindly providing a soft copy. I am thankful for her incisive comments as a discussant after the presentation of the paper in a conference.

somebody going to buy a loaf of bread, actually encompasses the far wider system of the whole world's grain market' (Levi, 1992, 96; Ghobrial, 2019, 14).

Jan de Vries has a different take. He does not agree with Levi's claims that the methods of microhistory seek 'fragments through which universal processes can be observed'. De Vries would call these 'grand claims', not shared by all (de Vries, 2019).

We have so far indulged briefly on a historiographical account of how some groups of historians or individuals have used time as a framework to analyse their chosen period and field of history. A definite choice between the long, the intermediate or the short term may not be necessary. Braudel's conceptualization of the *longue durée* has been influential, especially as it tended to be equated with the *Annales* school, though all *Annalistes* did not follow or practice this concept. Yet there had been other historians whose use of the long term would appear to be a little more nuanced. Studying an epidemic may call for using both the long-term and the short-term methods. Epidemics often had a prolonged impact or they recurred periodically. The remote origins of an epidemic, or its long-term impact would call for a method which may not suit the study of particular and immediate aspects of an epidemic in a given region at a given point of time. Studying the particular may call for a method other than the one used for the more general. The histories of the plague from ancient Greece to Europe, Asia and other regions would reinforce such a notion.

2.5 Plotting the Event: Looking Back at Plague in Europe

A very relevant context for the study of the pandemic is provided by the history of plague from the very ancient period. It may help to have a brief look at this history. The plague in Athens wrought great devastation. Starting in the second year of the Peloponnesian war, it continued for 4 years and took a heavy casualty in terms of human lives. The dead included Pericles, the great Athenian statesman, who became a victim of plague in 429 BCE. Thucydides, the historian, who was afflicted himself, has given an account of the ravages as the dead lay unburied and corpses filled the temples. The havoc of the pestilence reduced the population of Athens substantially. Thucydides also noted the demoralization it produced in Athens. He wrote of the practical and moral weaknesses which had disastrous impact. Athens lost the war which continued for a long period, but, as the historian noted, it led to the decline of the Athenian democracy. The plague had serious effects on the society including disrespect of laws and religious beliefs. In response, laws became stricter and more coercive. Non-citizens claiming to be Athenians were punished heavily. The plague, some have argued, contributed significantly to the decline of the Roman Empire as well (Bury, 1963, 407; Samaddar, 2021, 2–3).

Plague also overwhelmed a part of Europe between the 6th and 8th c. CE. This is now recognized as the first pandemic caused by the bacterium that later produced Black Death in the 14th c. Plague became a symbol of death and destruction. Bubonic plague had its origin in the East and was transmitted by fleas that in turn lived on rats. These made their way to Europe on the ships of Italian merchants. By 1347 it reached the Byzantium and Sicily, then Venice, Genoa, Marseilles, and Tuscany. Victims developed swellings at the point of flea bite and the purplish blotches—the '*buboes*'—gave the name *Bubonic* to this type of plague. Half the victims died. The pneumonic strain attacked the respiratory system and was even more fatal. There was a more deadly form—the septicaemic—where the victim did not show any symptoms at all. The Sienese chronicler Agnolo di Tura del Grasso wrote, 'The plague was a horrible and cruel event…almost everyone who witnessed it was stupefied by grief…People brought their own household to the ditches without priests; hundreds died day and night. … And I, Agnolo di Tura, known as the Fat, buried five of my children with my own hands …Nobody wept for the dead, since each was awaiting death'. Historians guess that 30% of the population (in some places almost 50%) was wiped out in Europe. South Eastern Europe, parts of West Asia, Italy, and Spain were severely affected (Holmes, 1990: 263–266). One of the obvious impacts of Black Death was demographic decline which started in the late thirteenth century in some regions. An estimate puts the total population in Europe in 1340 at 73.5 million, but in 1450 it came down to 50 million (Cipolla, 1981: 36). Disease as a demographic factor has not been adequately discussed. There is little evidence over a long period. Therefore, little attention was paid to the factor by historians until recent decades. The plague epidemics were the most spectacular and best-recorded phases of illness. But contemporary chroniclers were busy noting that the living was scarcely able to bury the dead.

The longer view would give a general perspective on movements and structures, but the experiences of men like Agnolo will remain buried in the past unless one puts the particular under the giant microscope. The plague obviously had deep psychological effects, but it is not easy for historians to unravel them. One impact was the suspension of conventional values and a decline in moral restraint, hedonistic abandonment and to this some have connected the questioning of authority and of religious truths. Among others were noticed rebellious spirits which became widespread a few decades later (England witnessed the peasant revolt of 1381; there was a *Jacquerie* in France in 1358, risings in maritime Flanders in 1382–4, for example) and development of new medical and intellectual interests (Holmes, 1990: 326) The plague returned with great frequency over the next few centuries. There was considerable economic impact as well. In much of Spain and Portugal, there was a crisis on the land; labour was scarce, wages rose, landlords were in temporary disadvantage. On the other hand, the governments tried to reverse these trends by legislation like the repeated Statutes of Labour in England against peasant mobility. Equally significant was the phenomenon of urban immigration in search of employment. The plague has been seen as a major force behind the general crisis of the fourteenth century.

Black Death in England in 1348 led to the beginning of the end of 'villein' system in England as one-third of the villages was wiped out. This enabled the villeins under the feudal system to try and improve their lot. There were desertions and migration to other areas for better terms of tenancy. In England, the long struggle led to the Peasant Revolt of 1381 (whose history was written by Rodney Hilton). Thus, the

Black Death in England eventually led to an early and fundamental change in the tenurial system.

The old village community in which families lived generation after generation upon the same land began to break up and a migratory class of labourers and peasants moving from one job and holding to the next arose. England witnessed the gradual disappearance of feudalism and the emergence of a differentiated, but relatively free peasantry on the one hand and the gentry on the other. In the long-term view, this led, inter alia, to structural changes in the economy and society facilitating industrialisation in England before any other country (Morton, 1984: 114–127).

Recent research has shown that in medieval England one person in every hundred was an immigrant. About 65,000 people came to the country between 1330 and 1550. The project on England's Immigrants undertaken by the universities of York and Sheffield details the names and occupations of those arriving from other parts of the British Isles and mainland Europe. Prof Mark Ormrod, the project director, said the influx was largely a result of the Black Death creating a labour shortage. 'We must remember that for a century or more after the Black Death the population of England was very low and there was plenty of work available. So people were coming from all across north-west Europe'. Prof Ormrod notes that many people were given a surname relating to their origin or trade after their arrival. 'Many people who today have names like Baker, Brewer, Smith or Cooper could actually be descended from immigrants' (BBC News, 2015).

Historians have also noted that the effects of Black Death played an important role in the early development of capitalism: Fuggers of Augsburg, the Stromers of Nuremberg, the Bladelins and Morels of Bruges, de la Poles of Hull. The Medici Bank did not possess a monopoly over the provision of credit in northern Europe and indigenous banking houses and financial syndicates, such as the English Wool Staplers of Calais, secured a larger share of the money market. Great wealth could be amassed in the northern world after the crisis of the fourteenth century, but it was very unevenly distributed (Holmes, 1990, 329).

2.5.1 *'Bacteriological Unification'*

A different perspective on time and space is offered by Emmanuel Le Roy Ladurie, who says that viewed from a great distance, from an international or intercontinental vantage point, the Black Death of 1348, can be reduced to a predictable episode in the overall process which was taking place between the fourteenth and sixteenth centuries. He would call it a 'bacteriological unification' of the planet. This, in turn, was conditioned by expansion of population in different continents of the globe, and the inevitable communication between the masses, as a result of the opening of the land and sea routes. Integration of Eurasia following the Mongol Empire of Genghis Khan, the opening of the silk route by the Genoese merchants, and the westward expansion in America increased the probability of massive waves of microbe infection carried west from the east; the Black Death was imported to Europe from Central

Asia via the Crimean port of Caffa (Ladurie, 1979: 112–113). The siege of Caffa was made by the Tatars, who were carrying the disease. Before retreating from Caffa, the General Khan Joni Beg catapulted the diseased bodies of the dead warriors over the city walls. This was probably the first instance of biological warfare.[2] In sheer panic, people fled in ships and boats from the Black Sea via the Straits and then the Aegean and the Mediterranean. A number of ships reached the Sicilian shores around October 1347. The plague travelled with them. The Sicilians found the ships full of dead bodies and sick people barely alive. The ships were pushed back into the sea, but the damage had already been done. The disease spread to the Sicilian port of Messina. By January, 1348 plague engulfed Italy. This is where the term 'quarantine' had its origin. It was stipulated that the incoming ships must sit at anchor for '*quaranto giorni*' (40 days). This is the source of 'quarantine'. Lawrence Wright asked Gianna Pomata, retired Professor of Johns Hopkins University, to compare Black Death to Covid-19 Pandemic, and her observation was that it was not 'in the number of death, but in terms of shaking up the way people think. The Black Death marked the end of the medieval period and the beginning of something else'. Wright says 'that something else came to be known as the Renaissance' (Wright, 2021). This exchange is germane to the conversation about the possibility of connected nature of the epidemics across time. There will be many such conversations, I feel, in the near future about the possible remote effects of the pandemic as well as its link to the past.

2.6 Disease Travels West from Europe

We may now turn to another and unique kind of epidemic introduced by the Spanish excursions into the New World. Eventually, Spain conquered Mexico and other countries of Central and South America and this led to the virtual extermination of the American Indian population. The action of the bacilli carried by the Spanish settlers between 1500 and 1700 was a major cause of loss of life in the conquered areas. Invasion of Mexico, for example, transformed the social and physical environment of the land, and the division of the country into governable units in the form of congregations that focused on agricultural production and conversion to Christianity—both of which brought people in much closer contact to one another, also with animals. Animals imported from the Old World were potentially disease vectors for illnesses of the New World. This had disastrous effects on the indigenous population. One estimate of the population of Central Mexico at the time of Spanish conquest puts it at 25 millions; a century later it was reduced to about 3% of that figure (Samaddar, 2020, 2; Habib, 1995, 11).

[2] Noted by Samaddar in *A Pandemic and the Politics of Life* (2021).

I have just aimed at an outline of some of the most serious plagues in early and late medieval history in Europe. There are several other instances of epidemiological disasters in different parts of the world where the notion of 'long' may be appropriately applied.

2.7 A Peep into Microhistory

I may now shift the attention to a microview of the plague in Italy presented by Cipolla and see the possibility of connecting the foregoing narrative, looking at the larger perspective and the micro 'event' in a small village. Cipolla explored the story of Monte Lupo, a small walled village in Tuscany about thirty kilometres from Florence during the plague epidemic of 1630–31 (Cipolla, 1979). He writes that the story of this village is exceptionally rich in documentation that allows the historian to capture the emotions, attitudes and behaviour of common people. He found that what happened during the epidemic in 'the microcosm of Monte Lupo threw unexpected light on the relationship between Faith and Reason, Church and State at a social level where such problems rarely surface in historical documents'. An important ingredient which coloured the outlook of many Tuscans of the time was a widely diffused anticlericalism which coexisted with deeply felt faith. He found that conflicts between the health authorities and the men of the Church were an everyday occurrence in the time of epidemics. The hostility was apparent even at the lower levels. The most frequent sources of conflict between clergymen and health authorities were the quarantine measures to which the clergy were not always willing to submit. Second, while for the Church God's anger was at the root of the scourge, the magistrates were also concerned with the 'miasmas', the 'vapours' the 'contagiousness' of the disease, no matter how the contagion operated. Administrative documents are revealing—when the plague was raging in 1630, the Grand Duke issued instructions to the health board. If anyone noticed a case of the disease, he should, (1) ensure that one dying of plague should not be buried in a Church, but in the countryside far from the high roads; (2) the moment the news of a sick man arrives, he should be carried to the pest house; (3) occupants of the house where the sickness has occurred must not leave the house; etc. In June 1631 five noblemen were appointed as commissioners general with high power to control and punish the recalcitrant. The resemblances with what has been happening after nearly 500 years are remarkable. Microhistory is capable of capturing the nuances of the times, particularly the emotions and attitudes, anguish and grief and sufferings at the grassroots level.

2.8 Variation in Space: Black Death in West Asia

Stuart Borsch and Tarek Sabraa have tried to estimate the mortality of the Black Death of 1348 for urban centres in Egypt, Syria and other areas of the West Asia and to use his data to quantify the migration of refugees fleeing from plague-stricken area (Borsch & Sabraa, 2016). They have discussed these in the context of the plague outbreak in Cairo, Alexandria, Gaza, Damascus, Aleppo, Homs, and Mecca by using quantitative methods. Between one-third and one-half of the inhabitants of Egypt and the West Asia in general were probably carried off by this outbreak. Plague, we are told, came back into the region not by a single trajectory, but in multiple directions on sea and over land. The sea journey carried plague bacterium to Constantinople, to the Aegean and to Alexandria and Cyprus in eastern Mediterranean, and then into the Caucasus and the Anatolian peninsula, and into Syria. Ibn Baṭuṭa reported on its arrival in Homs and Damascus. The plague struck Egypt and came to Cairo in the winter of 1348–9 and in that year also infected Arabia, decimating Mecca. Further southward, it reached Yemen, even as it spread westward through North Africa to Islamic Spain.

The inhabitants of Egypt were taken completely by surprise and knew next to nothing about this new and exceptionally lethal variant of plague that had suddenly appeared in their midst. It would seem that rural flight reached unprecedented proportions during this outbreak. This has been arrived at through trying to quantify urban plague mortality, one that factors in the death of rural migrants. Using sophisticated statistical methods they have arrived at the conclusion that the large incidence of death of urban paupers (people without property) from the plague outbreaks would imply that rural flight was substantial. This is an interesting story on rural migration in Egypt, and probably, in larger parts of West Asia.

2.9 In Lieu of a Conclusion

This essay has been essentially an exercise in historiography to understand the practitioners' ideas on what constitutes the 'long' in history. We have tried to put them in relief by considering other time frames used and conceptualized by practitioners. When one looks contemporaneously at a huge phenomenon like the pandemic of 2020, both the micro- and the *longue durée* approaches may provide useful tools to explore the complex, multi-layered phenomenon, with its local and global ramifications. Studying the Long 2020—the epidemiological aspect, the public health angle, the problem (should we say the tragedy?) of the migrant labourers, massive misgovernance, the impact of climate change, the emotional world of both the affected and of the caregivers in particular, to mention a few concerns, may deploy either one or the other of the methods. Emotions are difficult to record, but efforts may be made to capture micromoments, if possible. The losses, the lives lived in new ways, the negotiations, and the adjustments to a continuously changing reality are fascinating, if also challenging, subjects for the historians to explore. Literature, and a little imagination, might help in capturing the emotional world during the pandemic. One may recall the experience of Suryakant Tripathi 'Nirala', an eminent poet, during the Spanish flu of 1918–19 as recorded in his memoir, '*Kulli Bhat*' (English translation *A Life Misspent*, tr. Satti Khanna, Harper Collins). Nirala, born in Mahishadal in Bengal, went to Rae Bareilly, where his wife was staying with her parents at the time. On his way, he saw the Ganga full of dead bodies and on reaching her wife's home found her dead. Other members of the family followed. 'My family', he wrote, 'disappeared in the blink of an eye'. He also mentions the shortage of wood to cremate the dead. This explains why dead bodies were thrown into the river or buried on the river banks. The resemblance to what happened in UP more than a 100 years on is uncomfortably eerie (Gandhi, 2021). By a curious coincidence, the floating corpses on the Ganga a century later have been recorded in the book of poems, 'Shabbahini Gange' by Parul Kakkar. The book has attracted official censure as per newspaper reports. One may recall and compare the experience of Agnolo di Tura mentioned earlier. There are numerous ghost stories around Bengal villages to indicate the existence of a huge reservoir of collective memories relating to the impact of cholera and malaria epidemics taking heavy tolls. Sometimes whole villages were empty of human beings. This community memory is preserved in ghost stories like *Gadkhalir Haat* in its numerous versions (Mukharji, 2021).

Parallels will be found in the past, for example, in the sudden confrontation with the pathogen leading to knee-jerk response, to targeting the afflicted and to control their body to tide over the crisis. Even now this seems to be the approach so minutely analysed by Samaddar in his book, *A Pandemic and the Politics of Life,* a veritable running commentary of the long 2020.

References

Arendt, H. (1993). *Between past and future: Eight exercises in political thought*. Penguin.

Arrighi, G. (1994). *The long twentieth century: Money, power and the origins of our time.* Verso.

BBC News. (2015). England's medieval immigrants revealed by universities published 17 February 2015. https://www.bbc.com/news/uk-england-york-north-yorkshire-31462885. Accessed 2 June 2023.

Bernet, B. (2020). The post war Marxist milieu of microhistory. In B. Zachariah, L. Raphael, & B. Bernet (Eds.), *What's left of marxism.* Oldenbourg.

Borsch, S. J., & Sabraa, T. (2016). Plague mortality in late medieval Cairo: Quantifying the plague outbreaks of 833/1430 and 864/1460. *Mamlūk Studies Review, XIX, 2016*, 115–148.

Braudel, F. (1988). History and the social sciences: The *Longue Durée*. In M. Aymard & H. Mukhia (Eds.), *French studies in history* (Vol.1). Hyderabad.

Braudel, F. (1995). *Mediterranean and the Mediterranean World in the reign of Philip II (Vol. 1 & 2).* Berkeley

Bury, J. B. (1963). *A History of Greece, London.* Macmillan

Carrard, P. (1995). *Poetics of the new history, Fr. historical discourses from Braudel to Chartier*. Baltimore.

Cipolla, C. M. (1979). *Faith, reason and plague in seventeenth century Tuscany.* W.W. Norton and Company.

Cipolla, C. M. (1981). *Fontana economic history of Europe, the middle ages*. Collins/Fontana.
Crary, J. (2013). *24/7. Late capitalism and the ends of sleep*. London.
de Vries, J. (2019). Playing with scales: The global and the micro, the macro and the nano. *Past and Present, 242*(Suppl. 14), 23–36.
Eliot, T. S. (2004). Four quartets—Burnt Norton. In *Complete plays and poems* (p. 171). Faber and Faber.
Fryxell, A. R. P. (2019). Time and modern: Current trends in the history of modern temporalities. *Past and Present, 243*, 285–298.
Gandhi, G. K. (2021). Identical horror. *The Telegraph* (Kolkata).
Ghobrial, J.-P. A. (2019). Introduction: Seeing the world like a microhistorian. *Past & Present, 242*(14), 14.
Ghosh, A. (2021). Amitav Ghosh on Priya Satia's books: 'History has given us tools for upending dominant narratives'. *Scroll.in*. https://scroll.in/article/998495/amitav-ghosh-on-priya-satias-books-history-has-given-us-tools-for-upending-dominant-narratives. Accessed 2 June 2023
Habib, I. (1995). *Capitalism and history*. Paschim Banga Itihas Samsad.
Hartog, F. (2015). *Regimes of historicity: Presentism and experiences of time*. Columbia University Press.
Holmes, G. (Ed.) (1990). *The Oxford illustrated history of medieval Europe*. Oxford University Press (Paperback Edition).
Koselleck, R. (2004). *Futures past: On the semantics of historical time* (K. Tribe, Trans.). Columbia University Press.
Ladurie, E. L. R. (1979). *The territory of the historian*. The Harvester Press.
Levi, G. (1992), On microhistory. In P. Burke (Ed.) *New perspectives on historical* writing (p. 96). University Park.
Levi, G. (2019). Fall frontiers? *Past and Present, 242*(Sppl.14), 37–49.
Champion, M. S. (2019). A fuller history of temporalities. *Past and Present, 243*, 255–266.
Morton, A. L. (1984). *A people's history of England*. Lawrence and Wishart.
Mukharji, P. B. (2021). Mahamarir bhut (The ghost of the epidemic). *Anandabazar Patrika (Robibasariyo)*.
Ogle, V. (2019). Time, temporality and the history of capitalism. *Past and Present, 243*, 312–327.
Samaddar, R. (Ed.). (2020). *Borders of a pandemic: Covid-19 and migrant workers*. Mahanirban Calcutta Research Group.
Samaddar, R. (2021). *A pandemic and the politics of life*. Women Unlimited.
Satia, P. (2020). *Time's monsters: How history makes history*. Harvard University Press.
Tomich, D. (2011). The order of historical time: The *Longue Duree* and micro-history. *Almanac. Guarulhos, 2*, 52–65.
Wallerstein, I. (1974). *The modern world system* (Vol. 1).
Wright, L. (2021). Lawrence Wright traces the parallels between the Black Death and the COVID-19 pandemic. *Lit Hub*. https://lithub.com/lawrence-wright-traces-the-parallels-covid-19-pandemic/. Accessed 15 June 2021

Chapter 3
Locating the Diseased Body

Paula Banerjee

Abstract If we consider the last few decades as part of the long twenty-first century, it can easily be termed as the age of pandemics. The twentieth century closed with the AIDS epidemic and the twenty-first began with the SARS virus that was identified in 2003. The AIDS, the northern world decided began in Africa and the first known infections of SARS, it was speculated, appeared in Guangdong Province of China in 2002, so the world heaved a sigh of relief because it could now be logged as the Chinese pandemic. The SARS was followed by the swine-origin H1N1 in 2009, and this time it was Mexico. The world was caught up in H5N1 from Asia and then came H1N1. The trope that pandemics only affect poor countries lived on and the global North again remained under-prepared but happy that such diseases did not touch them. The diseased body was happily located elsewhere. It will not be remiss to say that this hunt for "Patient Zero," which today is more a metaphor than a real person, has been a recurring phenomenon in the last few hunts for the pandemic. In this paper I seek to address a few questions: (1) In any pandemic in the long 2020 why has finding the diseased body become such a crucial aspect of disease management? Is it more to do with ordering of society or rather fear of social disorder? (2) How did the idea of locating the diseased body come to exert such a strong influence on popular imagination? (3) What are the essential elements in this hunt for a diseased body? And why pandemics always lead to this hunt? (4) Is this a recent phenomenon? If not, then why has it acquired such significance in this present times?

Keywords AIDS · "Patient Zero" · SARS · China · USA

> When the next major pandemic strikes, it will be accompanied by something never before seen in human history: an explosion of billions of texts, tweets, emails, blogs, photos and videos, rocketing across the planets computer's and mobile devices. Some of these billions of words and pictures will have information, but many will be filled with rumors, innuendo, misinformation, and hyper-sensational claims. (Walker, 2016: 43)

P. Banerjee (✉)
Asian Institute of Technology, Bangkok, Thailand
e-mail: paulabanerjee44@gmail.com

MCRG, Kolkata, India

S. R. Chakraborty et al. (eds.), *The Long 2020*, India Studies in Business and Economics, https://doi.org/10.1007/978-981-99-4815-4_3

On 16th of March 2021, the killing of eight women of whom six were Asians by a 21-year-old white man, Robert Aaron Long, rocked Atlanta. (*The New York Times,* 17/3/2021) This came after a year of misinformation when the 45th US President, Donald J. Trump, and the right-wing media spread falsehoods about the causes of the origin and expansion of Covid-19 in the United States. The right-wing media gleefully quoted the former American President terming the novel coronavirus as "China Virus," or "Kung Flu." According to one media report, "Many have cited former President Trump as one of the top reasons for the widespread and rapid growth of violence against Asian Americans, especially since the outbreak of the COVID-19 pandemic." (Kai, 2021) This horrific incident and then the subsequent attacks on the older Asian population in the USA once again portrayed how a pandemic produces its own scapegoats. Hence it is not unfair to say that each pandemic in recent history has sought the original diseased body or bodies. Much of this investigation for the origin of the disease is crouched in scientific terms. This is not to challenge the scientific mind that might argue that an approximation of the origin of a disease can point to its remission or cure. But it cannot be denied that there is a politics that guides this investigation. Much of the public health policy in this long 2020 has been to seek a diseased body that is already a symbol of suspicion and alienation, so that it can be finally quarantined and contained. The long 2020 is in fact an age of "contagion" and containment. It is also an age of xenophobia that is built on an intense suspicion of the "other" from the "outside." The more technology makes the world connected the more there is suspicion of the "foreign" and efforts to contain it by multiplying borders. This paper intends to portray how the search for the original diseased body or patient zero has much to do with efforts to keep the unwanted out or safely contained. The perceived contagion therefore is not the disease but the 'first' carrier who is susceptible because of certain inherent weaknesses to foreign contagions from outside of one's borders.

3.1 Introduction

A few years before Covid-19, Richard A McKay in his book *Patient Zero and the Making of the AIDS Epidemic* wrote:

> In our daily lives we most frequently use words, stories, and images to interpret external phenomena and express our understanding of the world, and so it is vital to see these elements as an essential, constitutive part of our reality and not simply a neutral, natural label or a depiction of how things "actually" are in the world. (McKay, 2017: 6)

Patient Zero was a HIV positive flight attendant named Gaetan Dugas who got a job as flight attendant in Air Canada in 1974 and was both flamboyant and handsome. In 1980 Dugas suffered from Kaposi's sarcoma, a rare skin cancer. This later came to be known as "Gay cancer." Dugas participated in a study on cluster of gay men who had AIDS. This study was the basis for a 1987 book called *And the Band Played On.* In that book Dugas was marked as Patient Zero. The story of patient zero occupies only eleven pages in the book but the publicist asked the author, Randy Shilts, to pull out this case for the sake of sensational publicity. The publicist Michael Denneny to Shilts: "You pull this material out and present it to the New York Post, a miserably homophobic newspaper. This story has everything you want. It has beauty, it has depth, he's an airline steward and, best of all, a foreigner. They're going to eat it up." (Johnson, 2019) Dugas was shamelessly vilified long after his death as people accepted a "big lie" that he infected a huge number of people wilfully and without remorse. Dugas was both homosexual and a foreigner, and therefore he was the perfect prototype to be a scapegoat. Posthumously these charges against Dugas were proven fraudulent, but the lie persisted in popular discourse.

If we consider the last few decades as part of the long twenty-first century in it, we have witnessed multiple examples of contagion, containment and xenophobia. The twentieth century closed with the AIDS epidemic and the twenty-first began with the SARS virus that was identified in 2003. People spent days debating on the uncertain animal reservoir that ultimately infected humans. AIDS, the northern world decided, began in Africa and the first known infections of SARS, it was speculated, appeared in Guangdong Province of China in 2002 so the world heaved a sigh of relief because it could now be logged as the Chinese epidemic. The SARS was followed by the swine-origin H1N1 in 2009, and this time it was Mexico. The world was caught up in H5N1 from Asia and then came H1N1. Now the blame game was centred on another poor, impoverished exotic culture and the global North could easily blame another underdeveloped country albeit with a rich history but an impoverished economy.

The Middle East Respiratory Syndrome or MERS soon burst into the scene, and it broke at least one widely held assumption. Prior to this outbreak, the strange and exotic forests of Africa, and the crowded urban slums of Asia, where people lived crowded lives with their rats, chickens and swine were considered the two most important birthplaces for new human pathogens, but not anymore. However, the global North now argued that whatever happens in the Arab world stays among the Arabs so the "civilised" Western world forgot all about the disease and perpetrated the myth that all these diseases are foreign. Then came Ebola and although it attacked the rich and the poor alike but after all it originated in Africa. The world remained unconscious because if Europe and the United States were not affected then everyone could sleep peacefully. The diseased body was happily located elsewhere.

Much of the politics of ascribing the source of the disease has to do with questions of authority and representation. It will not be remiss to say that this hunt for "Patient Zero," which today is more a metaphor than a real person, has been a recurring phenomenon in the last few hunts for the pandemic. Locating the diseased body has now become an industry with fancy surveillance systems all in the name of science. As one report suggests:

> Contact tracing in an Ebola virus disease (EVD) outbreak is the process identifying individuals who may have been exposed to infected persons with the virus, followed by monitoring for 21 days (the maximum incubation period) from the date of the most recent exposure. The goal is to achieve detection and isolation of any new cases in order to prevent further transmission. (Senga et al., 2017: 1)

From this the leap to the original diseased body is but a short one. And herein begins my study.

In this paper I seek to address the history of embodying contagion among population groups that were already considered as different, inferior or alien. It did not happen unconsciously. I argue that there was a conscious will that categorised diseases on the basis of race, ethnicity or even nationality. Disease then became a determinative for who is part of the privileged community and who is not, who is preferred and who is not. In investigating the history of how the sickling disease has been located in the "black body" one social scientist made a relevant point. She said:

> I want to show how sickling became inscribed within a racialist discourse network, thus investing this network with a remarkable efficacy as a marker of racial difference. I will show how sickling came to be used in safe- guarding and [re]producing racial bodies and their differential signs; how sickling became employed as a litmus test to specify who is black and who is white and as an instrument for policing the boundaries between one group of people defined as black and another defined as white. My point is not to deny that certain diseases are present in some populations while absent in others but, rather, to identify the discourses that make it possible to account for such a distribution of disease in terms of race. Indeed, I want to argue that the discourse network within which a disease occurs is an integral part of that disease. (Tapper, 1995: 77)

In this paper I hope to take the argument even further. I argue that finding the diseased body has become so crucial in the long 2020 because this is how borders are re-inscribed and redrafted, and citizenship is [re] marked/produced. It is not incidental then that battles are habitually fought over race, ethnicity, political ideology, class and gender in times of epi/pandemic. The present pandemic is no exception and that is why movements such as "black lives matter," in the United States or restitution of rites of migrant workers in India acquire such immediacy and urgency. Hence the history of embodying pandemic in the long 2020 becomes critical. This paper traces such a history and recalibrates how contagions find its population groups for the purpose of marking who belongs and who does not.

3.2 How Diseases Were Embodied

In sum, the "poisonous quality" ("qualita velenosa") of the plague, as Ficino terms it in other parts of the text, passes more easily from the sick to the healthy when they share similar natures. In a way it is analogous to the transference of quality between similar elements—transferring to the second that unhealthy state which was already present in the first. (Katinis, 2010: 77–78).

Teodoro Katinis in one of his articles discussed how Marsilio Ficini was of the opinion about the plague in Florence in 1478–1479, that it spread from people to people faster if the two people were of "similar natures." It was the similarities between the two people that attracted the poison from one body to another and destroyed the "vital spirit" of an organism. The fact that disease needed a body to manifest itself was something that was obvious from antiquity but what Ficini's discourse contributed to was that certain bodies were more likely to "attract" the poison faster or more severely than the others. Therefore, it stands to reason that certain bodies were more fallible than the rest. From this the move to locate these bodies in certain geographical locales was but a short leap.

> A particularly striking aspect of the MSTree is the strong geographical clustering of populations (Supplementary Fig. 2). Isolates from China are scattered in multiple populations over ancestral branch 0, which evolved >2,600 ya, as well as branches 1 and 2, which split from branch 0 at least 728 ya. At the base of branch 0, Chinese populations
>
> 0.PE4 and 0.PE7 are intermingled with populations 0.PE1 through 0.PE3 from the Former Soviet Union. (Morelli et al., 2010: 3)

Bubonic plague, it was stated, originated from China through genomic sequencing and then spread to the Soviet Union. There are other scholars who argued that: "This transcontinental spread of *Yersinia pestis* could quite likely have occurred long before antiquity and have caused spread all the way back to China," but the popular discourse preferred China as the place of origin for the plague. (Wiechmann et al., 2012: 70) In the *Encyclopaedia Britannica* too this narrative found a space, "Having originated in China and Inner Asia, the Black Death decimated the army of the Kipchak khan Janibeg while he was besieging the Genoese trading port of Kaffa (now Feodosiya) in Crimea (1347). With his forces disintegrating, Janibeg catapulted plague-infested corpses into the town in an effort to infect his enemies."[1] This example, whether factual or not, portrays how diseases were not just embodied but how diseased bodies were then used as sources of threat. These threat perceptions then became the ground for redrawing borders.

Apart from the plague the other major disease that routed nations before the twentieth century was cholera. This disease was blamed on India. Debates in contemporary medical journals portrayed how national borders were redrawn around diseases. In one of these journals a doctor is quoted saying that:

> Thus, cholera is peculiar to India, yellow fever to America, intermittent fever to Africa, and so forth. He did not think that the carcasses of the animals sacrificed by the pilgrims to Mecca could account for the epidemic. Africa should, on these grounds, be constantly ravaged; and the plains of La Plata, where thousands of cattle were slaughtered, should be likewise infected. He was of the opinion that the malady should be combated in the very place of its origin; namely, India. The measures which the French Government recently suggested, should not be limited to Cairo or Constantinople, but be extended to India. ("Cholera", 1865: 447)

In another research work on cholera historian Asa Briggs argues how cholera or treatment of it created *cordon sanitaires* around different groups of people. He stated that:

> Differences of opinion about the value of *cordons sanitaires* tended to divide "conservatives" (particularly conservatives with military experience) and "reformers". Yet the reformers themselves were often divided too. In England Hume tended to dismiss all cholera precautions as alarmist he does not emerge well from the debates despite his professed concern for "civil liberties"- while Henry Warburton, philosophical radical and pioneer of medical

[1] https://www.britannica.com/event/Black-Death

> reform, made it clear that enlightened laissez-faire was not the same as "Turkish indolence". When George Robinson pressed as hard as he could for "gentle" control of cholera in the interests of commerce, Warburton retaliated that while "the mercantile interest was no doubt of great moment ... the public safety was a matter of permanent importance". In his view it was because of "mercantile activity and mercantile avarice and jealousy" that cholera had spread around the world. (Briggs, 1961: 83)

Thus experiences of plague and cholera and their interpretation by modern-day historians and social scientists show how the threat of the disease is transferred to the body that lodges it. Then the cause of disease becomes a marker of difference, whether they be national or ideological or philosophical, on the basis of which borders are redrawn. Hierarchies are created on the basis of these new borders. When borders of hierarchies are sketched, these were infused with notions of pollution and filth. Early modern medical journals equated contagion with filth. The *Moniteur* of France counselled the sick in the following manner. "The counsels are reduced to very simple precepts. These are scrupulous personal cleanliness, warm clothing, cleanliness in habitations, removal of filth of every kind, ventilation, ordinary regimen, the usual food, provided it be not prejudicial to health, and the absence of all excess." ("Cholera" 1865: 447) Clearly what was required was cleanliness and lack of excess, or in other words control. So the disease was equated with lack of or loss of control. Therefore medical policing was necessary and that expanded the role of state administration and brought it directly in control of bodies under its jurisdiction. As one commentator states, "All this necessitated the growth of local administrative machines and an expansion of state power, the invention of 'medical police' in fact. It also implied serious restrictions on individual liberty and provoked opposition for that reason, among others." (Slack, 1988: 433–434).

What made contagion so difficult to control was the understanding that contagion always appeared from foreign realms. As one historian specialising on the Ottoman Empire comments:

> Strikingly, the comparative notion of judging an 'other' civilisation as the origin of an epidemic disease was also not limited to European authors. Admittedly, even the ancient Greek Thucydides, the fabled 'father of history', contended that the plague that struck Athens in 430 BCE originated in East Africa and travelled to Greece via Egypt and Persia.31 Fourteenth-century European writers likewise believed that the Black Death came from central Asia. (Bulmus, 2012: 47-48)

What made diseases most threatening was its embodiment and its foreign origin. It is through embodiment that it became communicable or rather as some scholars call it a "contagion." According to them, "Contagion signifies the dangers circulating in social bodies and in populations—actual viruses and bacteria, 'contagious' morals and ideas, social dangers re-thought as bodily infectiveness." (Bashford & Hooker, 2001: 10–11) The word "contagion" is often contested and problematised by critical theorists as well as historians of medical sciences more specific and targeted, without necessarily discarding it. Pernick observes, "as contagion became equated with modern microbiology in mass culture, the term was dropped from the lexicon of medical science." (Pernick, 2002: 858–865) While the Latin root of the word etymologically referred to "touching," it also acquired a metaphorical currency during the period of European imperial expansion.

Before the twenty-first century there were as we see efforts to associate disease with undesirable bodies or undesirable lifestyles. But with the advancement of science, the embodiment of disease became associated with lodging the disease in population groups. Disease escaped the sanitarians and began to be explained by the germ theorists. These germ theorists were those who worked in laboratories and employed scientific means. These scientists had to work with those who could fund their studies and in the modern times the funders were largely administrators who governed the state, such as politicians and bureaucrats. Science then needed its patrons, and these were politicians with a motive. The motive to discriminate came from the notion that the contagion is always from the outside. Hence the effort to find patient zero became also an effort to find where it can be lodged and which population group can be held responsible.

3.3 HIV and Locating Patient Zero

In the nineteenth and twentieth centuries, understanding or studies of disease was progressively centred on the global north. What affected the Afro-Asian continents did not matter to what affected the north. It cannot be denied that there was a racial character to these understandings. Therefore the "Spanish" influenza of 1918 has often been termed as the "mother of all pandemics." (Chowell & Viboud, 2016: 13557) One of the most eminent epidemiologists of the present times, Anthony Fauci and his collaborator wrote:

> the 1918–1919 "Spanish flu" pandemic was among the deadliest public-health crises in human history, killing an estimated 675,000 people in the United States and an estimated 50–100 million people worldwide. This pandemic's explosive and still-unexplained patterns of rapidly recurrent waves and predilection to kill the young and healthy [5–7] cast an element of urgency… (Morens & Fauci, 2007: 1018)

Even though the American connection of this pandemic was unmistakable in popular parlance it was termed the Spanish flu and its World War I origins were constantly stressed. Even the *Encyclopaedia Britannica* says the following:

> The pandemic occurred in three waves. The first apparently originated in early March 1918, during World War I. Although it remains uncertain where the virus first emerged, it quickly spread through Western Europe, and by July it had spread to Poland. The first wave of influenza was comparatively mild. However, during the summer a more lethal type of disease was recognized, and this form fully emerged in August 1918.[2]

Therefore foreign origins of medical threats continued in popular tropes. For a long time after the Influenza of 1918 seemingly there were no pandemics affecting

---

[2] The Editors of *Encyclopaedia Britannica*, https://www.britannica.com/event/influenza-pandemic-of-1918-1919.

the northern world. Asia and Africa might be dealing with its viral fevers, malaria, diarrhoea, etc., but the West was contained. This sense of peace was shattered by HIV. In the early 1980s a disease with new and unusual symptoms began to appear in different parts of the world. In the United States a benign form of skin cancer called Kaposi's sarcoma, named after Moritz Kaposi, who discovered this disease in 1872, an affliction that was common among the elderly began affecting the younger population in cities such as New York and San Francisco. This disease was often accompanied by a new and virulent form of pneumonia. In the 1980s many of those affected were young homosexual men. Pundits trying to explain away the disease latched on to that fact and described it as a homosexual disease caused by sexual excesses practised by gay men. Again we can see stringent calls for controlling the aberrant and blaming them for sexual excesses. Cities such as San Francisco were devastated. A contemporary media outlet reported:

> In San Francisco much of the fear spawned by the disease is justified. Social and economic changes are transforming the city's homosexual community in response to the growing awareness of how AIDS is transmitted. Recently, business in bars, bathhouses and clubs that cater to men seeking anonymous sexual contact has declined markedly. At least two bath houses have closed. Others are posting public-health warning signs at the city's request. Conceded Hal Slate, owner of the Caldron, one of the estimated 300 homosexual clubs in San Francisco: "The sex business is, if you will excuse the pun, soft." The Caldron now posts signs advising patrons of supposed ways to maintain good health even while engaging in frequent, undiscriminating sex: "Spend more time with your partner," urges one sign. "Get to know him—before moving on to another."[3]

The gay community themselves became traumatised. The attack largely from the right wing kept mounting. Like any movements the attacks against the gay community found its most in/famous proponent in Jerry Falwell. In July 1983 Jerry Falwell's newsletter, *The Moral Majority Report*, had a picture on its cover showing a typical American family, with the headline, "Homosexual Disease Threaten American Family."[4] Falwell made many outrageous remarks of which most in/famous was, "Aids is not just God's punishment for homosexuals, it is God's punishment for the society that tolerates homosexuals," and "The idea that religion and politics don't mix was invented by the devil to keep Christians from running their own country." (Reed, 2007) Falwell continued his diatribe against the gay community influencing millions and his moral majority movement attracted 6.5 million followers. In 1984,

> Falwell called the gay-friendly Metropolitan Community Church "a vile and Satanic system" that will "one day be utterly annihilated and there will be a celebration in heaven." Members of these churches, Falwell added, are "brute beasts." Falwell initially denied his statements, offering Jerry Sloan, an MCC minister and gay rights activist $5,000 to prove that he had made them. When Sloan produced a videotape containing footage of Falwell's denunciations, the reverend refused to pay. (Blumenthal, 2007)

Following Falwell there were many others who condemned and vilified the homosexual community. There were other religious denominations that attacked the homosexual community with virulence. In a message to Veronica Leuken, the Lady and

---

[3] https://archive.macleans.ca/article/1983/8/1/a-crisis-of-mounting-aids-hysteria

[4] AIDS (1983), https://hivaids.omeka.net/items/show/9.

Lords of the Roses stated: "My children I shall not allow the scientific world to find a cure for AIDS because of the horrible nature of what brings on this disease called AIDS. It is being flaunted now as though the good were to be stomped upon and the bad shall receive the glory."[5] The lethal nature of the disease and the attacks on the homosexual diseased bodies drove many to hide the disease. Also it shifted attention from the heterosexual transmission of the disease and mother-to-child transmissions. Even as early as in 1984 when testing was symptomatic and not systematic, there were 2848 cases in New York City. Among these over a thousand (1010 is the number) were heterosexual men and women. One reviewer complained that even the CDC was biased against homosexuals. He said, "the CDC's so-called hierarchical presentation does accomplish one thing: it de-emphasises and under-represents every patient characteristic *except* homosexuality. One cannot help suspecting a theological mind-set behind this statistical misrepresentation of reality: That which is most 'sinful' is presumed also to be the most dangerous." (Lauritsen, 1993: 16)

There were some push-backs to these attacks. One book that became very popular was Alan Cantwell's *AIDS and the Doctors of Disease*. In it Cantwell made the fantastic claim that the deep state in conjunction with the market infected the homosexual population of the United States. He elaborated upon his meeting with another doctor Robert Strecker, who was of the opinion that gay men were injected with the virus when they volunteered to take part in an experiment in Hepatitis B vaccine trials in New York (Cantwell Jr. 1988). Such discourse might have challenged the reasons why homosexual men were getting afflicted with the disease but it did not challenge the notion that AIDS was a gay epidemic. When it became known that other population groups were also getting affected by the disease the narrative was changed somewhat. In the next story it was the central African primates that were the cause of the disease. It apparently jumped species and then entered the black African population. Then the virus travelled to Haiti and after attacking the heterosexual population there it latched on to gay men in Manhattan. There were a lot of inconsistencies in this narrative but it did attract popular attention. There were media reports that pushed back on attacks faced by homosexual men. When people went on a frenzy about children who were born in households with AIDS risk there were witch hunts against homosexuals living therein. In one report it was stated:

> What the media failed to report, however, was that most important AIDS researchers and government health officials in the United States immediately cautioned against drawing conclusions from incomplete news reports on the article which did not sufficiently emphasize the fact that each of the eight children lived in households where one or both parents were immigrants from Haiti or the Dominican Republic or were intravenous drug users.[6]

When the attack was diverted from the homosexual community, it was predictably directed towards the foreign element such as people from Haiti and Dominican Republic in this case. According to the CDC, by 1983 there were 15 European

---

[5] Message of Our Lady and our Lords to Veronica Leuken, "AIDS-Plague From God: I shall Not Allow a Cure, " Roses, 21 August 1985, https://wellcomecollection.org/works/e7qc88kx accessed on 13 September 2021.

[6] https://archive.macleans.ca/article/1983/8/1/a-crisis-of-mounting-aids-hysteria

countries, seven Latin American countries, Canada, Zaire, Haiti, Australia and Japan all reported the presence of HIV-positive patients in their countries.[7] But somehow it was the Haitians or the Africans who were blamed.

The United States was not the only country where blame was put on the outsiders for HIV and AIDS. In the USSR also there were similar efforts but this time the blame apparently lay with the West. Pyotr Nikolayevich Burgasov, the former deputy minister of public health, chief state public health physician of USSR in 1985 said:

> AIDS is a dangerous disease; it must not be underestimated. No cases of this disease have been reported here in our country. The reason for this is that the problem is largely a social one, since it is connected with sexual promiscuity—this, alas, is tolerated in certain circles in the West, but it is unnatural for our society … Nevertheless, we are carefully studying all aspects of the new disease, for we do not live in isolation in the world. (Fesbach, 2006: 7)

For a minister of the former Soviet Union of course it was the West that was to blame. By denying the existence of HIV/AIDS in his country he was essentially driving an already vulnerable population underground. There is no doubt that even before the Soviet Union collapsed HIV had invaded the Soviet lands simply because the disease had little to do with culture or mores but for political purposes it made a good copy to blame the West. A social scientist, Murray Feshbach commented: "When officials did admit that some of these behaviors existed in the Soviet Union, they placed the blame on foreigners and Western countries for "infecting" Soviet citizens, contaminating Soviets with their social ills, and, according to a disinformation campaign, producing the HIV virus in a laboratory to attack the world." (Ibid: 8) Much of this was not surprising as in the long 2020 origin of disease was always dependent on political will. And the political will used these narratives of origin to further their interest. Apart from foreigners in Russia the intravenous drug users were also vilified, which proves our contention that it was either the foreigners or the deviants who were blamed for epi/pandemics.

As for Europe one study describes that, "of the first few hundred cases of AIDS diagnosed in Europe, about half occurred among patients coming from central Africa, mostly from Zaire. Over the following years, the epidemiology of HIV-1 infection in Kinshasa would be described in great detail by a group of American, Belgian and Congolese researchers known as Project Sida, based at Hospital Mama Yemo." (Pepin, 2011: 6) The European story of origin, like its American counterpart, focussed on Africa as the place of origin of HIV/AIDS. But there was no mention of Haiti. Although studies on Africa often concentrate on trying to prove why Central Africa can be considered as the source, such proofs are tenuous, usually done by scholars from outside the region. The proof is often the presence of a certain variety of chimpanzees. Whatever may be the source, this dependence on theories about AIDS originating from primates makes it easier for people to think of it as a deviance.

Even in the case of India HIV/AIDs was thought of as an aberration. In 1985 a young microbiologist, Sellappan Nirmala under the guidance of her mentor, Suniti Solomon tested women from Chennai's red light area and found the dreaded virus present among six sex workers. I have written extensively on this in other volumes.

---

[7] https://www.publichealth.org/public-awareness/hiv-aids/origin-story/

(Banerjee, 2010: 160–197) For our purposes it will suffice to quote Nirmala who later commented to BBC that:

> The press at the time wrote that HIV was a disease of the "debauched West" where "free sex and homosexuality" were prevalent. Indians, on the other hand, were portrayed as heterosexual, monogamous and God-fearing.
>
> Some papers even remarked smugly that by the time the disease reached India, the Americans would have found a cure for it.
>
> Also, the city of Chennai and the surrounding Tamil Nadu region were considered especially traditional societies. Hundreds of samples, collected from the supposedly more promiscuous city of Mumbai, had already been tested at the virology institute in the western city of Pune and no positive results had turned up so far. (Pandey, 2016)

In India, although the homosexual community was not blamed the sex workers were equally threatened as a community and equally discriminated against. This overzealous attention to sex workers, especially those who catered to men from across the border, diverted attention from other affected category. The foreign origin of AIDS was stressed in the case of India as well. (Sharma et al., 2019)

This single-minded attention to certain "aberrant" groups and efforts to focus on the foreign element was extremely detrimental to many at-risk groups. The UNAIDS Fact Sheet from 2020 clearly states the following:

> Every week, around 5000 young women aged 15–24 years become infected with HIV.
>
> In sub-Saharan Africa, six in seven new HIV infections among adolescents aged 15–19 years are among girls. Young women aged 15–24 years are twice as likely to be living with HIV than men. Around 4200 adolescent girls and young women aged 15–24 years became infected with HIV every week in 2020.
>
> More than one-third (35%) of women around the world have experienced physical and/or sexual violence by an intimate partner or sexual violence by a non-partner at some time in their lives.
>
> In some regions, women who have experienced physical or sexual intimate partner violence are 1.5 times more likely to acquire HIV than women who have not experienced such violence. (UNAIDS 2021)

These population groups were not studied in the initial period. The purpose of locating the original diseased body was neither to advance research nor to find who was at risk. I contend that the purpose of this exercise was to blame certain "deviance" and "secure" the borders so that social unrest could be kept at bay. These were also years of right-wing resurgence with Margaret Thatcher in England and Ronald Reagan in the United States. The purpose was to mark the 60 s and 70 s as years of left-wing excesses and "debauchery" that resulted in dreaded "afflictions." With a missionary zeal the intention was to protect the borders against any unwanted and foreign influence. The threat therefore was always from the outside. As in much of the long 2020 experiences from the years of HIV/AIDS were to shape future discourses on public health. After all, the entire world got its Patient Zero because of the HIV/AIDS epidemic and the tragedy of Gaetan Dugas exemplified the falsity and politics of this quest. But this did not save the countries that were severely affected from inevitable destabilisation or the lesson that. But the quest to find the original diseased body continued. As the politics in the United States portrayed this quest merely led to marking the hated homosexual community as diseased thereby making them pariah. After all, Reagan was not going to help the same community, vilifying whom he came to power. Patient Zero just strengthened the case for Reagan and the "moral majority" to ignore a disease that would eventually kill thousands of Americans and millions the world over.

3.4 Flu and Blame Game

Recent UNAIDS reports state that 1997 can be considered as the peak of the HIV/ AIDS epidemic. (Ibid) In the new millennia the sensation of AIDS gave way to other public health sensations, and much of these were different forms of flu or flu-like epidemic beginning with SARS, Avian Flu, Swine Flu, MERS and Ebola. As I have mentioned earlier for many of these diseases the West or the global north had ready answers of who to blame. The SARS was a result of Chinese excesses. It was extensively argued that the disease must be a result of the Chinese exotic food habits and lifestyle and so the Atlantic world had nothing to worry as this disease was of foreign origin. Among the first group of people infected with SARS 1 were food handlers, chefs and one person who sold live animals to the market. But none of the early cases were peasants or poultry farmers who dealt with livestock. (Xu et al., 2004) But there was little evidence that, "Acute Respiratory Syndrome (SARS), a previously unknown virus believed to have emerged from the wet markets of Guangdong province before spreading into major cities," or was a result of Chinese excesses. (Stanway, 2020) Later media reports blamed certain kinds of bats but even then there were doubts. One report suggests:

> Later surveys revealed large numbers of SARS-related coronaviruses circulating in China's horseshoe bats (Rhinolophus)2—suggesting that the deadly strain probably originated in the bats, and later passed through civets before reaching humans. But crucial genes—for a protein that allows the virus to latch onto and infect cells—were different in the human and known bat versions of the virus, leaving room for doubt about this hypothesis.[8]

However, the myth of Chinese wet markets persisted. China remained the rogue country that helped to cover up a virus that killed hundreds and had the potential to kill thousands. Although it was said that in April 2003 China started cooperating with WHO and in late April: "The Beijing mayor and health minister were held responsible for the initial covering up of the disease and were sacked." (Hung, 2004: 24–25) Even then the popular perception that China was responsible for SARS persisted.

Interestingly H1N1 was a flu-like disease that did not originate in China but apparently travelled from Mexico. The WHO raised the Pandemic alert to Phase 6 on 11 June 2009. Beijing had detailed plans of combatting the virus by maximising intervention to reduce morbidity and mortality of the Chinese people with minimum

[8] Bat cave solves mystery of deadly SARS virus—and suggests new outbreak could occur (2017).

disruption of essential services. The whole structure was built around dealing with "imported cases." The method was described by the Chinese as:

> We implemented border entry screening (BES), ILI screening in hospitals, medical follow-up of travelers from overseas, and quarantine of close contacts. Public health workers conducted rigorous epidemiological investigations on each imported case (including detected subclinical infections), subsequently tracing and placing close contacts, whose residence fell within the jurisdiction of Beijing, under quarantine in designated hotels that were rented by the government as quarantine stations. Throat swabs for testing were collected from each close contact before quarantine and after clinical symptoms occurred during the quarantine period. This provided us with a good opportunity to describe the characteristics of imported cases of 2009 HINI influenza and to assess the effectiveness of public health intervention measures. (Zhang et al., 2012: 933)

Interestingly the one time that a flu epidemic that was not globally blamed on China, made Chinese officials target people from across the border, largely those coming from North and South America.

The next flu epidemic of 2012 was said to have originated in Saudi Arabia. When two people with MERS were detected in the United States the Arab world was blamed for it. The advisory from CDC about people with increased risk among others were those who had exposure to camels.[9] The fear of MERS persisted and news of new mutations made people even more nervous. Intermittent news such as these kept trickling in: "In 2017, one Middle East respiratory syndrome (MERS) patient in Riyadh was responsible for directly infecting 16 patients, leading to an outbreak that infected 44 people in the surrounding area in just over a fortnight."[10] Before the MERS had run its course the Ebola burst on the scene. The WHO declared Ebola a public health emergency of international concern in August 2014. Again it was Africa that was to blame. There were over 28,000 infected and over 11,000 dead in the three countries of Guinea, Sierra Leone and Liberia. Liberia and Sierra Leonie were trying to build a public health system after years of civil war. Fears stigmatised not just the diseased but also the health workers and people with other major illnesses stayed away from health centres and became progressively ill and often died. Yet the disease was eroticised in the racist propaganda and African rituals were blamed for the spread of the disease even when it was discovered in Spain and the United States. One Indian journalist analysing the global media said that:

> in their very framing, global health agencies that laid claim to being the international arbiters of "safe and dignified burials" implied local practices of caring for the Ebola-deceased (and living) were backward, primitive and detrimental to the virus's elimination. Global media reportage racially exoticised the African "natives" and characterised their "traditional burials" and "funerary rituals" as "super spreaders". Local religious and tribal beliefs were thus rendered antithetical and unethical from the point of view of international health agencies and modern Western media. (Pandhi, 2021)

These exotic twists in narratives reinforced the foreignness of the origin of these diseases. For the global North that designed the discourse on public health the

---

[9] https://www.cdc.gov/coronavirus/mers/index.html

[10] The rapid journey of a deadly MERS outbreak (2019).

diseased body remained either the deviant or the exotic and foreign. Pandemic was always an outside threat.

3.5 A Full Circle: Covid-19 and the Diseased Body

On 5 August 2021 Governor De Santis of Florida declared "Joe Biden has the nerve to tell me to get out of the way on COVID while he lets COVID-infected migrants pour over our southern border by the hundreds of thousands." (Kessler, 2021) Such sentiments sent shock waves through the international human rights community. When Joe Biden and Kamala Harris won the Presidential and Vice Presidential elections in the USA in November 2020, there was a sense of jubilation among human rights groups in much of the underprivileged world. This was because there were feelings among these groups that the Biden administration would be different from that of Donald Trump at least as far as immigration policies are concerned. Thousands of unaccompanied minors appear every year on the US-Mexico border. Donald Trump and his administration famously termed them as "national security threat." Most of these unaccompanied minors are coming from the turbulent Central American states. According to many analysts Trump's policies amounted to a humanitarian crisis. But why do these children keep coming? "Experts say the reasons for migration are varied. Poverty, gang crime and natural disasters are some reasons that migrants may feel pushed to leave their home countries. Pandemic-related job losses could be adding to the surge...."[11] But notwithstanding the pandemic this migration has been happening for over half a century and the political conditions in Central and South America points to the fact that this migration will not abate in the recent future. One cannot deny that the unsettled condition in these countries is to a large extent due to American policies in the region. Therefore, it was heart-rending for many when Kamala Harris visited Guatemala in June 2021 and declared: "I want to be clear to folks in this region, who are thinking about making that dangerous trek to the US-Mexico border, do not come, do not come."[12] The pandemic made the situation even direr but these migrants were not the superspreader but rather the "normal" American lifestyle and the right wing that blamed liberal excesses for all public health hazards continued to be responsible for the persistence of Covid-19.

When first Covid-19 was detected in Wuhan China the American President, Donald Trump, refused to consider it to be of any threat. He reiterated American strength and preparedness. Yet when the disease spread he blamed the Asian community for the dreaded disease who were then targeted by the general population. Then he started blaming migration through the southern border. He with the help of right-wing media tried to argue that the Coronavirus itself was a conspiracy of "fake news." His message as reported in National media:

[11] Child migrants: Massive drop in children held by border officials (2021).

[12] Kamala Harris tells migrants "do not come" during talks in Guatemala (2021).

> President Donald Trump on Monday claimed the worsening coronavirus outbreak in the United States is a "Fake News Media Conspiracy," saying the nation has the most cases in the world only because "we TEST, TEST, TEST."
>
> "Corrupt Media conspiracy at all time high," Trump said in a tweet Monday morning. "On November 4th., topic will totally change," he added, referring to the day after the presidential election.[13]

Another international media outlet informed:

> The astonishing first key finding of a study by the Ithaca, New York-based Cornell University says United States President Donald Trump was "likely the largest driver of the COVID-19 misinformation 'infodemic' ". The study said that not only did "Trump mentions [comprise] 37.9% of the overall misinformation conversation", but that this was "well ahead of any other topics".[14]

American administration and right-wing media for years have marked the diseased body as deviant. The exotic foreign lifestyle was always blamed for the introduction of the disease into their island. For the perpetuation of the disease the deviants and their excesses, supported by "left-wing," liberals were blamed. As a result of this the conservatives were not willing to accept the truth that without any precaution, even a "normal" American and Christian lifestyle can still lead to the disease and its consequent morbidity and mortality. It is true that the Covid-19 proved more lethal for the poor or the minorities because they were more likely to be in the front line of Covid-19. But since the total number of deaths is 7.61 lakhs by 14 November 2021 it stands to reason not all of these can be either exotic foreigner or those with deviant lifestyle.

In case of the latest Omicron variant of Covid-19 too, the Global North countries who have relatively managed to control the spread of Covid-19 immediately imposed travel bans to and from South Africa simply based on the fact that the variant was first detected in the continent.[15] According to Tulio de Oliveira of Centre for Epidemic Response and Innovation, the fact that the variant was first detected by South African scientists does not necessarily assert that it originated there. (Zubașcu, 2021) In fact, the early detection of the mutations in the spike protein by South African scientists deserves credit because it lets other countries take precautions against the variant faster. As the South African foreign affairs ministry said, "This latest round of travel bans is akin to punishing South Africa for its advanced genomic sequencing and the ability to detect new variants quicker." This tabooing and ostracisation of South Africa and previously, India for the Delta variant, and China for Covid-19 are instances of the First World trying to shut out poorer countries and ensuring their safety while trying to make Covid-19 an entirely third-world problem like Polio was for ages.

---

[13] Lovelace (2020).

[14] Trump Falls Victim to COVID-19 Misinformation That Study Says He Spread the Most (2020).

[15] Covid: South Africa 'punished' for detecting new Omicron variant (2021).

3.6 Conclusion

Contagious diseases have always evoked fear among any population. In the long 2020 these fears found a body in the perception of the global North that has set the international narrative on public health. The HIV/AIDS crisis set the stage for responses of the global North towards the diseased body. The diseased body was a deviant body it was also a "dangerous" body. The body was often a symbol for a group of people who had the propensity to spread the disease faster and further. Often that body appeared from across the border and hence migrant bodies were considered as vehicles for the contagion. If such a false and politicised narrative led to the death of a few thousand then they were collateral damages. Often these deaths were the results of targeting of groups and that was justified because these groups were marked as different and as harbingers of all that ails the society.

Most of the world followed the narrative that was developed in the global North. Disease was always from foreign lands and the diseased body was a contagious body. Just as Patient Zero the original diseased body was also a myth. But that myth was a conscious political construction. That myth was created so that the political status quo was not disturbed. Those who suffered were told that they were suffering because of providence or because of their life choices. So the public health choices that they made were their responsibility. The minority all over the world realised the unfairness of such construction. For the first time the Covid-19 pandemic challenged this. The jury is still out on how this episode will conclude.

References

A crisis of mounting AIDS hysteria. *Dateline San Francisco*, 1 August 1983. Maclean's archive, https://archive.macleans.ca/article/1983/8/1/a-crisis-of-mounting-aids-hysteria. Accessed 15 Sept 2021.

AIDS. (1983). *Moral Majority Report*. https://hivaids.omeka.net/items/show/9. Accessed 5 Nov 2021.

Banerjee, P. (2010). *Borders, histories, existences: gender and beyond*. Sage Publications.

Bashford, A., & Hooker, C. (2001). *Contagion*. Taylor and Francis.

Bat cave solves mystery of deadly SARS virus—and suggests new outbreak could occur. (2017). *Nature*. https://www.nature.com/articles/d41586-017-07766-9. Accessed 7 Nov 2021.

Black Death. Encyclopaedia Britannica. https://www.britannica.com/event/Black-Death. Accessed 14 June 2021.

Blumenthal, M. (2007). Agent of Intolerance. *The Nation*. https://www.thenation.com/article/archive/agent-intolerance/. Accessed 6 Aug 2021.

Briggs, A. (1961). Cholera and society in the nineteenth century. *Past & Present, 19*.

Bulmus, B. (2012). *Plague, quarantines and geopolitics in the Ottoman Empire*. Edinburgh University Press.

Cantwell Jr., A. (1988). *AIDS and the doctors of death: An enquiry into the origin of AIDS epidemic*. Aries Rising Press.

Child migrants: Massive drop in children held by border officials. (2021). *BBC*. https://www.bbc.com/news/world-us-canada-56405009. Accessed 10 June 2021.

Cholera. (1865). *The British Medical Journal, 2*(252), 447. https://www.jstor.org/stable/25205066. Accessed 16 Aug 2021.

Chowell, G., & Viboud, C. (2016). Pandemic influenza and socioeconomic disparities: Lessons from 1918 Chicago. *Proceedings of the National Academy of Sciences of the United States of America, 113*(48).

Covid: South Africa 'punished' for detecting new Omicron variant. (2021). https://www.bbc.com/news/world-59442129. Accessed 12 Dec 2021.

Fesbach, M. (2006). The early days of the HIV/AIDS epidemic in the former Soviet Union. In J. L. Twigg (Ed.), *HIV/AIDS in Russia and Eurasia* (Vol. 1). Palgrave Macmillan.

Global HIV & AIDS statistics—Fact sheet. (2021). *UNAIDS*. https://www.unaids.org/en/resources/fact-sheet. Accessed 6 Nov 2021.

HIV and AIDS an Origin Story. *PublicHealth.org*. A Red Ventures Company. https://www.publichealth.org/public-awareness/hiv-aids/origin-story/. Accessed 10 Oct 2021

Hung, H. (2004). The politics of SARS: Containing the perils of globalization by more globalization. *Asian Perspective, 28*(1).

Influenza pandemic of 1918–19. *Encyclopedia Britannica*, 7 Jul. 2020. https://www.britannica.com/event/influenza-pandemic-of-1918-1919. Accessed 2 Nov 2021.

Johnson, B. D. (2019). How a typo created a scapegoat for the AIDS epidemic. *Macleans*. https://www.macleans.ca/culture/movies/how-a-typo-created-a-scapegoat-for-the-aids-epidemic/. Accessed 8 Aug 2021.

Kai, J. (2021). How trump fueled Anti-Asian violence in America: Trump's encouragement of white supremacy and his strident anti-China rhetoric proved a toxic combination for Asian Americans. *The Diplomat*. https://thediplomat.com/2021/06/how-trump-fueled-anti-asian-violence-in-america/. Accessed 7 Aug 2021.

Kamala Harris tells migrants "do not come" during talks in Guatemala. (2021). https://www.youtube.com/watch?v=bpGitFIzamQ, Accessed 3 Aug 2021.

Katinis, T. (2010). A humanist confronts the plague: Ficino's Consilio contro la Pestilentia. *MLN, 125*(1).

Kessler, G. (2021). DeSantis's effort to blame Biden for the Covid surge in Florida. *The Washington Post*. https://www.washingtonpost.com/politics/2021/08/06/desantiss-effort-blame-biden-covid-surge-florida/. Accessed 12 Aug 2021

Lauritsen, J. (1993). *The AIDS war: Propaganda, Profiteering and Genocide from the Medical-Industrial Complex*. Asklepios.

Lovelace, Jr. B. (2020). Trump claims the worsening U.S. coronavirus outbreak is a 'Fake News Media Conspiracy' even as hospitalizations rise. Health and Science, CNBC. https://www.cnbc.com/2020/10/26/coronavirus-trump-claims-the-worsening-us-outbreak-is-a-fake-news-media-conspiracy-even-as-hospitalizations-rise.html. Accessed 10 Oct 2021.

McKay, R. A. (2017). *Patient zero and the making of the AIDS epidemic*. Chicago University Press.

Middle East Respiratory Syndrome (MERS). Centre for Disease Control and Prevention, https://www.cdc.gov/coronavirus/mers/index.html Accessed 6 Nov 2021.

Morelli, G., et al. (2010). Phylogenetic diversity and historical patterns of pandemic spread of Yersinia pestis. *Nature Genetics, 42*(12), 1140–1143. https://doi.org/10.1038/ng.705

Morens, D. M. and Fauci, A.S. (2007). The 1918 Influenza Pandemic: Insights for the 21st Century, *Journal of Infectious Diseases*, 195 (7)

Pandey, G. (2016). The woman who discovered India's first HIV cases. *BBC News*. https://www.bbc.com/news/magazine-37183012. Accessed 16 Sept 2021.

Pandhi, N. (2021). Ebola, COVID-19 and the Moral Injury of Dignity. *The Wire*. https://thewire.in/health/ebola-covid-19-moral-injury-dignity. Accessed 10 Oct 2021.

Pepin, J. (2011). *The origins of AIDS*. Cambridge University Press.

Pernick, M. S. (2002). Contagion and culture. *American Literary History, 14*(4).

Reed, C. (2007). The Rev Jerry Falwell: Rabid evangelical leader of America's 'moral majority'. *The Guardian*. https://www.theguardian.com/media/2007/may/17/broadcasting.guardianobituaries. Accessed 5 Oct 2021.

Senga, M., et al. (2017). Contact tracing performance during the Ebola virus disease outbreak in Kenema district, Sierra Leone. *Philosophical Transactions*: *Biological Sciences, 372*(1721)

Sharma, A. L., Singh, T. R., & Singh, L. S. (2019). Understanding of HIV/AIDS in the international border area, Manipur: Northeast India. *Epidemiology and Infection, 147*, e113. https://www.ncbi.nlm.nih.gov/pmc/articles/PMC6518467/pdf/S0950268818003564a.pdf. Accessed 6 Nov 2021.

Slack, P. (1988). Responses to plague in early modern Europe: The implications of public health. *Social* Research, 55(3).

Stanway, D. (2020). The shadow of SARS: China learned the hard way how to handle an epidemic. *Reuters*. https://www.reuters.com/article/us-china-health-sars-idUSKBN1ZL12B. Accessed 10 Nov 2021.

Tapper, M. (1995). Interrogating bodies: Medico-racial knowledge, politics, and the study of a disease. *Comparative Studies in Society and History, 37*(1).

The New York Times. (2021). 8 Dead in Atlanta Spa Shootings, with fears of Anti-Asian Bias. https://www.nytimes.com/live/2021/03/17/us/shooting-atlanta-acworth. Accessed 19 March 2021.

The rapid journey of a deadly MERS outbreak. (2019). *Infectious Disease* (p. 54). https://media.nature.com/original/magazine-assets/d42473-019-00422-y/d42473-019-00422-y.pdf. Accessed 7 Nov 2021.

Trump Falls Victim to COVID-19 Misinformation That Study Says He Spread the Most. *The Wire*, 2 October 2020. https://thewire.in/world/donald-trump-coronavirus-misinformation. Accessed 6 Nov 2021.

Walker, J. (2016). Civil society's role in a public health crisis. *Issues in Science and Technology, 32*(4).

Wiechmann, I., et al. (2012). History of Plague. *RCC Perspectives*, No. 3.

Xu, R., et al. (2004). Epidemiologic clues to SARS origin in China. *Emerging Infectious Diseases, 10*(6). https://www.ncbi.nlm.nih.gov/pmc/articles/PMC3323155/pdf/03-0852.pdf. Accessed 6 Nov 2021.

Zhang, Y., et al. (2012). The characteristics of imported cases and the effectiveness of outbreak control strategies of pandemic influenza A (H1N1) in China. *Asia Pacific Journal of Public Health, 24*(6)

Zubașcu, F. (2021). Do not blame South Africa for the Omicron variant. *Science Business*. https://sciencebusiness.net/news/do-not-blame-south-africa-omicron-variant, Accessed 12 Dec 2021.

Chapter 4
Structure, Agency, Temporality: Revisiting Historical Analyses to Study the Contemporary

Kaustubh Mani Sengupta

> *It was the best of times, it was the worst of times, it was the age of wisdom, it was the age of foolishness, it was the epoch of belief, it was the epoch of incredulity, it was the season of Light, it was the season of Darkness, it was the spring of hope, it was the winter of despair...*
> *(Charles Dickens, A Tale of Two Cities)*

Abstract The pandemic brought forth issues of health, economy, and the state in a way that it became imperative to delve into the past to analyse the present and ascertain the bleak future. In this essay, I will discuss a few methodological issues that can help us understand the year 2020, the sufferings of the working population, the crisis in the economy, and the varied social, political, economic, and epidemiological responses that we encountered. These are methods that historians have used to analyse various moments of the past—be it collective action, everyday situation, common mentality at times of war, famine, or epidemic. I suggest that an understanding of these methodological issues may help us grapple with the complexities of the ongoing crises and situate them in a historical context. As a historian, I want to hesitantly propose certain ways through which we can try and make meaning of the events that unfolded during the last year and a half; events or issues which are still making headlines today. Needless to say, these are nothing but tentative theoretical propositions to analyse contemporary issues. To situate 2020 in a historical frame, I will focus on three crucial elements that historians and social scientists have dealt with in great detail regarding their craft. These are: (a) the question of structure, event, and agency; (b) the question of time and temporality; and (c) the question of everyday life in history and relating it to the concerns of state, politics, and bio-power in the present context.

K. M. Sengupta (✉)
Department of History and Archaeology, Shiv Nadar Institution of Eminence, Delhi NCR, India
e-mail: kaustubh.sengupta@gmail.com

S. R. Chakraborty et al. (eds.), *The Long 2020*, India Studies in Business and Economics, https://doi.org/10.1007/978-981-99-4815-4_4

Keywords Historical methods · Social history · Timescale · Everyday life · Bio-power

We are living in strange times. There's very little wisdom, light, or hope, it seems. Our generation in India has not witnessed the tumultuous events of the twentieth century that had shaped the destiny of our parents. We are the quintessential children of a neoliberal India; an India with rising GDP as well as increasing social inequalities. Suddenly, the pandemic put a halt to the march of the nation. People had to press the pause button. And, as if waking up from a long slumber, equally suddenly, we were confronted with long march of a different kind: migrant workers trudging across the highways to return to the safety of their homes in desperate, uncertain times. The unbelievable images of the migrant workers circulating during the first few months of the nationwide lockdown in early 2020 in India came as a rude shock to the social media-savvy urban middle class who were happily posting cooking videos and images of leisure readings. The pandemic brought forth issues of health, economy, and the state in a way that it became imperative to delve into the past to analyse the present and ascertain the bleak future.

In this essay, I will discuss a few methodological issues that can help us understand the year 2020, the sufferings of the working population, the crisis in the economy, and the varied social, political, economic, and epidemiological responses that we encountered. These are methods that historians have used to analyse various moments of the past—be it collective action, everyday situation, common mentality at times of war, famine, or epidemic. I suggest that an understanding of these methodological issues may help us grapple with the complexities of the ongoing crises and situate them in a historical context.

The essay will not deal directly with the happenings of the harrowing days of 2020–21; this is not an exercise in writing the history of the present. Writing contemporary history is never an easy task, as the basic premise of an historian's job demands a temporal distance. Samaddar has reminded us, "You burn your hands when you attempt to write current history; current history is a reflection of current times but in a historical frame. More than recalling past histories as the necessary backdrop, the present itself has to be framed as 'history', or as the philosopher said, 'event as history'." (Samaddar, 2021, xi) As a historian, I want to hesitantly propose certain ways through which we can try and make meaning of the events that unfolded during the year 2020 and events or issues which are still making headlines today. Needless to say, these are nothing but tentative theoretical propositions to analyse contemporary issues. To situate 2020 in a historical frame, I will focus on three crucial elements that historians and social scientists have dealt with in great detail regarding their craft. These are: (a) the question of structure, event, and agency; (b) the question of time and temporality; and (c) the question of everyday life in history and relating it to the concerns of state, politics, and bio-power in the present context.

Let me elaborate. Studying the myriad happenings since March 2020, we are confronted with the issue of social response to a biological threat. This social response was determined by the existing state of knowledge, which kept on changing, and as we learnt more about the virus, we kept on altering our stance and confronted it from new angles. All these were underlined by certain common understanding of the virologists regarding the transmission of the virus. However, as we have noticed, people reacted to the pandemic in ways ranging from nonchalance to bordering on obsessive–compulsive disorder. The hurriedly announced lockdown and the attendant hardships of the millions laid bare the apathy of the neoliberal state for its poor citizens. The inadequacies of public health system, lack of provision of food and shelter, or the absence of basic sanitary facilities became evident throughout the nation. People were forced to march along the highways to go back to their home or had to wait in long queues to get some ration. Daily wage suddenly got stopped for many workers. They lost their jobs almost overnight. The scamper to return to the 'safety' of the village home often stemmed from the apathy of the urban employer. I believe to understand these myriad responses—both from the point of view of the state and the people—we can revisit some of the debates among social scientists and historians regarding the efficacy of structural analysis vis-à-vis human agency.

Related to the issues of structure, event, and agency are the notions of time and temporality. Different historians have studied the theoretical understanding of time, and its relationship to the narrative structure of the historian's craft. While Braudel spoke of three levels of temporal dynamics in analysing historical processes, a school of German historians first alerted us to the possibilities of studying human actions through the idea of *Alltagsgeschichte* or the 'history of everyday life'. This mode of analysis, I believe, has particular relevance to the trials and tribulations of the numerous migrant workers trudging across the subcontinent during the first lockdown in early 2020. It also alerts us to the new possibilities carved out by the hapless population; they shifted vocations and made ingenious use of limited resources. It is in the same vein we can recall Arrighi's definition of 'long' as proposed in his book *The Long Twentieth Century*. Arrighi writes, "consecutive systemic cycles of accumulation overlap, and although they become progressively shorter in duration, they all last longer than a century: hence the notion of the 'long century', which will be taken as the basic temporal unit in the analysis of world-scale processes of capital accumulation." (Arrighi, 1994, 6–7) In our case, 2020 is not over yet. We are indeed dealing with a 'long year' that, some would argue, structurally started way before March 2020.

The last issue pertains to one of the central themes of the present period—that of state, collective politics and bio-power. Invoking Michel Foucault, Agamben's early critique of Italy's COVID policies as a direct intervention in the lives of the people—reducing them to 'bare life'—did not find much takers in the left-liberal circles (Agamben, 2021). Rather, ultra-conservatives became champions of 'COVID is just a flu' and 'no vaccine' campaign. In a curious turn of events, left-liberal and centrist dispensation were much more cautious in their approach to the pandemic. They vociferously argued for a 'scientific' temper among the ordinary population, with regular washing of hands, wearing proper mask, and maintaining physical distance. The state in India, however, utterly bungled the situation with the sudden announcement of nationwide stringent lockdown. The plight of the migrant workers made as much headlines as the news related to health and mortality. In these rather bleak times, voluntary groups came forward and facilitated an economy of care providing food and shelter to the destitute. A new type of public power was enunciated, which Samaddar has termed as 'bio-politics from below'. In the last section, I will look at some of these arguments. Starting with a discussion of the historical analyses of 'everyday life' and 'microhistory', the section will look at some of the basic questions of our times and make an appraisal of present crises.

4.1 Structure and Agency in Historical Analyses

Though there are certain apprehensions in judging the current crisis against any and every human crisis—medical or otherwise, we can discern certain structural elements in the history of various societies that bind the periods of crises. In case of India, as Chhabria has mentioned, "Using…historical analysis, we learn that the production of widespread poverty, the resultant malnourishment and hunger, and the neglect of public health investments *together* form the conditions under which India's real public health disaster is created time and time again." (Chhabria, 2020) Samaddar also notes "the *structural* inability of the neoliberal post-colonial regime to ensure the safety of life is evident." (Samaddar, 2021, 134, emphasis in original) Further, analysing the present situation, in their volume *India's Migrant Workers and the Pandemic,* Bandyopadhyay et al. write

> The current crisis needs to be understood as a conjuncture and cannot be reduced to a question of tackling a menace from outside. Externalizing the virus and the migrant as an 'outsider' will not help us address the crisis. The book is a plea to treat both the spread of the virus and the migrant as intimate to the capitalist mode of production. The book goes on describing the current crisis as a combination of an epidemiological (the breakdown of the public health infrastructure), an economic (recession and the collapse of the global supply chains) and a political (authoritarianism and centralization of power) crisis. (Bandyopadhyay et al., 2021, p. 5)

As we know, the plague epidemic of the 1890s brought in strict quarantine measures and an extremely interventionist state. David Arnold stresses the similarity between that era and the present crisis, mentioning that, "Then, as now, the middle classes could save themselves by self-isolating…insulated by the privileged distancing of caste, class, and gated communities, while for the poor, self-isolation was (and is) a fantasy. Then, as now, the slum dwellers and the migrant poor were doubly victimized—by disease and by loss of livelihood." (Arnold, 2020) Similarly, during the Bengal famine, millions died in the countryside, while Calcutta was closely guarded. "Famine and war had…transformed the geo-political importance of Calcutta. Millions had died—and continue to die—of deprivation and disease, so that Calcutta, the colonial war effort, and Capital could thrive…. 'Belonging' to Calcutta meant 'priority', which, in turn, meant survival." (Mukherjee, 2015) These instances show that epidemic crises were combination of medical emergency, faulty public health system, hunger, poverty, and malnutrition, with coercive agrarian relations and drought leading to famine.

In March 2020, with the sudden lockdown in India, huge number of migrant workers faced severe hardship. They were forced to move from their places of work in metropolitan cities to the 'safety' of their homes in various villages and small towns. The measure which was supposed to restrict mobility, paradoxically, created a train of people across highways. Bandyopadhyay et al., succinctly described the cruel situation these wretched souls had to endure in the following words:

> The disturbing image of thousands of men, women and children walking along the highways under the scorching sun and bleeding feet became a standard and a familiar image of the national lockdown. This image resembled primitive on-foot mass exodus which destroyed the self-image of modernity in the twenty-first century….In this way, the national lockdown unfolded as a massive paradox. The act of immobilization entailed an act of unimaginable mobility of labouring bodies across the nation, leading to the absolute breakdown of lockdown. A policy to immobilize led to unforeseen mobility of people which the country had never witnessed after the Partition saga. If lockdown was a gigantic boundary-making exercise, the migrants' exodus was its political response as it broke those boundaries. (Bandyopadhyay et al., 2021, pp. 3–4)

For them, a structural understanding of the present situation is essential. It reveals the logic of historical context and offers us theoretical tools to grasp the contemporary. It has been observed that "The lockdown period witnessed a severe fall in the standard of living of the working class, a sizeable section of which was constituted by the internal migrants. As production and services shrunk in the cities and the industrial centres, the internal migrants lost employment. In certain sectors, government policies before the lockdown increased precarity. The lockdown played havoc when married to such legacy issues." (p. 2)

Taking cue from these observations, let me briefly recall the historical methodology deployed by the social historians to understand the nature of social structure and collective action. For a prolonged period, there have been heated debates between proponents of structuralist analysis of society and historians arguing for human agency. During the 1960s–70s, a group of British Marxist historians alerted us to the possibilities of structural analyses of popular discontent. Hobsbawm, in his famous articulation on pre-industrial rebels, mentions that "they are *pre-political* people who have not yet found, or only begun to find, a specific language in which to express their aspirations about the world. Though their movements are thus in many respects blind and groping, by the standards of modern ones, they are neither unimportant nor marginal." (Hobsbawm, 1959, p. 3) Rescuing the submerged voices from the 'condescension of posterity', a group of Marxist historians started to look for ordinary people in European history before the advent of industrial economic structure when well-defined antagonism between the capitalist and the proletariat was yet to form. This search for a 'history from below' brought forth an array of writings on various aspects of social banditry, urban mobs, or food riots during the period of transition from feudalism to capitalism in western European countries. Men and women of these movements were not born in the world of capitalism; rather, as Hobsbawm mentions, "they come into it as first-generation immigrants, or what is more catastrophic, it comes to them from outside, insidiously by the operations of economic forces which they do not understand and over which they have no control…revolutions or fundamental changes of law whose consequences they may not understand, even when they have helped to bring them about." (Ibid. 4) These historians show that social banditry stemmed from a moral claim. The movements were reformist, not revolutionary. "Its ambitions [we]re modest: a traditional world in which men [we]re justly dealt with, not a new and perfect world." (Ibid, 7) Banditry was mainly rural in origin. For Hobsbawm, "Social banditry has next to no organization or ideology, and is totally inadaptable to modern social movements." On the other hand, the riots in the city, or the urban mob has been defined as 'the movement of all classes of the urban poor for the achievement of economic or political changes by direct action—that is by riot or rebellion—but [here also, Hobsbawm mentions] as a movement which was as yet inspired by no specific ideology'.

However, not everybody writing in this vein subscribed to this view. Notable exception is George Rude. Studying the revolutionary crowds in history, Rude has shown that they were anything but inchoate mob—'far from being social abstractions, [they] were composed of ordinary men and women with varying social needs, who responded to a variety of impulses, in which economic crisis, political upheaval, and the urge to satisfy immediate and particular grievances all played their part.' These men and women 'were impelled by specific grievances and by motives other than those of loot or monetary gain.' Moving away from his materialist explanation of crowd action, Rude in his later writings sought to incorporate ideology as an important element of popular protest. He locates two levels of ideas: the 'inherent' ideology of the group and the ideas coming from outside. For pre-industrial protest movements, Rude sees popular ideology as 'not a purely internal affair and the sole property of a single class or group…It is most often a mixture, a fusion of two elements, of which only one is the peculiar property of the 'popular' classes and the other is superimposed by a process of transmission and adoption from outside.' In this internal/external division, however, Rude makes an important observation: 'there is no such thing as an automatic progression from 'simple' to more sophisticated ideas…one cannot simply describe the second as being 'superior' or at a higher level than the first.' The 'derived' notions get 'grafted onto the 'inherent' notions and beliefs and the new popular ideology' takes shape as an amalgam of the two (Rude, 1995).

Thus, the two most important features of this strand of scholarship are the insistence on the pre-political character of the movements and an effort to understand the insurgent's beliefs—either as an absence of ideology, having only some moral claims [Hobsbawm], or viewing it as a curious mix of inherent and outside knowledge. These analyses were a challenge to the old-school political history. As one commentator has noted, "What made social history so compelling was not so much the pulling down of the historiographically mighty from their seats…as the emergence of a historical discipline grounded in tough-minded structural analysis." (https://archives.history.ac.uk/makinghistory/resources/articles/social_history.html) However, social historians have long debated the efficacy of an exclusively structural analysis, arguing instead for an understanding of historical processes in terms of human agency and actions. One of the most famous diatribes against structural analysis came from Thompson in his polemical tract against Althusserian Marxism. Thompson was especially critical of Althusser's total disregard for human 'experience'. For Thompson, Althusser's structuralism spoke of 'stasis', which departed widely from Marx's notion of historical-dialectical method, and had no means of explaining contradiction, class or change. (Thompson, 1978) Thompson, one of the most celebrated postwar British Marxist historians, always sought to understand people's consciousness, saw class as a relationship, and analysed it as a process, amply testified by the very title of his magnum opus. Similarly, Raphael Samuel once mentioned that "As a pedagogic enthusiasm, and latterly as an academic practice, social history derives its vitality from its oppositional character. It prides itself on being concerned with 'real life' rather than abstractions, with 'ordinary' people rather than privileged elites, with everyday things rather than sensational events." (https://www.historytoday.com/archive/what-social-history).

These were also reactions against the structuralist understanding of history as proposed by the French *Annales* historians, especially by Fernand Braudel and his notion of different temporal cycles. I will discuss the issue of time in historical writing in the next section. Here, let us just mention that Jacques Ranciere once wrote about the waning of interest among French historians regarding working-class movements, and noted that they became much more interested in 'static history', "which is rich in descriptions of climate, population, eating habits, epidemics, births and deaths but eschews the history of struggle of the workers and others on the grounds that such history…is nothing but 'superstructural' illusion, 'ideology'." (Rude, 1981, 66) This brief survey reveals the contradictions and complexities of social history as it has evolved over the years. The question of structure and agency could not be resolved. As Reinhart Koselleck commented, "The processual character of modern history cannot be comprehended other than through the reciprocal explanation of events through structures, and vice versa.…The interrelation of event and structure must not be permitted to lead to the suppression of their differences if they are to retain their epistemological object of disclosing the multiple strata of history." (Koselleck, 2004, 110) Similarly, in his review of the field of study, William Sewell surmised that.

> Although they were probably writing more from professional instinct than from considered theoretical scruples, social historians have demonstrated how, in a great variety of times and places, structures are in fact dual: how historical agents' thoughts, motives, and intentions are constituted by the cultures and social institutions into which they are born, how these cultures and institutions are reproduced by the structurally shaped and constrained actions of those agents, but also how, in certain circumstances, the agents can (or are forced to) improvise or innovate in structurally shaped ways that significantly reconfigure the very structures that constituted them. (Sewell, 2005, 128)

This dual nature helps us rethink the ways through which we can conceptualize the present crisis. The state of the workers and labourers in these neoliberal times suddenly came to the fore due to the pandemic. The glittering cities and shimmering billboards occlude the deep divide in society. Suddenly, the threat of contagion and diseased body created spatial boundaries whereby mobility was circumscribed and distancing was promoted. Cities turned into closely guarded spaces, with various confinement zones and varying curfew hours. Fear of unsustainable pressure on the public health system pushed the authorities to contain people within strictly monitored spaces. For Bandyopadhyay et al., "The migrants' question became a social question the moment they were on the move." (p. 3)

Following Chandavarkar, I suggest studying the pandemic not as "a single, integrated phenomenon", but rather as a phenomenon that represents and signifies "different things to different people." More than focusing on discrete events of the plague in Bombay, Chandavarkar looked at the manner of their construction. He mentioned that "The historical process of their construction not only illuminates wider relationships between social groups and between state and society, but it can also be argued that the constituent events of an epidemic upon which historians focus might be grasped most firmly when they are acknowledged to be, separately and discretely, a function of the very process of its construction." (Chandavarkar, 1998) Recalling Sewell's understanding of social history, we find that he is particularly keen on the dynamism of structures. He writes,

> Structure is dynamic, not static; it is the continually evolving outcome and matrix of a process of social interaction. Even the more or less perfect reproduction of structures is a profoundly temporal process that requires resourcefulness and innovative human conduct. But the same resourceful agency that sustains the reproduction of structures also makes possible their transformation—by means of transpositions of schemas and remobilizations of the old. Structures, I suggest, are not reified categories we can invoke to explain the inevitable shape of social life. To invoke structures as I have defined them here is to call for a critical analysis of the dialectical interactions through which humans shape their history. (Sewell, 2005, 151)

4.2 Time and Temporal Scale

For an historian, the understanding of social situation as a blend of both systematic elements and individual agency brings forth the crucial element of time and temporality in a narrative. To make sense of the present crisis, we must acknowledge the different experiences of time of different groups of people. While preventive mechanisms like 'social distancing' were spatial measures, the plight of the migrants brought forth temporal dimension of the situation. The nights on the empty roads were no doubt qualitatively different from middle-class households. In the Indian context, the term 'social distancing' was an unfortunate neologism. As Harsh Mander mentions,

> Caste is an extreme and inhuman form of social distancing that we have practiced for millennia. Indeed, 'social distancing' mimics many age-old caste prohibitions: keeping distance, refusing to touch, not sharing utensils, denying entry into one's home....Politicians, policy makers, scientists, journalists, celebrity artistes, business leaders—every popular public figure, almost without exception, used the phrase and promoted the practice over and over again, all of them unmindful of the fact that they were thus further normalizing a civilizational apartheid. (Mander, 2021, p. 20)

Soumyabrata Choudhury also notes, "Social distancing is a spatial prescription. It is not meant to be a temporal distance between different social individual. Which is what it has turned out to be…." (Choudhury, 2020) The conquest of space by time—as embodied by the introduction of the railways in the nineteenth century—was cruelly reversed at one stroke. Workers from metropolitan cities found themselves on endless railway tracks, were chased away from platforms, and were forced to sleep on tracks which turned fatal on quite a few occasion. However, in some instances, the loss of regular livelihood forced the working population living in the cities to innovate. Hawking and peddling in middle-class neighbourhood became quite prominent. The daily rhythm of the economic life of the city changed substantially as these mobile vendors became an important part of the commodity circulation. Tracing and tracking these various experiences, temporal disjunctions, and spatial trajectories, the historian could only think of the different ways in which historical narratives have represented human engagement with time and temporality. Apart from standardized clock time—the hegemonic 'modern' sense of passage—different societies had their own notion of temporality which often sat at odds with the scientific accuracy of the clock. On Barak in his book on the introduction of various 'Western' technologies in modern Egypt shows how two concepts of time got established in the everyday lives of the people. 'Western time' became associated with standard clock time while 'Egyptian time' was seen as 'a substandard approximation'. Further, he shows that how "The country's modernizing classes understood the slowing down of colonial modernity as Egyptian and its acceleration as Western. They experienced modernity as moving swiftly ahead yet always remaining one step behind." (Barak, 2013, p. 2).

These notions of different temporality animate much of colonial India's modernity as well, where specific groups of people became a part of 'politics of time' with the European at the apex of the civilizational ladder. As Barak further elaborates, and which resonates with other colonial societies, "Modern science and technology have provided a yardstick that allowed Europe to reveal its assumed superiority vis-à-vis its colonies. Nineteenth-century European supremacy was brought into relief with technical gauges provided by the new transportation and communication networks that welded together the metropole and colonies, offering a continuum along which the East could be demonstrated to be spatially peripheral and temporally backward. Difference and hierarchy often found their source in comparability, connectivity, and commensurability." (Barak, p. 2) As an example, we can discuss briefly Prathama Banerjee's skilful analysis of the Santal rebellion in during the mid-nineteenth century. She shows how the neat depiction of the *hul* within a singular narrative of cause and effect hides the complex notions of temporality and everydayness that informed the Santal articulation of the *hul*. Banerjee argues, "by making the rebellion into an event, chronology—as a purely formal succession—was to overdetermine and defuse what were clearly temporal contradictions between Santal practices and the colonial-modern teleology." (Banerjee, 1999, 210) And the efforts of the state and the Bengali middle class, searching for its own historicality, ensured that the Santal uprising was a mere aberration in the course of progress for the nation—an evidence of the 'primitive' excess. The Santals were supposed to be temporally behind the Bengali society—they were the 'primitive within' for the Bengali middle-class intelligentsia, and "[t]o the Bengali author of history, the 'primitive' rebellion thus appeared as the theoretically absurd moment of the past rebelling against the present." (Ibid) Banerjee's whole enterprise rests on the unpacking of this 'politics of time', and thus for her, the Santal rebellion was not merely a challenge to the nexus between merchants, moneylenders and the state, but also the assertion of a critique of the 'disciplining of time into chronology' and 'reduction of temporal acts into synchronic and cumulative knowledge'. (Banerjee, 2004).

It is this 'disciplining of time into chronology' that is at the heart of historian's enterprise. Any historical narrative is a sequential systematization of occurrences that produces cognition. As Koselleck has described, "Chronological accuracy in the arrangement of all elements contributing to an event is...a methodological postulate of historical narrative. Thus, for the meaning of historical sequence, there is a *threshold of fragmentation* below which an event dissolves into unrelated incidents. A minimum of "before" and "after" constitutes the significant unity that makes an event out of incidents." (Koselleck, 2004 [1979], 106) Without going into the raging debates between proponents of narrative character of history and their critics, we might look at one specific reaction against the narrativist thesis. This is crucial for our understanding of the ways in which historians have viewed time and temporality.

Reaction against the narrative character of history—with a supposed belief in little or no distinction between history and fiction—rose in the French historiography, particularly from the historians of the *Annales* school. For them, narrative history was simply the history of political events. This "l'histoire événementielle", history of events was only a part of entire historical project, according to Braudel. Fernand Braudel embarked on a grand project of 'total history', collapsing the disciplinary boundaries of different subjects of the social sciences and incorporating concepts of sociology, economics, geography, etc. Braudel conceived of different levels of temporality in historical studies. He introduced the concept of *longue duree* which is concerned with changes over a period of 2000 or 3000 years. It "is an inquiry into a history that is almost changeless, the history of man in relation to his surroundings. It is a history which unfolds slowly and is slow to alter..." (Braudel, 1980, 3). The notion of different timescale for different occurrences come from the recognition of two other phenomena—the conjuncture and the event. As Braudel put it, "Over and above this unfaltering history (i.e. the *longue duree*), there is a history of gentle rhythms, of groups and groupings..." (Ibid) This is the conjuncture—the pace of change is faster than that of the *longue duree*. Then comes the event—"A history of short, sharp, nervous vibrations." (Ibid).

Paul Ricoeur has argued that even in the 'structural' history of Braudel there are 'quasi-events' leading to 'quasi-plots' and the presence of 'quasi-characters' who always refer back to a narrative structure. In this connection, we can bring in Lawrence Stone, who speaks of a 'revival of narrative' after a period of 'new history' in post-war era which denounced narrative history as story-telling. (Stone, 2001) By narrative, the 'new' historians mainly meant the organization of material in a chronologically sequential order with a content of a single coherent story with some sub-plots. The subject of such history was seen to be essentially political which is descriptive rather than analytical. Marxist ideology and social science methodology influenced historians, who now became interested in societies and not individuals, and were striving to produce a 'scientific history'. Stone identifies three strands in this effort for 'scientific history'—Marxist, French ecological/demographical model and American 'cliometric' methodology. Stone discerns a revival of narrative arising from the widespread disillusionment with the economic deterministic model of historical explanation. Historians started to focus on society and culture groups and even the will of the individuals. These were now seen as potential causal agents of change besides the impersonal forces of material output and demographic growth. Also, an antipathy towards the quantitative history was perceived. The practitioners of the 'new history', the members of the *Annales* school, also turned their attention to the individual with their study of the *mentalité*. The effort to discover what was going on inside people's minds in the past and what it was like to live in the past inevitably led them back to the use of narrative. There was wider use of anthropological methods and this, in place of sociology and economics, was one of the most influential causes for the revival of narrative among the 'new historians', according to Stone.

In recent years, there has been a revival of the Braudelian vision with the rise of global history as a distinct methodology. Historians like Jurgen Osterhammel have been compared with Braudel for writing tomes on transformations of the world in the modern era. These new histories of connections and comparisons have both spatial and temporal dimensions. On the other hand, environmental histories have embraced 'global and planetary scales' (Chakrabarty, 2021). Guldi and Armitage have made an impassioned plea for 'big history' in their *History Manifesto.* They argue that to be relevant to public discourse, historians need to engage with big issues and present a roadmap for the future by analysing long-term trends from the past. They are hopeful that new *longue duree* trends are making a comeback in historical studies. But this is not an unqualified return to the old Braudelian framework. As they mention, "The new *longue duree* has emerged within a very different ecosystem of intellectual alternatives. It possesses a dynamism and flexibility earlier versions did not have. It has a new relationship to the abounding sources of big data available in our time—data ecological, governmental, economic, and cultural in nature, much of it newly available to the lens of digital analysis." (Guldi & Armitage, 2014, p. 9)

4.3 From Big History to Small Voices

The dynamism of the new history, as recognized by Guldi and Armitage, also pushes us to look for human agency and actions and analyse them as part of larger narratives. The temporal dimension of these actions was brought forth by the practitioners of *Alltagsgeschichte* or 'history of everyday life' in Germany. Studying the experience of common people 'History of everyday life' tried to develop a qualitative understanding of the lives of ordinary men and women. One of the best-known practitioners of the field, Alf Ludtke describes the project in the following words: "At the center…are the lives and sufferings of those who are frequently labelled, suggestively but imprecisely, as the 'small people.' It involves their work and nonwork. The picture includes housing and homelessness, clothing and nakedness; eating and hunger, love and hate." (cited in Eley in Ludtke 1995, p. ix) The repetitiveness of daily activities, the uneventful chores of ordinary people, the silent sufferings of the common folk—all these became a part of historian's gaze. In a sense, Ludtke and others were looking for "people without history". The experience of the multitude in their everyday settings gave new meanings to the notions of work and play, struggle and leisure, the ordinary and the exceptional. They borrowed from various traditions and disciplines, most notably from the anthropologists and the 'history from below' approach of the British Marxists, with their own modifications. As Ludtke mentions, "A decisive impetus for all inquiry into the history of "the many" was provided by the thesis that rebellious "mobs" do not act irrationally but consistently follow the lights of their own rationality, honed by experience. E. P. Thompson has developed this perspective using the example of the logic or "moral economy" of plebeian crowds in English towns during the eighteenth century, with notable results." (Ludtke, 1995, pp. 21–22).

A similar tendency of focusing on ordinary folks was found in the post-war Italian historiography. Giovanni Levi and Carlo Ginzburg, among others, started writing 'microhistory', a term denoting the life and worlds of individuals. In his celebrated book, *The Cheese and the Worms,* through the views of a single person Gizburg builds a whole corpus of cultural activities. (Ginzburg, 2013). The agency of human beings was restored once again in history, in sharp contrast to the structural history of Braudelian paradigm. As some critics observed, there is a risk of succumbing to the anecdotes, to the history of events in this way of writing, but for Ginzburg 'it is not an inevitable risk'. Microhistory is not simply presenting the ideas of an individual—his/her ideas can be seen as indicative of the culture of which the individual is a part. Describing the methodology, Ginzburg writes,

> even a limited case…can be representative: in a negative sense, because it helps to explain what should be understood, in a given situation, as being "in the statistical majority"; or, positively, because it permits us to define the latent possibilities of something (popular culture) otherwise known to us only through fragmentary and distorted documents, almost all of which originate in the "archives of the repression".

Ginzburg was against the notion of a homogenized version of 'collective mentality' which was espoused by *Annales* historians like Lucien Febvre and Jacques Le Goff. For him, the crucial argument against following the methods of these historians arises from the fact of this 'collective mentality' which imparts in these histories a 'classless character'. His endeavour differs specifically in this respect. Instead of 'collective mentality' he prefers to use the term 'popular culture', which he admits is unsatisfactory in some cases. In spite of that, he carries on with 'popular culture', since it entails a concept of class structure, which, "even if conceived in general terms, is still a big advance over classlessness." Also, Ginzburg does not view culture as a latent, unchanging, static stream of emotion and values which generally corresponds to the temporality of a *longue durée.* Rather, for him, culture has certain dynamism, and popular culture, as has already been discussed, had a circular relationship with the dominant cultural patterns. Microhistory's tendency of looking at the scraps rather on larger entities has been seen as the typical expression of "postmodernist historiography" by Ankersmit (Ankersmit, 1989). But, Ginzburg is not willing to term his craft as postmodern since there is an insistence, according to him, on the context, "exactly the opposite of the isolated contemplation of the fragmentary advocated by Ankersmit." (Ginzburg et al., 1993).

Without going into various critiques of microhistory as an approach—whether it is possible to capture the culture of a group by studying an individual, or the relationship between oral and written records, or the problems associated with the very term 'popular culture'—we can have some useful insights from the methods of Levi and Ginzburg. Even in these times of global and connected histories, a group of historians in the pages of *Past and Present* have argued for blending global with microhistorical tools so that we can have context-specific analyses. Here the everyday becomes important. As we are aware, numerous articles and newspaper reports have documented the sufferings and misfortunes of the working population during the lockdown period and afterwards. These are invaluable sources for future historians. These everyday occurrences give us individual experiences which can elucidate the hidden structural elements of society when studied from a distance. As Koselleck once said, "What is today a methodological reflection on the nature of structural history can easily belong to the daily experience of former generations. Structures and their transformation are detectable empirically so long as their temporal span does not exceed the memory of contemporary generations." (108).

Terming the present collective action and the economy of care of solidarity groups across various levels as 'bio-politics from below', Ranabir Samaddar has argued that with the failure of the neoliberal state to provide for the downtrodden, a new kind of political moment has arrived. He notes, "the crisis of life produces, and must produce, political responses. Bio-politics from below is not so much about the 'below' as it is against the 'above', and about multiple scales—local, community, state, national, as well as occupation-centric. These multiple scales speak of the need for a new kind of public power." (Samaddar, 2021, 133) And this new type of public power will value "care as the guiding principle of organising society, which will be treated as commons." (Ibid. 135) For Samaddar, the march of the migrants, defying the lockdown, was a classic bio-political act from below: "Such a radical act was a completely novel form of strike; it combined protest, refusal to play the economy game of the rulers, an irresistible urge to find other locations of life and survival, of despair and hope." (Ibid. 172).

In his recent book, Chinmay Tumbe has studied past moments of epidemics to situate the present crisis. He argues that with the rise of large-scale industry, capitalist world economy, colonial mode of exploitation, warfare, and long-distance trade in the nineteenth and twentieth centuries, the period from 1817 to 1920 can be termed as 'age of pandemics', following Hobsbawm's famous 'age of' series. Analysing the effects of cholera, plague, and influenza on human history during the last couple of centuries, Tumbe tries to understand and situate COVID-19 'in the rear-view mirror'. He identifies certain crucial elements that come to the fore during any pandemic. He terms them as origin myths; pandemic politics; economics, epidemiology and the environment; pandemics and migration; the stages of a pandemic; and remembrance.

(Tumbe, 2021) One can surely follow these issues to understand the present moment. On the other hand, we can look at certain structural elements beyond the specific study of pandemic to situate the humanitarian crises. Here, I think, Guldi and Armitage's suggestion might be helpful. They prescribe the following:

> Building on earlier models of the *longue duree*...we set forward three approaches that history offers to those in need of a future: a sense of destiny and free will, counterfactual thinking, and thinking about utopias. Those freedoms of history...set aside historical thinking from the natural-law models of evolutionary anthropologists, economists, and other arbiters of our society. They are a crucial remedy for a society paralysed by short-term thinking, because these future-oriented tools of history open up new patterns of imagination with which to understand possible futures." (Guldi and Armitage, 10)

They focus on the efficacy of new data sets enabled by the information technology of the present era. They show "how scholars, businesses, activists, and historians are using new datasets to aggregate information about the history of inequality and the climate and...project new possible futures." (Ibid. 12) For Guldi and Armitage, this is a new beginning in terms of data, and historians will have a major role to play in utilizing these big data. This is an important issue. As Tumbe mentions, "When COVID-19 broke out in early 2020, the ignorance of the history of pandemics outside Europe, especially in India, was stunning. While writing this book, I am continually struck by the paucity of first-person accounts in the Age of Pandemics." (Tumbe, 2021, 193) New archives—collating reports from administration, private bodies, newspapers as well as ordinary people's recounting—need to be formed for the future historian. We need to be aware of the idea of different temporalities—both in the sense of the long-term similarities and differences, as well as the experiential dimension of a period of crisis.

4.4 Conclusion

Several observers are pretty aghast at the way the situation unfolded in India and elsewhere during 2020–21. As Mander exasperatedly writes, "This should be a moment of introspection, a recognition of the collapse of our moral centre as a nation and as a people. In coming months and years, as so many crises converge in a confluence....will we at last learn lessons of solidarity, equality and justice?" (Mander, 2021, pp. 203–04) This is a grim situation, no doubt, but as Samaddar has mentioned, bio-politics from below gives us a new sense of public power. He finds moments of solidarity and care among the community members of the Dharavi or the municipal awareness programme of Kerala. We must also recognize the resilience of ordinary folks in times of extreme hardships. People survived tumultuous events during the last century. People adapt to new situations with dexterity. In a similar vein, may we ask if moments of crises open up new possibilities, forcing people to be flexible in their livelihood choices? The plague of 1898–99 actually gave the workers some bargaining power with the mill owners in Bombay. The present situation is vastly different, no doubt, but can we think along similar lines? If not, then how has our economic system changed over these years? Can crises become an opportunity? An opportunity to conceive a new sense of politics, ethics, and care? Here again, we come back to the issue of comparison, long-term trends and spatial articulations where different locations have produced distinct experiences, where people have responded in a variety of ways.

References

Agamben, G. (2021). *Where are we now? The epidemic as politics*. Rowman and Littlefield.

Ankersmit, F. R. (1989). Historiography and postmodernism. In *History and theory* (Vol. 28, No. 2).

Arnold, D. (2020). Pandemic India: Coronavirus and the uses of history. *Journal of Asian Studies, 79*(3), 569–577.

Arrighi, G. (1994). *The long twentieth century: Money*. Verso.

Bandyopadhyay, R., Banerjee, P., & Samaddar, R. (2021). *India's migrant workers and the pandemic*. Routledge.

Banerjee, P. (1999). Historic acts: Santal Rebellion and the temporality of practice. *Studies in History, 15*, 2.

Banerjee, P. (2004). *Politics of time: 'Primitives' and history-writing in a colonial society*. Oxford University Press.

Barak, O. (2013). *On time: Technology and temporality in modern Egypt*. University of California Press.

Braudel, F. (1980). *On history*. University of Chicago Press.

Chakrabarty, D. (2021). *The climate of history in a planetary age*. Primus Books.

Chandavarkar, R. (1998). Plague panic and epidemic politics in India, 1896–1914. In R. Chandavarkar (Ed.), *Imperial power and popular politics: Class, resistance and the State in India, c. 1850–1950*. Cambridge University Press.

Chhabria, S. (2020). Manufacturing epidemics: Pathogens, poverty, and public health crises in India. *The India Forum* (Issue: June 5, 2020) (Manufacturing Epidemics | The India Forum).

Choudhury, S. (2020). *Now it's come to distances: Notes on Shaheen Bagh and coronavirus, association and isolation*. Navayana.

Ginzburg, C., Tedeschi, J., & Tedeschi, A. C. (1993). Microhistory: One or two things I know about it. *Critical Inquiry, 20*(1):10–35.

Ginzburg, C. (2013 [1976]). *The cheese and the worms: The cosmos of a sixteenth-century Miller.* Johns Hopkins University Press

Guldi, J., & Armitage, D. (2014). *The history manifesto*. Cambridge University Press.

Hobsbawm, E. (1959). *Primitive rebels*. Free Press.

Koselleck, R. (2004). *Futures past: On the semantics of historical time*. Columbia University Press.

Ludtke, A. (1995). *A history of everyday life: Reconstructing historical experience and ways of life*. Princeton University Press.

Mander, H. (2021). *Locking down the poor: The pandemic and India's moral centre*. Speaking Tiger.

Mukherjee, J. (2015). *Hungry Bengal: War, famine and the end of empire*. Harper Collins.

Rude, G. (1981). Review: The 'poverty of theory' debate. *Saothar, 7*, 62–68.

Rude, G. (1995). *Ideology and popular protest*. University of North Carolina Press.

Samaddar, R. (2021). *A pandemic and the politics of life*. Women Unlimited.

Sewell, Jr., W. (2005). *Logics of history: Social theory and social transformation*. University of Chicago Press.

Stone, L. (2001). The revival of narrative: Reflections on a new old history. In G. Roberts (Ed.), *The history and narrative reader*. Routledge.

Thompson, E. P. (1978). *The poverty of theory and other essays*. Monthly Review Press.

Tumbe, C. (2021). *The age of pandemics, 1817–1920. How they shaped India and the world*. Harper Collins.

Chapter 5
The Island of the Day After: Digital Epidemiology, Artificial Intelligence and a Biopolitics of Future

Iman Mitra

Abstract As some commentators have observed, one of the major differences between the influenza pandemic of 1918 and the COVID-19 outbreak can be sought in the relatively faster response time in the latter case. For any other epidemic or pandemic in the past, the response from the medical professionals, researchers, pharmaceutical companies and the governments came only after the spread of the disease entered a critical stage. Even though the response time is quicker this time, it is certainly not because we know more about the virus or viruses that have caused the pandemic. We must note that the knowledge of the disease in the case of a global pandemic such as this assumes a seemingly loose, flexible form, which is different from other forms of knowledge that can afford meticulous reflection and offer conjectures. Once the speed of the circulation of knowledge becomes more important than the accuracy of its content, we enter the domain of logistics. In this paper, I am interested in exploring the logistics of knowledge production during the pandemic, which, I shall argue, springs from an intersection of economic rationality and epidemiological reason under the rubric of neoliberalism. I shall study this logistical imagination at the moments of the convergence between economics and epidemiology, both as epistemic constellations as well as technologies of intervention. Moreover, as we shall see, it inaugurates an era of digital epidemiology based on artificial intelligence and machine learning that reshapes some of the earlier notions and practices of governmentality.

Keywords Digital epidemiology · Economics · Medical market · Artificial intelligence · Governmentality

As some commentators have observed, one of the major differences between the influenza pandemic of 1918 and the COVID-19 outbreak can be sought in the relatively faster response time in the latter case. For any other epidemic or pandemic in

I. Mitra (✉)
Department of History and Archaeology, Shiv Nadar Institution of Eminence, Delhi NCR & MCRG, Kolkata, India
e-mail: iman.mitra@snu.edu.in

S. R. Chakraborty et al. (eds.), *The Long 2020*, India Studies in Business and Economics, https://doi.org/10.1007/978-981-99-4815-4_5

the past—be it the bubonic plague in India in the 1890s or the AIDS in the 1980s—the response from the medical professionals, researchers, pharmaceutical companies and the governments came only after the spread of the disease entered a critical stage: "In almost every epidemic in history there has been a substantial delay between its emergence and the development of a widely agreed-upon representation of its scale, distribution and overall dynamic" (Engelmann, 2020). One can blame the inadequacy of human knowledge in deciphering the cause of the disease as the primary reason of the delay—for long the reason of the influenza pandemic was held to be a bacterial infection—but that cannot be the only reason. Even though the response time is quicker this time, it is certainly not because we know more about the virus or viruses that have caused the pandemic. In order to understand what is happening, we need to adjust our concept of knowledge itself—the knowledge that facilitates a quicker response time—and the networks that produce such knowledge. In ways more than one, this is an epistemological question. We must note that the knowledge of the disease in the case of a global pandemic such as this assumes a seemingly loose, flexible form, which is different from other forms of knowledge that can afford meticulous reflection and offer conjectures only when all the personal and collective misgivings about rigour and objectivity are satiated. The knowledge that must be in circulation to defeat the pandemic is required to have a frenetic agility that saves a lot of lives by being quickly discernible and applicable and cannot be traded for the stoic composure usually expected of the scientific expert of an earlier generation. Once the speed of the circulation of knowledge becomes more important than the accuracy of its content, we enter the domain of logistics. In this paper, I am interested in exploring the logistics of knowledge production during the pandemic, which, I shall argue, springs from an intersection of economic rationality and epidemiological reason under the rubric of neoliberalism. I shall study this logistical imagination at the moments of the convergence between economics and epidemiology, both as epistemic constellations as well as technologies of intervention. Towards the end, I shall also engage with the question of a more appropriate politics of life that these logistical manoeuvres may indicate.

5.1 The "War" Against COVID-19

I am borrowing the concept of logistics from Benjamin Bratton's brilliant introduction to a new edition of Paul Virilio's *Speed and Politics* (Bratton, 2006: 7–25). Talking about Virilio's notion of modernity, which is logistical in the sense that it deals with everything that makes a war "possible", Bratton defines logistics as "the preparation for war through the transfer of the nation's potential to its armed forces in time of peace as in times of war." (ibid: 7). Bratton's definition of logistics is significant for our discussion in many ways. One, the concept-metaphor of war has been predominant in the response discourse on COVID-19 (PTI, 2021; Raman, 2021; Zee Media Bureau, 2021). Masood Ahmed, a former IMF economist and the President of the Washington-based think tank, the Center for Global Development, has recently opined that the US is losing the "global war" against the pandemic by not considering this a "national security issue": "Imagine if 600,000 Americans and 4 million worldwide had been killed in a terrorist attack, and 50,000 were still being killed every week. Would our response look like what we are doing to fight COVID-19 across the world? The fight against COVID-19 is a global war but policymakers are not behaving accordingly" (Ahmed, 2021). Ahmed's appeal as the head of one of the influential think tanks is replete with what seem like war metaphors but we shall be mistaken to take them only as metaphors. His intention is probably noble, which is to draw the attention of the US government to the continuing loss of lives and resources in the rest of the world and ask them to consider the pandemic not only as an issue of domestic priority but also as one deserving building of international solidarity and support networks. However, his rhetoric not only equates the viral spread with the terrorist attacks that have previously led to military intervention but also points to a particular type of preparedness, which can only emerge out of perceiving the situation as that of a perpetual war:

> A year into the pandemic, four of the leading international agencies have set up a joint task force—I'd prefer that they think of it as a war-room—to try and produce a coordinated global response. As their largest and most important shareholder, the US should ask them for a global battle plan by September 1 [2021] and to nominate a single official who has the authority and accountability to deliver. That plan needs to have an authoritative monthly delivery plan for vaccines, logistics for getting those vaccines to each country in need, support to ensure those countries will have the capacity in place to deploy the vaccines when they arrive, and a war-footing effort to scale short- and long-term vaccine production in every available factory worldwide (ibid).

The four members of the joint task force are, of course, the IMF, the World Bank, the World Health Organization and the World Trade Organization. The task force now has its own website that tells us that its aim is to "vaccinate at least 40% of people in every country by the end of 2021, and at least 60 per cent by mid-2022."[1] Only a third of the 35 billion dollars of projected funding for this operation has been collected as of 30 July 2021, a joint statement by the leaders of the institutions informs us (Multilateral Leaders Task Force, 2021). The eighth meeting of the task force took place in March 2022 where, after a consultation with the CEOs of the leading vaccine manufacturers, UNICEF, and Gavi, the Vaccine Alliance,[2] the leaders admitted that the prolonging of the pandemic was caused by the "unequal access to COVID-19 vaccines, tests and treatments": "23 countries are yet to fully vaccinate 10% of their populations, 73 countries are yet to achieve 40% coverage and many more are projected to miss the 70% target by middle of this year" (Multilateral Leaders Task Force, 2022). The situation would improve, they argued, when "sustained investment in geographically diversified manufacturing capacity and new technologies for vaccines, therapeutics, and diagnostics" would

[1] https://www.covid19taskforce.com/en/programs/task-force-on-covid-19-vaccines. Retrieved January 10, 2023.

[2] Initiated by the Bill & Melinda Gates Foundation, Gavi, the Vaccine Alliance, has WHO, UNICEF, and the World Bank as its core partners to reach vaccines to the children of low-income countries all over the world (https://www.gavi.org/our-alliance/about). Retrieved January 2023.

be made available by working with the "leading vaccine manufacturers in exploring and undertaking new partnerships" and solving the logistical bottlenecks like lacking health care infrastructure and slow delivery mechanisms (ibid).

5.2 Epidemics and Modern Governmentality

But that is not the entire issue. Ahmed makes it clear—it is the undecidedness of the global leaders that is affecting the whole process: "It's time to stop "passing the parcel" at every international meeting and take a decision at the upcoming G20 summit to do what it takes to combat the worst health and human security risk in almost a century" (Ahmed, 2021). The undecidedness is argued to be coming from the lack of preparedness or the unwillingness to get into a combat-ready mode, although there exist a lot of manuals on this preparedness to fight global pandemics, especially the ones like influenza, which can spread fast by contact (Fukuda et al., 2009; Prior, 2006; The US Department of Homeland Security Contributors, 2006). Many of these guidelines were drawn after the 2005 Avian epidemic, popularly known as the bird flu epidemic. Apart from insisting on the public–private partnerships in the time of such an emergency, these guidelines also call for the integration of the pandemic plans into the "national emergency preparedness plans, frameworks and activities" and the use of the preparedness in strengthening "the basic and emergency health related capacities" (Fukuda et al., 2009: 19). The preparedness, therefore, would have a long-term goal and can act as a model for any kind of government of emergencies. The twist is that the notion of emergency is quite a stretchable one and, as we know from Michel Foucault's lectures on *Security, Territory, Population*, it was the management of the emergency outbreaks of smallpox in Europe in the eighteenth and nineteenth centuries through inoculation, variolisation and vaccination, which contributed to a species politics of human life and bodies called biopower (Foucault, 2019). Foucault lists four principles of what he calls the "medical police"—the security apparatus in the context of managing smallpox but extendable to other epidemics—*case* ("a way of individualizing the collective phenomenon of the disease"), *risk* (identifying the levels of risk among individuated cases and calculating the probable outcomes of treatment or inoculation), *danger* (distinguishing groups and zones on the basis of calculated relative degrees of risk) and *crisis* (the "phenomenon of sudden, circular bolting that can only be checked either by a higher, natural mechanism, or by an artificial mechanism") (ibid: 60–61). Unlike in the case of leprosy where the segregation between the sick and the healthy would do the trick, the new apparatus of medical governance "takes all who are sick and all who are not as a whole, that is to say, in short, the population, and it identifies the coefficient of probable morbidity, or probable mortality, in this population, that is to say the normal expectation in the population of being affected by the disease and of death linked to the disease" (ibid: 62). Identifying the patterns of the normal in the distributive logic of the population, as Foucault has consistently argued, is the cornerstone of modern governmental power. This would not have been possible without the development of statistics not only as a discipline but also as an apparatus of mitigating uncertainty in terms of risk as subject to probabilistic calculations. The development of epidemiology as a medical science based on such calculations is tantamount to accepting the model of managing emergency as a general model of the procedural deployment of governmentality.

In the same lectures, Foucault talks about three sites of development of security apparatuses in the eighteenth century: town, scarcity and epidemics. These three sites, he shows, are characterised by the movement, exchange and contact of three corresponding phenomena identified as "problems": street, grain and contagion. In other words, "they all more or less turn on the problem of circulation" (ibid: 64). It is no longer the safety of the sovereign and his territory that is at stake, but the security of the population. Ensuring smooth dispersal and distribution of things by diminishing the risks therein becomes the object of government. Once again, that brings us to the question of logistics as explained by Bratton: dispersal of resources in the preparation of war during peacetime. The epidemiological reason, hence, works in the service of this dispersal and the modernity thus envisaged looks like "a world in motion, expressed in translations of strategic space into logistical time, and back again" (Bratton, 2006: 7). In the context of a viral epidemic, the strategic space can be represented as the intersection of the trajectories of the virus and its probable carriers. Everyone, for that matter, is a probable carrier—the population. The models of epidemiology make predictions of these intersections and appear as what Lefebvre calls the spaces of representation (Lefebvre, 1991: 33, 38–39). The strategic part lies in the desire to turn these spaces of representation into representational spaces—from spaces conceived to spaces lived—a governmental prerogative. By trying to modify the trajectories of the future intersections, the predictive models attempt to secure the present, which is nothing but future in retrospect. I would like to argue that the back-and-forth translations of strategic space into logistical time is nothing but this realisation of the present as a retrospective future—a problem of circulation, which is legible in terms of the problem of response time. In the rest of the paper, we shall see how, in the case of COVID-19, the predictive modelling of the pathways of the pathogen draws upon the convergence between the futurisms of economic and epidemiological reasons in the twenty-first century.

5.3 Digital Epidemiology

As it was pointed out in the beginning, the response time against the spread of the Novel Coronavirus has been unprecedentedly fast. The key to that is what Lukas Engelmann, a historian of epidemics and epidemiology, is calling digital epidemiology, which offers:

> near-real-time surveillance of the epidemic, cum-pandemic, while it keeps emerging. Circumventing dated and excruciatingly slow reporting chains from front-line physicians to laboratories to national reporting institutes and clearing centres to the World Health Organization, the disruptive promise of digital epidemiologists is attractive. Any ongoing epidemic

> could be inferred directly and seamlessly from the global data exhaust, collected from what people do and what traces they leave online. (Engelmann, 2020)

The inferring does not need to be done by humans. Nearly a week before the first WHO notification came about a "flu-like outbreak in China", BlueDot, a Canadian health-monitoring platform warned its clients of an epidemic in the making (Niller, 2020). BlueDot's success has been amply celebrated by a section of the media, which advocates AI technology and machine learning. Eric Niller from *Wired* wrote about BlueDot and its founder, Kamran Khan, on 25 January 2020—even before the virus got its more familiar nomenclatures. Titled "An AI Epidemiologist Sent the First Warnings of the Wuhan Virus", the article echoes Khan's view that the governments often fail to disseminate timely information about medical crises. "We can pick up news of possible outbreaks, little murmurs or forums or blogs of indications of some kind of unusual events going on", he tells *Wired* (Niller, 2020). Collating data from different private and public sources—Khan is not very trusting of social media though—is not the end here. BlueDot has developed a "disease surveillance analytic program, which uses natural-language processing and machine learning techniques to sift through news reports in 65 languages, along with airline data and reports of animal disease outbreaks" (Niller, 2020). It is the primary analysis—finding patterns, connecting dots, deciphering signals—that makes the "AI epidemiologist" look like a thinking android from the pages of science fiction. The sifting of data itself does the first—and definitely more cumbersome—job of reducing noise in the information. By the time, humans take over to do more refined, second-order analysis, the strategic space of knowledge production is already somewhat defined. The task now is to initiate translations between this strategic space and logistical time.

The website of BlueDot gives us some idea about how these translations take place. The website describes the company as "ahead of the curve throughout the pandemic".[3] Being ahead of the curve means also being able to look back and predict the curve. The website also tells us that BlueDot was one of the earliest to recognise the emerging risk, which they communicated to their clients like the Canadian government, Air Canada and ASEAN among many. Their team also published the "first scientific paper on COVID-19"; their data suite delivers "near-real-time intelligence to governments, hospitals and airlines, revealing COVID-19's movements"; their focus reports successfully predicted India and Brazil as the new epicentres of the pandemic long before the said countries started experiencing the second wave. All these claims, irrespective of being true or false, point to an urgency with which the nodes of circulation could be mapped and forecast. The first scientific paper in question was published in the *Journal of Travel Medicine* on 14 January 2020, only five days after the WHO sent out its first notification (Bogoch et al., 2020: 1–3). The paper was submitted on 8 January, revised on 9 January, and accepted on 10 January—unbelievably fast response time for any academic journal. In this paper, Kamran Khan and his associates "evaluated 2018 travel data generated from the International Air Transport Association (IATA) to quantify passenger volumes originating from the international airport in Wuhan, China, between January and March, inclusive" (ibid: 1). The

[3] https://bluedot.global/. Retrieved January 10, 2023.

authors correlated this data with the Infectious Disease Vulnerability Index (IDVI) of the regions to which these flights took off for gauging and distinguishing the degrees of susceptibility. "The IDVI score is a validated tool to estimate a country's capacity to prepare for and manage infectious disease threats", the authors inform. "The score is based on metrics from the following seven domains: demographic, health care, public health, disease dynamics, political (domestic), political (international) and economic" (ibid: 4). Incidentally, the index was prepared by Melinda Moore, Bill Gelfeld, Adeyemi Okunogbe, Christopher Paul in a 2017 paper titled "Identifying Future Disease Hot Spots" on behalf of the RAND Corporation and published in their medical journal *Rand Health Quarterly* to help the "Department of Defense, the Department of Health and Human Services (e.g., through the Centers for Disease Control and Prevention), the U.S. Agency for International Development, and the international community more broadly" for targeted actions against future infectious disease outbreaks (Moore et al., 2017: 5). As we know, the RAND Corporation is another US-based think tank—much larger than the Center for Global Development and heavily funded by the government—which basically works as a research and analytical wing of the US Armed Forces.

The analysis of the air traffic data to predict the pathway of the virus is a novel approach not merely because of its ingenuity or the fact that one it can bypass the bureaucratic bottlenecks of governmental information. It takes the discipline of epidemiology to the domain of big data analytics, artificial intelligence, machine learning and deep tech. Add to that the correlation with IDVI—the preparation of which involved the resources of the RAND Corporation, an organisation that specialises in logistical research in the most pertinent sense that Bratton has used it. In a way, these strategies follow the four-pronged security apparatus of case, risk, danger and crisis but the empirical field out of which this apparatus seeks its rationale is quite different from the earlier times. Rather than the older regimes of census and survey modalities where the data was collected and worked upon as an objective mass of unruly observations, the regime of big data and AI focuses on interfacing between disparate elements, logics, and knowledge systems whereby the data itself acquires an experiential sovereignty—a mnemonic autonomy where prediction becomes identical with analysis and not its incidental consequence. In machine learning, the predictions are made not simply by making causal connections between pre-existing trends and current situations. It happens by re-presenting the future, as if the present is a fulfilment of the potential of the future, and not the other way round. Every time we complete a sentence with the words predicted to us by the writing software, we make the future part of our present. It is the same promise of a futuristic present, which brings epidemiological reason close to the economic rationality of business decisions and investments in futures—the world of finance, so to speak.

5.4 Socialisation of Risk

It is not surprising that, in the recent years, AI-based modelling has become quite popular in the economic discipline. As one observer points out, the increasing use of AI will finally heal the heartache to which the economists have subjected themselves for long, namely that the discipline, however empirically sound or deductively profound it may look, is still not considered a natural science (Niyazov, 2019). Although theories like the theory of rational expectation assume a mechanical human agent unperturbed by irrational desires or subjective biases, the predictive power of the discipline in the face of the randomness of individual or institutional behaviours seems minuscule. The problem is, of course, the human mind, which seldom practices straight thinking. Making predictions about anything that involves human thinking—making predictions with human thinking—is, therefore, impossible: "economists had failed to predict 148 of the past 150 recessions" (ibid). On the other hand, left to artificial intelligence, many of these problems will be solved, as the algorithms can analyse human sentiments without getting sentimental themselves: "AI algorithms can also analyze how media headlines influence sentiments about the economy. In fact, JPMorgan already uses an algorithm that tracks the effects of President Trump's tweets on financial markets. [...] Central banks and fiscal authorities, by knowing when a recession hits, will be more effective and rapid in enacting monetary and fiscal tools, thereby mitigating the effects of business cycles" (ibid). The best thing is that these programmes do not need any human intervention after a point. By way of machine learning, they can programme themselves.

This is the ultimate neoliberal fantasy. Phillip Mirowski, while talking about the centrality of the market principle in the neoliberal imagination of social engineering, tells us how, for most of the neoliberal thinkers like Hayek or Milton Friedman, the market is a giant information processor with a mind of its own (Mirowski, 2009: 440). "The price system transmits only the important information and only to the people who need to know", Milton Friedman and Rose Friedman once remarked (Friedman & Friedman, 1980: 15). The discriminatory intelligence of the price system is analogous to the predictive powers of the algorithm as both tend to prioritise. In a recent book on how an economics based on AI improves business decisions, Ajay Agarwal, Joshua Gans and Avi Goldfarb write that the AI is a prediction technology, which does not presume the absoluteness of truth or accuracy while dishing out information; it keeps on predicting which information will suit the purpose of an inquiry: "Alexa [the AI patented by Amazon] doesn't "know" the capital of Delaware. But Alexa is able to predict that, when people ask such a question, they are looking for a specific response: "Dover"" (Agarwal et al., 2018: 15). One can understand how this makes the lives of decision-makers in business easy. If they can already predict what the clients want—even before they know themselves, like in the case of BlueDot and its clients—failure is an impossibility. The biggest epistemic contribution that AI has made is changing the face of knowledge that seeks to minimise uncertainty. In this new epistemic universe, to know is to predict what others want to know/need to know. Or, even better, what they should know. This is precisely the logic of the algorithms that predict the ads, which would channel our desires, and hence, purchasing decisions. The world of making the future by way of predicting it is the world of finance. According to Randy Martin, we inhabit this world by socialising risk: by adopting the logics of financial instruments like securities and derivatives in our everyday decisions—sometimes bundling together and sometimes separating the risky from the not-so-risky—we as able neoliberal subjects distinguish ourselves as risk-takers from those who are at risk (Martin, 2007). This will involve a particular type of deliberation on future—a deliberation familiar to us—the way one can make the future their present: "Contingencies of the future are to be lived out in the present, blurring the distinction between the not-yet and the now" (ibid: 3). It will sound even more familiar when we shall see how the same logic permeates the new imperial wars of preemption: "Enemies are to be defeated before they can make their antagonism manifest" (ibid). It is not a coincidence, as we have seen before, that the war on terrorism for the last two decades will be invoked time and again in the war against the virus. They both follow the same logic of preemption—"by converting potential threats into actual conflicts", transferring "future uncertainties into present risk".[4] The uniqueness of the response to COVID-19, therefore, springs from this convergence between epidemiological and economic reasons that shape the neoliberal subject of our time.

5.5 Agamben's Anxiety

One can stop here and announce the end of the liberal order, which for long had championed the linear chronology of both politics and epistemology—the former as the domain of progression of democratic rights and the latter as the field of disciplinary evolution. Or, one is tempted to ask what lies ahead of us politically and epistemologically. Evidently, we have arrived at a crossroads. From the dry theories of rational expectation, we have moved to the thrilling universe of science fiction. In Steven Spielberg's adaptation of Phillip K. Dick's novella, *Minority Report* (released in 2002), a group of police officers called the "precogs" apprehend the criminal even before the crime is committed. This is the level of efficiency, which is expected from the back-and-forth translations of strategic spaces and logistical times where the pathway of the virus must be predicted in a futuristic timescale of its circulation. In Spielberg's film, it is done with something called "foreknowledge." We are as if living in a world of foreknowledge. Add to that the issue of medical surveillance and what we have is a chilling description of a dystopia where all our movements and desires are already mapped in the mechanic unconscious of an all-pervasive entity without any sentiment or ethical consideration.

In a series of articles over the last couple of years, Giorgio Agamben has emerged as the prophet of this seemingly inescapable doom. In a foreword to a collection of

---

[4] "By converting potential threats into actual conflicts, the war on terror transfers future uncertainty into present risk" (*ibid*).

these articles, he makes clear that he is drawing upon his own theories of bare life and state of exception to criticise the direction of the changes that are taking place in our social and political lives—changes that are more imposed than organic: "The defining feature, however, of this great transformation that they are attempting to impose is that the mechanism which renders it formally possible is not a new body of laws, but a state of exception—in other words, not an affirmation of, but the suspension of, constitutional guarantees" (Agamben, 2021: 8). In a way, he seems right. The laws that are usually invoked to declare a lockdown or curtail people's movements and interactions have been in existence for a while and were used before in various other "exceptional" situations of calamitous possibilities, natural disasters or even epidemics. As we already know, the segregation of the diseased from the healthy based on estimates calibrated to reduce the risk in the circulation of bodies and things has been a regular feature of modern governmentality. What concerns him is the scale of the operationalisation of what he calls "biosecurity": "the government apparatus that consists of this new religion of health, conjoined with the state power and its state of exception—an apparatus that is probably the most efficient of its kind that Western history has ever known" (ibid: 9). One may point out that, although it has been unknown to the Western history, the histories in the erstwhile colonies have witnessed such efficiency quite frequently. One may also take it from here to argue that it was in the colonies where the West had perfected these apparatuses. The security apparatuses that send chills down the spines of the Western intellectuals—"a sanitation terror and a religion of health" (ibid: 8) —were all deployed routinely during the epidemics in British India, most notably during the plague epidemic in the late nineteenth and early twentieth centuries (Arnold, 1993). Peculiarly, what Agamben has once diagnosed as an essential attribute of the Western bourgeois democracies—the monopoly of the state over declaring war against its own subjects—seems like a breach of promise to him now. It will not be a mistake to read in all this an anxiety that was truly unfamiliar to the Western intellectuals till date—that of the suspension of a political will, which was so far exclusively available to the individuated citizens of the West. In so many words, Agamben expresses his dismay in an interview: "It does not surprise me that Italy is at the moment spearheading the development of a technology of governance that, in the name of public health, renders acceptable a set of life conditions which eliminate all possible political activity, pure and simple" (Agamben, 2021: 34).

Agamben is not alone in this anxiety. "The hypothesis that we are experiencing the end of a world—the world of bourgeois democracy that is built on rights, parliaments and the division of powers—is now spreading widely", he writes in another article (ibid: 35). Ironically, he finds a lot of supporters in the political right who also find the "despotism" of the "security state" infringing personal freedom. The curious accord between the interlocutors on both sides of the political spectrum signals how flimsy their ideological differences are and how limited their vocabularies of discontent could be. The problem lies in the articulation of politics itself as an attempt to enhance agentive sovereignty of the individuated self. This view would see any other political action as suspect as that would call for going beyond the agenda of respecting personal freedom and a sociality based on exchange relations, both emanating from the ideal of private property. The biopolitics that Agamben finds unacceptable threatens the status quo of self-congratulatory liberalism, wrings dry the nostalgia of a just state based on parliamentary democracy and exhausts the rhetoric of collective accountability where the collective is merely a sum of individual citizen subjects. Perhaps the time has come to reinvent the collective, reimagine politics and redefine democracy. For that, one needs to turn the futuristic biopolitics that we have described so far on its head.

5.6 A Biopolitics of Future

Benjamin Bratton in an incisive polemic against the position taken by Agamben and his supporters' points out many of its fallacies. The "negative biopolitics" of Agamben, which asks us to treat any scientific attempt at mapping the movement of the virus as coercive and politically undesirable, is doing more harm than good, according to him (Bratton, 2021). Contrary to that is his own notion of a "positive biopolitics" that deserves our attention. Rather than making calls for going back to a less entangled and more natural past, Bratton suggests that we should review the meaning of these entanglements and discover our own positions within them: "Entanglement is the baseline, not the exception" (ibid: 1).Viewing the pandemic from this perspective allows us to think of a politics that exists at a planetary level and come up with solutions that are not localised or spontaneously laissez-faire. First of all, he wants us to think of this moment not as a state of exception but "more as revealing *pre-existing conditions*" (ibid: 7; author's emphasis). Many of these conditions originate in the suspicion of technological interventions that may supposedly affect the individuality at the core of human sociality. The first task, therefore, is to delink sociality from individualism by adopting what Bratton calls an "epidemiological view of the society", which, among other things, teaches us to see it as "a population of contagion nodes and vectors" (ibid: 33). This shift in perspective from private individuation to public transmissibility offers a fresh description of the society conducive to information technology, albeit with a positive spirit: "Each organism is a transmission medium for information—from ideas to viruses—and is defined by who and what each is connected to and disconnected from" (ibid). Here Bratton invokes Foucault's lectures on biopolitics to argue that it is a misconception of this biopolitics that treat the medical governance only as technologies of surveillance lacking any possibility of a positive species politics. The epidemiological view renders the life of the body not as private, incommunicable or subjective as many interlocutors like Agamben would think. Rather "a realist and materialist conception of the human body as a biochemical assemblage and collective human intelligence as the collaboration of such creatures working in concert" (ibid: 38) is possible to imagine from the same framework and that would lead to a collectivisation of "risk"—not as "a private algebraic decision" but "as a plural and intersubjective set of relations" (ibid: 34).

It is not difficult to understand the difference between collectivisation of risk and its socialisation as discussed by Martin previously. In the case of socialisation of risk, the individual risk-taker makes some calculations to maximise the present potential of an uncertainty in the future whereas, in the case of its collectivisation, the risk is distributed among a large group of people in terms of their interconnectivity. Two things are important to note: (1) the interconnectivity is subject to an understanding of the human body as a biochemical assemblage where the humanity is not an exclusivist essence but a site of cohabitation of many life forms including the virus; (2) the concept of risk is still a product of collection and interpretation of information but the nature of this information is radically different from the one we observe in the case of socialisation of risk. Here we take note of the need for creating what Bratton calls a "sensing layer"—testing and tracking in the most extensive manner in the present context: "To have more widely available testing is to have more accurate sensing, which means better models, which means a better public health response" (ibid: 41). Modelling the virus is seeing the world in a particular way "outlined by specific visual vernaculars of what constitutes risk, pattern, curve, prediction and recommendation" (ibid: 48) so that one can gauge the risk more objectively and start working on its mitigation. It is a logistical manoeuvre in which the translation of the strategic space (represented in the symbolic order) into a logistical time of intervention is the principal goal but this intervention must happen at a planetary scale or it will be ineffective. Hence, one must leave behind the understanding of data as some kind of tool to predict individual consumption preferences and private behaviour and venture into an archival paradigm focused on "very long-term, multivariate samples of relevant phenomena over very long periods of time" (ibid: 149) Although Bratton is not explicit on this, he does not seem to mind the use of AI and machine learning technologies in this archival paradigm, especially since he insists on the self-correcting and self-forming aspect of the biosocial that may emerge from this politics of life—a biopolitics of future, which is more inclusive and less conceited, more entangled and less individuated, more collective and less personal. "Per Derrida, the archive is a promise to the future that the present time will make itself accountable", he writes. "It can also be a technology to ensure that the future is even possible" (ibid: 151–152). Rather than re-presenting the future, this is a move towards refuturing the present.

5.7 The Real Conflict

It is evident that this overhaul of the data politics will call for many other systemic overhauls. For one, the relationship between the state and capital must be redefined so radically that it will need to upend almost all the existing modalities of production, distribution and circulation. Rob Wallace in a timely rejoinder reminds us that the pandemic is a symptom of much deeper inequalities and more intense perversions inhering the global circuits of capital that keep on "destroying regional environmental complexity that keeps virulent pathogen population growth in check" (Wallace, 2020: 54). "The underlying operative premise is that the cause of COVID-19 and other such pathogens is not found only in the object of any one infectious agent or its clinical cause", he adds, "but also in the field of ecosystemic relations that capital and other structural causes have pinned back to their own advantage" (ibid: 55). The conflict, therefore, is not between the pathways of the virus and that of the humans, but between the self-accumulative drive of capital and the self-corrective ethics of a biosociality that should not distinguish between the risk-takers and those who are at risk—between the entrepreneurs, big pharma, agro-capitalists, and the philosophers who are sitting in their air-conditioned bubbles of privilege and making profits or passing judgements (speculating, all of them, in their respective ways) and the migrant workers and the care workers who are at the frontline of this biopolitical resistance and fighting for a more secure and equitable future.

References

Agamben, G. (2021). *Where are we now? The epidemics as politics*. Eris.

Agarwal, A., Gans, J., & Goldfarb, A. (2018). *Prediction machines: The simple economics of artificial intelligence*. Harvard Business Review Press.

Ahmed, M. (2021, July 28). *The US is losing the global war against COVID-19—and that is a national security issue*. Retrieved January 10, 2023, from https://www.cgdev.org/blog/us-losing-global-war-against-covid-19-and-national-security-issue

Arnold, D. (1993). *Colonizing the body: State medicine and epidemic disease in nineteenth-century India*. University of California Press.

Bogoch, I., Watts, A., Thomas-Bachli, A., Huber, C., Kraemer, M., & Khan, K. (2020). Pneumonia of unknown aetiology in Wuhan, China: Potential for international spread via commercial air travel. *Journal of Travel Medicine, 27*(2), 1–3.

Bratton, B. (2006). Logistics of habitable circulation. In P. Virilio (Ed.), *Speed and politics* (pp. 7–25). Semiotext(e).

Bratton, B. (2021). *The revenge of the real: Politics for a post-pandemic world*. Verso.

Engelmann, L. (2020, March 6). *#COVID19: The spectacle of real-time surveillance*. Retrieved January 10, 2023, from http://somatosphere.net/forumpost/covid19-spectacle-surveillance

Foucault, M. (2019). *Security, territory, population: Lectures at the College de France, 1977–78*. Palgrave-Macmillan.

Friedman, M., & Friedman, R. (1980). *Free to choose: A personal statement*. Harcourt Brace Jovanovich.

Fukuda, K., Harmanci, H., Park, K., & Chamberland, M. (2009). *Pandemic influenza preparedness and response: A WHO guidance document*. Nonserial Publication.

Lefebvre, H. (1991). *The production of space*. Basil Blackwell.

Martin, R. (2007). *An empire of indifference: American war and the financial logic of risk management*. Duke University Press.

Mirowski, P. (2009). Postface: Defining neoliberalism. In P. Mirowski & D. Plewhe (Eds.), *The road from Mont Pelerin: The making of the neoliberal thought collective* (pp. 417–455). Harvard University Press.

Moore, M., Gelfeld, B., Okunogbe, A., & Paul, C. (2017). Identifying future disease hot spots: Infectious disease vulnerability index. *Rand Health Quarterly, 6*(3), 5.

Multilateral Leaders Task Force. (2021, July 30). *Joint statement of the multilateral leaders task force on COVID-19 vaccines, therapeutics, and diagnostics for developing countries following its second meeting*. Retrieved January 10, 2023, from https://www.worldbank.org/en/news/statement/2021/07/30/joint-statement-on-second-meeting-of-task-force-on-COVID-vaccines-therapeutics-and-diagnostics-for-developing-countries

Multilateral Leaders Task Force. (2022, March 7). *Eighth Meeting of the multilateral leaders task force on COVID-19, 1 March 2022: "Third consultation with the*

CEOs of leading vaccine manufacturers" Joint statement. Retrieved January 10, 2023, from https://www.worldbank.org/en/news/statement/2022/03/07/eighth-meeting-of-the-multilateral-leaders-task-force-on-covid-19-1-march-2022-third-consultation-with-the-ceos-of-leadi

Niller, E. (2020, January 25). *An AI epidemiologist sent the first warnings of the Wuhan virus*. Retrieved January 10, 2023, from https://www.wired.com/story/ai-epidemiologist-wuhan-public-health-warnings

Niyazov, S. (2019, November 10). *How A.I. will redefine economics*. Retrieved January 10, 2023, from https://towardsdatascience.com/how-ai-will-redefine-economics-ec305e3cb687

Prior, S. (2006). *Preparing for a pandemic influenza: A primer for governors and senior state officials*. National Governors Association.

PTI. (2021, May 8). *War against COVID to be fought collectively, with public participation: Jitendra Singh*. Retrieved January 20, 2023, from https://economictimes.indiatimes.com/news/india/war-against-covid-to-be-fought-collectively-with-public-participation-jitendra-singh/articleshow/82481160.cms?from=mdr

Raman, R. (2021, April 21). *India's war against Covid-19*. Retrieved January 10, 2023, from https://www.hindustantimes.com/opinion/indias-war-against-covid19-101618913917918.html

The U.S. Department of Homeland Security Contributors. (2006). *Pandemic influenza preparedness, response, and recovery guide for critical infrastructure and key resources*. U.S. Department of Homeland Security.

Wallace, R. (2020). *Dead epidemiologists: On the origins of COVID-19*. Monthly Review Press.

Zee Media Bureau. (2021, October 3). Retrieved January 10, 2023, from https://zeenews.india.com/india/war-against-covid-19-not-over-it-can-return-with-vengeance-aiims-task-force-chief-2399261.html

Part II
Global and Local Response to 2020

Chapter 6
Global Capitalism and Corona Pandemic—In Search for Radical Solution

Byasdeb Dasgupta

Abstract Global capitalism's instability is inherent in its nature and structure. In fact, Corona pandemic triggered the third capitalist crash in the global economy in the present century. May be the crash was anyway inevitable, but the Pandemic has aggravated the dimensions of the crash hitherto unknown. The crash even though aggravated by the Pandemic is systemic in nature. The system is not infallible. Rather, the inherent tendency of capitalism as an economic system is to produce recurring crashes and the radical solutions to that sickness of the system are beyond the imagination of the politics as it is practised today in various parts of the world—mainly in the garb of liberal democracy. Three basic problems can be attributed to global capitalism as an economic system. Firstly, the economic space of capitalism as it is ruled by several capitalist enterprises is undemocratic. And this undemocratic nature of capitalism in the economic sphere keeps it away from the general well-being of the majority. The second problem associated with global capitalism is its inherent tendency of generating crash or crisis every four to seven years which damage the enterprises and the economy—rather, the majority of the enterprises and the current Pandemic is no exception. Thirdly, capitalism in general and global capitalism in particular generate inequalities of wealth and income which widen further at the time of crash or crisis. This chapter on global capitalism and Corona pandemic will make an attempt to decipher these basic three problems of capitalism as an economic system and would try to see if any radical solution is plausible in terms of reforming the system as Keynes advocated at the time of Great Depression during 1930s.

Keywords Capitalism · Liberal democracy · Economic crisis · Crash · Great depression · Keynes

Global capitalism's instability is inherent in its nature and structure. In fact, Corona Pandemic triggered the third capitalist crash in the global economy in the present century. May be the crash was anyway inevitable, but the Pandemic has aggravated the

B. Dasgupta (✉)
Department of Economics, University of Kalyani, and MCRG, Kolkata, India
e-mail: byasdeb@gmail.com

S. R. Chakraborty et al. (eds.), *The Long 2020*, India Studies in Business and Economics, https://doi.org/10.1007/978-981-99-4815-4_6

dimensions of the crash hitherto unknown. The problems that are associated with the current global capitalism in this age of neoliberal globalization remain unresolved. The crash even though aggravated by the Pandemic is systemic in nature. The system is not infallible. Rather, the inherent tendency of capitalism as an economic system is to produce recurring crashes and the radical solutions to that sickness of the system are beyond the imagination of the politics as it is practised today in various parts of the world—mainly in the garb of liberal democracy. Three basic problems can be attributed to global capitalism as an economic system. Firstly, the economic space of capitalism as it is ruled by several capitalist enterprises is undemocratic. A small minority at the top including owners, board of directors and major shareholders makes all the decisions (particularly with regard to appropriation and distribution of the surplus) in every enterprise, but this minority is not accountable to the majority who are the employees of these enterprises. This is a contradiction inherent in any society shaped by capitalism where the political is based on so-called liberal democracy, but the economic is undemocratic. And, this undemocratic nature of capitalism in the economic sphere keeps it away from the general well-being of the majority. This is the first problem that capitalism has inherited from its predecessors like feudalism as an economic system. The second problem associated with global capitalism is its inherent tendency of generating crash or crisis every four to seven years which damage the enterprises and the economy—rather, the majority of the enterprises and the current Pandemic is no exception. May be the magnitude of the crisis has been widened by the Corona episode. In mainstream economic theory, this is referred to as business cycles. Thirdly, capitalism in general and global capitalism in particular generate inequalities of wealth and income which widen further at the time of crash or crisis. This present Pandemic is a very good example that the wealth of the top one per cent of population in terms of wealth and income has increased manifold during this pandemic while many commonplace went income less and jobless. So, the capitalism's problems including lack of economic democracy, lack of stability and lack of equality when we look at them at times of Corona Pandemic bring into fore global capitalism as a sick system.

The present work on global capitalism and Corona Pandemic makes an attempt to decipher these basic three problems of capitalism as an economic system and would try to see if any radical solution is plausible in terms of reforming the system within capitalism as Keynes advocated at the time of Great Depression during 1930s.

Global capitalism as an economic system continues to exist with recurring crises as mentioned above. Following class-focused approach, one can envisage any society as ensemble of various processes and/or sites which are overdetermined in Althuserian sense.[1] For the sake of simplicity, we can distinguish these processes/sites as

[1] The philosophy of overdetermination negates the logic of determinism which is structured by cause-and-effect relationship between two or more variables. For example, the statement "X causes Y" implies that the causal relationship is running in certain determined relation. If there are three variables such that "X causes Y" and "Y causes Z," then by the transitivity relation "X will cause Z" also, not otherwise. Note that here in this system of three variables X is not caused either by Y or by Z. So, in the system it remains absolutely pre-determined, exogenously given. On the other hand, the logic of overdetermination tells us that X, Y and Z are overdetermined implying that each

economic, political, cultural and natural and these processes/sites mutually constitute each other. There are various contradictions and push and pull factors among these processes/sites which shape a society. When we analyze any economic system (say, feudalism, capitalism), we cannot ignore the overdetermined constitution of such system by these different processes/sites—namely, economic, political, cultural and natural. No single site/process is pre-given and none is more important than the others. Each is equally important in shaping an economic system. So, the space of economic is constituted by the overdetermined presence of economic, political, cultural and natural. And at certain juncture of history, each one of these four processes/sites takes certain nuances and stances which help to shape an economic system. This way of looking at the economy and economic system differs from the essentialist or reductionist envisioning of economy *a la* classical Marxism, as the base and political and cultural as the superstructure. So, while analyzing global capitalism as an economic system, we need to be very careful in taking care of the different meanings produced by the non-economic processes/sites in influencing the shaping of (global) capitalism as an economic system.

At the current juncture the economic, which concerns the global capitalism is undemocratic as the decision-making mechanism within a capitalist enterprise is in the hand of few (productive) capitalists and not in the hand of the majority—the direct producers who produce the surplus value which is appropriated and distributed by the (productive) capitalists. And this needs a political sanction and a cultural environment which provide the necessary conditions of existence and reproduction of capitalist class processes without which capital accumulation and profit generation at large scale are not possible. The garb of liberal democracy thus garners support to global and local capitalist enterprises, while the latter remain undemocratic as the performers of surplus value do not have any voice in appropriation and distribution of those surplus that they generate again and again.

As mentioned above, one of the basic features of global capitalism is its recurring crisis (which in mainstream neoclassical economics) is defined as business cycles where booms are followed by recessions almost as a rule. And most of the time capitalism accuses certain factor external to it as responsible for such downturns. This time this external is Corona pandemic. The pandemic has ruined the economy for the general milieu and the most unique feature of the pandemic is (which distinguishes it from other externals occurred earlier in history) the fact that it has posed a public health threat—to which both capitalists and direct producers are susceptible. So, the

mutually constitutes each other. Each influences others and in turn gets influenced by the others. Each variable is cause of the other variables and also the effects of the others. So, the there is no unidirectional causality as in deterministic relation where X gets reduced to Y and Y gets reduced to Z, and hence, X ultimately gets reduced to Z. Such reductionism is absent in an overdetermined system. For a critical appreciation of overdetermined reality and contradictions in it, see Althusser (1962). Society is a space—rather an overdetermined space where natural, economic, political and cultural mutually constitute each other and this inter-relationships between the four sites of the society occur dynamically over time and space, as a result of which there is always dynamic transformation in the societal spaces in contradictory manner. The space of economic is constituted in terms of three basic activities of consumption, production and distribution—each one of which is inseparable from the other when viewed from the perspective of overdetermined reality.

question is how the global capitalism is tackling this public health threat or is there any solution available within global capitalism to cope with this threat?

Or the other basic query is whether global capitalism is considering the current pandemic as a new avenue of generating surplus, capital accumulation and reaping super-normal profits?

The present work makes an attempt to address these two basic questions afflicting the global capitalism in the context of ongoing public health crisis. The work is designed to proceed in the following way. Firstly, an attempt will be made to understand the present crisis in economy in particular and global society at large. The moot question is whether the present crisis would have been averted if the outbreak of pandemic was not there? Or is it the case that the "global" is constituted in such a manner that a crisis would have been inevitable irrespective of the fact whether there was pandemic or not? To answer these two questions one need to envisage global capitalism and the public health threat as produced by the Corona from non-essentialist viewpoints as we have already mentioned that the global or society for that matter including the economic (as a system) is overdetermined constitution by economic, political, cultural and natural. This is so because nothing is pre-given as base and the history of capitalism too is not linear as generally claimed. Hence, the understanding of the present crisis as is claimed to be consequence of pandemic needs to be analyzed from the global economic, political, cultural and natural so to say as they are in the present time point.

Second question with which we are concerned with in the present work is whether global capitalism envisages the pandemic as new vistas for generating more surplus, capital accumulation and profit mongering? If so, what is analytical link of the global capitalism with the pandemic in furthering or strengthening the factors responsible for the recurrent reproduction of capitalist class processes worldwide? There is a need for some analytical verification of the present facts in the current context in this regard. How does capitalism, as a system extracts more and more surplus and thus accumulates more and more wealth for handful few capitalists—productive as well as unproductive?

Related with the second question just mentioned above is the question of widening income and wealth inequality which is a basic feature of global (and also local) capitalism in the garb of so-called liberal democracy. Does pandemic give way to widening inequality with which capitalism (global as well as local) has continued to survive for centuries? This is an issue as already some established facts have indicated the same and which needs to be analytically posed. Why cannot capitalism survive with an egalitarian distribution of income and wealth or what prevents capitalism to do so and how pandemic fuels the capitalism's lust for inequality? Is it at all possible to have an egalitarian stance of economy with the present global capitalism and how pandemic has corroborated the widening gap between the performers of surplus value and the appropriators of such surplus?

Finally, we want to conclude the work with the question whether any solution to the present crisis of the society in general and economy in particular plausible keeping the economic system in the global capitalism as it is? Or whether there is a need for a radical solution to the recurring economic crisis (and also to the public health threat as posed by the pandemic)? A radical solution which may cure the sickness of the system? Now, the question of "radical" may usher utopia. Now, some may argue that a reformulated capitalism with the state playing larger role (as was envisaged by Keynes in view of the Great Depression of the 1930s) may bring an end to such recurrences of the crises as are occurring in capitalism with periodic gaps in a systemic manner. Our question is whether that is also feasible under global capitalism or whether global capitalism in this age of neoliberalism would allow such reforms to happen (as it happened in the shape of New Deal in the USA in 1940s)? Does global capitalism require another New Deal to address the problematic of the pandemic-induced crises or whether such is not feasible in this age of neoliberalism? And that raises the question of search for "radical" solution to the present pandemic-hit economy and society.

The work is mostly analytical in understanding the concrete reality of the connection between global capitalism and pandemic, which will be supported by empirical facts as and when necessary. The basic entry point of the analysis will capitalist class process which is an economic process and we will proceed in terms of non-essentialist perspective while deciphering the overdetermined constitutivity of that economic process with other non-economic processes, as in this work the economy is not posed as base and political and cultural as superstructure—a departure from the classical Marxism. In our class-focused rendition, the basic concern is whether it is the sickness of the system which is global capitalism that matters—be it Corona or not, and hence, there comes the search for radical solution. And we are also concerned with the proposition whether this "sick" system can be reformed or not in terms of a New Deal, and even if it is possible, whether neoliberal globalization would allow such Deal? These are some of the queries in terms of which we make an endeavour to search for "radical" solution to the sickness of the system. Or is it the case that "There is no alternative" (TINA) to the present global capitalism in this neoliberal age? So, just some stimulus or rescue packages for the time being!

The entry point of our analysis is class-focused Marxist theory as propounded by Resnick and Wolff (1987). So, we begin with a brief description what is meant by non-essentialist class-focused Marxist rendition of society at large and economy in particular in which class questions become quite significant.

6.1 Class-Focused Marxist Theory and Global Capitalism

Class-focused Marxist approach differs from the orthodox/classical Marxism in the sense that where in the latter class is understood as noun it is regarded as an adjective, as a process in the former. Whereas class is defined with reference to the ownership of means of production in the orthodox Marxism, it is defined as a process based upon surplus labour in class-focused Marxist approach. The entry point of analysis in class-focused approach pertains to surplus labour defined as the excess labour (time) performed by direct producer over the necessary labour (time). According to Marx, those who perform surplus labour are direct producers. So, the term *direct producer* here is connotation of owners of labour power. Class as a process is performation, appropriation, distribution and receipt of surplus labour. In terms of performation and appropriation of surplus labour, one can define fundamental class process, and in terms of distribution and receipt of surplus labour, one can define subsumed class process. Those who occupy subsumed class positions offer necessary and fundamental conditions of existence and of reproduction to the fundamental class process. Fundamental and subsumed processes are inter-related in overdetermined manner implying that each mutually constitutes each other. An individual may occupy at the same time different class positions—fundamental as well as subsumed. For example, a capitalist owner of a factory belongs to the fundamental class process as appropriator of surplus labour, and at the same time, he may occupy subsumed class position as money lender to another fundamental class process. Viewing class as process in this sense opens innumerable possibilities of different class forms. Broadly, we can distinguish two principal class forms in any society at a time—(a) exploitative class process and (b) non-exploitative class process. As per Marx, exploitation is appropriation of surplus labour by non-performer of such labour in a production process. One can at least distinguish between four different types of exploitative class processes, viz. capitalist, slave, feudal and communistic (in which surplus labour is performed by the members of community but appropriated by one member only). Similarly, we can identify three different non-exploitative class processes, viz. communistic (where surplus labour is appropriated by all the members of community), communistic and independent (where a single individual performs surplus labour and appropriates his/her surplus labour). Therefore, at least six different class processes are possible at a time in a space. This immediately negates the idea of class-based society and its linear transformation in terms of historical materialism of the orthodox Marxism. Capitalist class process differs from the other processes as the surplus labour in this class process gets converted into surplus value through market. Production in capitalist class process is meant for market. Process of capital accumulation in capitalist class process refers to the recurring generation of surplus value.

Now, the question is why exploitation as an economic category so much emphasized in Marxian analysis? First of all, exploitation means looting of surplus labour by non-performer of such labour, which is unethical as any looting is. Secondly, those who appropriate surplus labour also take the decision of its distribution. In fact, viewing a production process on the basis of class process also signifies that distribution in the society is intrinsically related to production. Surplus labour gets distributed to those who occupy the subsumed class positions and provide necessary and fundamental conditions of reproduction of the concerned fundamental class process again and again. Surplus may get distributed, for example, to the supervisory staff and managers in the factory, to the suppliers, to the creditors including banks, to the shareholders of the firm as dividends, to the government as tax, to the distributors as commission, to the labour contractors of the firm, and a portion may be retained as undistributed, which in the terminology of finance is known as retained earnings. Profit of a firm is a part of surplus that is distributed. Surplus is not profit. In our understanding, pattern of distribution is crucial for the type of needs, viz. consumption choices and preferences, that will be generated in the society. Production of those commodities will occur whose need is more.

The world has witnessed over the last three centuries enormous expansion in the capitalist class process that is production for the market. The sole criterion of such class process is to generate as much surplus value as is possible. The basic characteristic of such production is greed of the capitalist producers—greed which finds its expression in (money) value term more and more wealth accumulation. More is always better as far as money value of such wealth accumulation is concerned. And in order that money value of wealth is maximized capitalist production processes relied upon excessive use of natural environment which was hitherto unseen. Also, any capitalist class process strives to find new avenues of generating surplus and mongering profit—be that new avenue be a public health threat like Corona Pandemic.

How does the nature of class processes matters for a public health threat. Now, in our understanding economic use of a public health threat (as it is in the form of Corona today) and also, the construction of that threat crucially hinges upon the kinds of needs which are generated and sustained over time in the society. Pre-industrial society has different genres of need than the post-industrial one. In post-industrial society, need is proportionately more for industrial goods than for primary goods. For example, post-industrial society with the advent of science and technology has more needs of a particular type of industrial goods—that is the pharma goods and a Pandemic generates more needs of pharma and related goods and services. This need finds its expression in the sphere of market in terms of demand for various categories of industrial products in general and health-related goods and services in particular. The latter is more so when a public health threat occurs like the present Corona Pandemic. Not all categories of need for industrial products are essentially harmful for natural environment—neither from the point of view of production nor from the point of view of consumption.[2]

If we take a close look at the evolving pattern of industrial goods since the inception of Industrial Revolution in Europe and later in other parts of the globe, we come across two distinct trends. *First*, the production of consumer durables and products such as health-related goods and services increased more sharply than the non-durables.[3]

[2] For example, the need for jute products can be cited, whose production hardly entails any environmental problem nor there is any threat to natural environment when jute products are consumed. Rather, both jute production and consumption are environmental friendly as jute is a bio-degradable product. But the need for jute over the years in the post-World War II era has been replaced by the need for synthetic or plastic material which harms employment—both when produced as well as consumed. Environment pollution is generated when such material is produced and also when such material is consumed as they are non-bio-degradable.

[3] Durable products have always posed some threat to the environment, if not at the level of production, but at the level of consumption definitely. Several instances in this regard are available. Of them the most noteworthy is the greenhouse effect caused by emission of CFC gas by refrigeration products. In fact, the problem is global as it is causing depletion in the ozone layer leading to global warming and threatening the very life-support system which natural environmental system provides to the living organisms including human beings in earth. Despite several efforts at the global level to reduce such emissions and to bring it down to socially tolerable limit are in vain as that would mean

And the class processes associated with such production are mostly capitalist as these entail production for the markets and appropriation of surplus is performed by the non-performing capitalist owners. They are mostly large firms and need huge market to sell their products worldwide. And accordingly, they push their products in the markets by advertisement and other customer-friendly services. Also, to keep in mind the fact is that new need is continuously generated and sustained. The new need owing to Corona Pandemic is a classic example of it and it is going to be sustained because the threat of Corona will be there for the years to come. But one noticeable fact is that a need which is related with a public health threat gets into the market with active support of the state, and in the present case, it is the neoliberal states all over the world. The state support is crucial but note that (at least in the Indian case) the onus is befalling on the individuals and private parties for the treatment of Corona and even in the case of vaccination private bodies are encouraged so that if some can afford they can take vaccine by paying price. And it can be claimed that in the future when the threat of the Pandemic wanes out, an individual has to go to a private party to take the vaccine by paying a price. Thus, on a sustained basis need is generated. Need for such products increased over time with the change in life forms in the post-industrial society where such products become the integral part of modern lifestyle. And in the future, it is sure that the modern development of pharma industry including the R&D therein will be mostly in terms of creating more and more new needs of medicines and other products and services pertaining to Corona virus. The crux of the argument here is that more is the pharma production for Corona virus, more is the need and more is the generation of effective demand in the market for the treatment and/or prevention of Corona virus. The class process involved in pharma manufacturing is neither non-exploitative nor non-capitalist. They are exploitative capitalist. Such class processes not only will produce more medicines and related goods and services for Corona neglecting perhaps the other necessary goods and services required for public health at least in the global South as the scope of surplus generation and profit mongering will be more in Corona-related production than the economic production for other public health threat in the global South. Also simultaneously through its distribution of surplus generates the desired need for them in the market. Hence, to address one public health threat, other similar threats at present may be ignored as the present threat with its uncertain future provides more scope for surplus appropriation by the productive capitalists all over the globe which is distributed between different unproductive capitalists as well who are providing the necessary condition of reproduction of such fundamental class processes on a sustained basis. And the neoliberal state is playing a supportive role in creating the new market instead of creating public healthcare system. The onus is befalling on the private capitalist enterprises in which few multinational pharma companies are playing dominant role.

Second distinct trend with the emergence of Corona threat is the growth of many services for which commonplace affected with the virus is paying exorbitant prices

---

ending production of refrigeration products, which are mostly produced by the large corporations all over the world and the lion's share in that production is borne by the multinationals.

as these services for them are essential and there is separate market for these services. Sellers of these services are charging high price as in economic sense they are essential and these services are price inelastic. First of all with the growth of these services extraction of extra surplus has increased at increasing rates. This is posing the problem for the future affordability of such services by the commonplace. But being essential in nature these productions may cause tremendous economic pressure on the commonplace. This is a classic case of unequal exchange and capitalism prefers such exchange as they ensure more surplus and hence, more profit. Most of these productions are for the markets and for the sole objective of reaping as high return from investment as possible, which warrants surplus value generation over time at increasing rates. And this is possible theoretically through an exploitative capitalist class process where once again the distribution pattern corroborates simultaneously the ever-increasing need of these products including services.

The above analysis is an attempt to understand how with the outbreak of the Pandemic, new needs are created thus skewing also the needs for other public health necessities (as the latter at the moment does not entail scope for super-normal capital accumulation and wealth generation for handful few in the globe). The other gets devalued. Modern society thrives on markets. And markets thrive on need. Type of need is the resultant of the distribution process typical to a particular class process. The predominant class process in the modern society is capitalist one, which gave way to a distribution process conducive to the emergence of particular need necessary for the further reproduction of such class process.

We have so far hinted upon just one type of class process. The class process whose entire focus is on surplus accumulation by non-performer of such surplus and thereby, accumulate more and more capital. In doing so, they not only plunder the surplus labour of the direct producers but also plunder the need of other health threats—double plundering. Today in the mainstream economics development is treated from the perspective of capital—capital accumulation and discretionary wealth generation, and this Pandemic is no exception. It is a capital-centric view from the perspective of generation of typical return on investment. So, the stress is on increasing productivity of capital to reproduce again and again for Corona and like in the form of generating fear among the commonplace regarding the uncertain consequence of any public health threat. The mainstream does not find any fault with the kind of need which relishes the growth of modern industrial society. It does not question the distribution which sustains such need. It simply finds fault with one of its factors of production, viz. labour, as labour has to become the risk-bearing factor (as the conditions of labour—particularly migrant ones indicate with the surge of the Pandemic and long lockdown therefore). Productivity enhancement of labour remains the sole means to solve the problem even at this time (which is vindicated by the attempt of the Indian state to introduce new labour codes). In this sense, the social relations of production matter as the threat of Pandemic gets longer and longer.

It is not our claim that whatever is non-capitalist is good for labour—the performer of surplus labour (value). Space of non-capitalist is divided between exploitative and non-exploitative. But two things merit attention in this regard one of which is relevant for the public health. First some of the non-capitalist class processes are exploitative and some non-exploitative. Exploitative non-capitalist class processes entail skewed distribution, and in our understanding as distribution gets more and more skewed, need for new goods is more. Given the experience of South, one can comment that capitalist class processes do extend support to exploitative non-capitalist process. It is evident in terms of coexistence of feudal class process in Indian agriculture along with capitalist class process. To our understanding exploitative non-capitalist class process helps the cause of capitalist class processes by generating need for modern industrial products including the pharma and related goods and services.

Secondly, there are some traditional production processes in the non-capitalist space, in which protection of natural environment is integral part. Many of the community-based production processes of tribal societies fall in this category. The predominant industrial society has always undervalued such non-capitalist space, which is otherwise ethical in our rendition, as lacking other, under-developed and uncivilized. This brings us to the discussion of capitalo-centricism from the perspective of the natural which is grossly neglected at the present moment.

Let us now take a look at a typical capitalist class enterprise which will help us to understand the sources of generating wealth including capital accumulation in the present global order characterized by neoliberal globalization.

That productive capitalists personify capital as appropriators and distributors of surplus value do not mean that an enterprise with capitalist fundamental class process will be simply reduced to the moment of capitalist appropriation. An enterprise is much more complex. First the appropriated surplus value (SV) is not kept by the productive capitalist but is distributed as subsumed class payments to different agents/institutions who provide a range of conditions of existence. Here ΣSV (sum of appropriated surplus value) = ΣSSCP (sum of subsumed class payments). In order to reproduce itself, the enterprise must distribute its surplus in such a way as to satisfy a number of conditions of existence, Such conditions comprise economic processes (such as exchanging commodities in the market or using part of capital for furthering the process of accumulation of capital), political processes (such as paying the managers or paying the state to keep the workers and unions under control), cultural processes (such as paying for advertisement) and natural processes (such as paying for keeping the work environment pollution free). Those who are receivers of subsumed payments (SSCP) include to name a few, banks, merchants, state, landlords, managers, etc. Thus, the enterprise is no longer an economic entity reducible to class. It is rather an overdetermined and contradictory site of class process and its constitutive economic, cultural, political and natural processes. Second, an enterprise is also constituted by the receipt of the subsumed class payments in exchange for providing numerous conditions of existence to fundamental class processes of other enterprises. For example, the above-mentioned enterprise may be providing finance capital to other enterprises (capitalist or non-capitalist) in order to, say, enable those enterprises to purchase its means of production against which they would have to make a certain amount of subsumed payments. Such payments enter into the capitalist enterprise's balance sheet as subsumed class revenue or as ΣSSCR. In order to produce these conditions of existence, the enterprise will be incurring expenditures (for example, maintaining staff who deal with loans) to the amount ΣX. $\Sigma\text{SSCR} = \Sigma X$. Finally, the capitalist enterprise may be receiving non-class revenues for providing non-class conditions of existence as well. Loans for home building to its productive and unproductive workers would be an example of such activity. Since such loans secure no fundamental class process, the revenues derived from such loans reflect non-class processes. We add such non-class revenues as ΣNCR. To reproduce the conditions of such revenue generations, expenditure of ΣY is incurred. $\Sigma\text{NCR} = \Sigma Y$. We thus get a picture of the capitalist enterprise in terms of revenue (left-hand side) and expenditure (right-hand side):

$$\sum \text{SV} + \sum \text{SSCR} + \sum \text{NCR} = \sum \text{SSCP} + \sum X + \sum Y, \quad (6.1)$$

Let us further note that Eq. 6.1 can be used for depicting any enterprise, whether capitalist or non-capitalist. For example, a change in the manner of appropriation from, say, capitalist to communist, would change the class nature of the enterprise from capitalist to communist.

A global capitalist enterprise in terms of the accounting frame is the one which appropriates surplus in one geographical space and distributes such surplus in another geographical space. Not only that in terms of receiving subsumed class revenue and incurring expenditures for them, geographical spaces may be different. Same is true for non-class revenue.

Now, in the context of the present Corona Pandemic, the fact is that a global capitalist enterprise (and also a local capitalist enterprise) has secured or appropriated surplus values (SV) and also, non-class revenues (NCR). For example, Indian pharmaceutical companies producing Corona vaccines have received hefty sum from the Indian state apart from the prices paid by the Indian state to purchase the vaccines. These revenues of the pharma companies from the Indian state fall in the category of non-class revenue and the selling prices received by these companies for selling vaccines are the exchange values in money form from which surplus value is accumulated, and thus, also capital is accumulated in an expanding reproduction perspective *a la* Marx. It may be asserted that given the present trend of global and local large capitalist enterprises, a part of the retained earnings or revenues get invested in the financial instruments offered by other (financial and/or non-financial) entities to make subsumed class revenue at a very high rate in the immediate short run. This is a typical feature of capitalist enterprises under the neoliberal globalization for the last three decades. Hence, at a time when the real economic activities are reeling under deep recession due to Pandemic-related lockdown, some capitalist enterprises are able to generate huge revenues and profit from the surplus, subsumed class revenues and non-class revenues.

6.2 Corona Pandemic and Rising Inequality

As mentioned at the outset, that global capitalism is characterized by the persistence of inequality of income and wealth. And this gets more widened when a crisis or downturn occurs. The present Pandemic is no exception in this regard as there is now some studies which vindicate the widening of the inequalities as the productive and unproductive labour loses their jobs and livelihood and so experiences contraction in their income and wealth on the one hand and increasing wealth accumulation for handful billionaire (productive and unproductive) capitalists on the other hand. In this regard, we refer the report titled The Inequality Virus by Oxfam (2021) which indicated that the pandemic might lead to an increase in inequality in almost all the countries of the globe at once. As per the report around two millions people all over the world have died and hundreds of millions were drawn below the poverty line and at the same time many of riches including corporations did thrive. To our understanding, this inequality is the result of an economic system which is exploitative in class-focused term and does work for a few (productive) capitalists, not for the majority—many of whom are the creators of wealth as direct producers in capitalist class processes all over the world.

Given the above picture of widening inequality as indicated in Oxfam (2021), it is a question just not of inequality in income and wealth; it is also a question of inequality which arises and gets further widened during the Pandemic in terms of gender, race, caste and class. The class connection to inequality can be easily verified from the accounting framework of a typical global capitalist enterprise depicted in the previous section of this paper. But it is just simply not class-based exploitation; it is also a question of increasing degree of oppression—be it gender oppression, be it racial oppression, be it caste-related oppression (as in India). All these forms of exploitation and oppression (viz. class and non-class based) overdetermine each other as a result we find more class-based exploitation (i.e. more degree of unpaid labour) where gender, racial, caste-based oppressions and like continue to persist. To put it differently, say, gender-based oppression paves the way for more class-based exploitation on the one hand and the class-based exploitation paves the way for more gender-based oppression. As a consequence, more is the discretionary wealth accumulation from revenues accrued in the form of surplus value or subsumed revenue or non-class revenue. The financial crisis of 2008 saw the billionaires to lose their wealth and also saw widening inequality. But billionaires of the globe had to wait for a longer time to get back the volume of wealth equal to the pre-financial crisis period. But this time they had just to wait for nine months! And their magnitude of wealth surpassed even the pre-pandemic level as we come to know from the Oxfam report. This is also indicated in the report titled the Global Risk Report published by the World Economic Forum (2021). One noticeable feature of the Corona time is the stock market boom despite downturn in real productive activities which is a paradox in terms of the logic of mainstream neoclassical economics.

Labour anyway is the risk-bearing factor of production (not the capital) under neoliberal globalization characterizing the present day global capitalism. As the

Pandemic broke out and lockdowns announced in almost all parts of the globe it is the labour (both migrant and non-migrant labour) in the formal and informal sector lost their jobs, livelihoods and earnings. The stories of reverse migration of labour from the cities to their villages in India are now well documented in the media (Dasgupta, 2022). On the other hand despite close down of real economic activities wealth accumulation went on unabated through financial channel and also through newly opened up productive channels like that of the pharma sector. It is profit which remained the main driving force of the pharam sector—especially those which are producing medicines and related drugs for the pandemic. For example, as reported in Chintan (2021), Moderna which was founded only 11 years ago could succeed to have a skyrocketing revenue growth of 8300%, Novavax by 1810%, Pfizer by 68%, AstraZeneca by 23% and Johnson & Johnson by 17%. All these could happen courtesy to the upsurge of the Corona Pandemic which took away livelihoods, earnings and jobs of countless productive and unproductive labour all over the globe. This is capitalism, and as Wolff (2020) called, it is the sickness of the system called capitalism which is perhaps incurable within without some radical solutions which we will deliberate upon in the last section of this chapter. But before that let us analytically understand the main driver of global capitalism that is profit.

6.3 Global Capitalism, Corona and Profit Mongering

Profit depends on overdetermined and contradictory processes over who gets what. But earning of modern corporations ensue from other than their own production process that is fundamental class process consisting of performance and appropriation of surplus labour (value) mentioned above. Modern firm can earn from subsumed class positions that is capitalist can earn from franchise, stock, bond. Similarly, the board members of any corporation can take multiple class positions and it can affect every process within the enterprise. Now using the above class Eq. (6.1), we can see this:

$$\sum \mathrm{SV} + \sum \mathrm{SSCR} + \sum \mathrm{NCR} = \sum \mathrm{SSCP} + \sum X + \sum Y, \qquad (6.1)$$

where $\sum SV$ = Surplus Value produced and appropriated within the enterprise.
$\sum SSCR$ = Subsumed class revenue.
$\sum NCR$ = Non-class revenue.
$\sum SSCP$ = Sum of subsumed class payments.
$\sum X$ = Sum of payment made to secure SSCR.
$\sum Y$ = Sum of payment made to secure NCR.

Left-hand side of Eq. (6.1) represents the revenue side of enterprise, while the right-hand side its expenditure required to reproduce the conditions of existence of the components in the revenue side, which we have already delineated above.

$\sum$ SSCP reflects subsumed class payments made by the enterprise to ensure the surplus value (SV).

Now,

$$\mathrm{SV} = \mathrm{SC}_I + \mathrm{SC}_O + \mathrm{SC}_C + \mathrm{SC}_R, \tag{6.2}$$

where SC_I = Subsumed class distribution to its internal management or bureaucracy.

SC_O = Subsumed class payments to owners.

SC_C = Subsumed class payments to lenders and financiers.

SC_R = Subsumed class payments to the rest of the condition providers.

Alternatively,

$$\mathrm{SC}_I = \beta\mathrm{SC}_I + (1-\beta)\mathrm{SC}_I, \tag{6.3}$$

where $\beta\mathrm{SC}_I.$ = Share of net earnings distributed to management for accumulation.

$(1-\beta)\mathrm{SC}_I$ = Share distributed to management for securing other social process internal to the enterprise.

Now, putting Eq. (6.3) in (6.2) and then (6.2) in (6.1), we get,

$$\beta\mathrm{SC}_I = \mathrm{SV} + \mathrm{SCR} + \mathrm{NCR} - \left[(1-\beta)\mathrm{SC}_I + \mathrm{SC}_O + \mathrm{SC}_C + \mathrm{SC}_R + \sum X + \sum Y\right]. \tag{6.4}$$

Now, $\beta\mathrm{SC}_I = \Delta C + \Delta V$, dividing Eq. (6.4) by $C+V$ with C being the constant capital and V the variable capital

$$\frac{\Delta C + \Delta V}{C+V} = \frac{\mathrm{SV} + \mathrm{SCR} + \mathrm{NCR}}{C+V} - \frac{\left[(1-\beta)\mathrm{SC}_I + \mathrm{SC}_O + \mathrm{SC}_C + \mathrm{SC}_R + \sum X + \sum Y\right]}{C+V}. \tag{6.5}$$

From Eq. (6.5)

$$\hat{K}^* = \hat{\rho} - \hat{\lambda}. \tag{6.6}$$

$$\hat{\rho} = \frac{\mathrm{SV}}{C+V} + \frac{\mathrm{SCR}}{C+V} + \frac{\mathrm{NCR}}{C+V}. \tag{6.7}$$

$$\hat{\rho} = \rho + r_1\alpha_1 + r_2\alpha_2. \tag{6.8}$$

Here, $\hat{\rho}$ is the complex rate of profit which is generated from the income accruing from class and non-class positions.

Weighted return to subsumed class position ($r_1\alpha_1$), weighted return to non-class position ($r_2\alpha_2$) and the rate of surplus value appropriation in fundamental class process (ρ) are the source of profit for any local or global corporate firm.

This we have taken clue from the seminal work of Resnick and Wolff (1987), which helps us to understand the actual reasons which led to the expansion of capital during the Pandemic, while the real economy is in crisis, but the enterprises of the billionaires are not.

From this equation of complex rate of profit (Eq. 6.8), it is discernible that the sources of profit are many—just not the class relations; it is beyond that. For instance, during the Pandemic period, global pharma companies dealing in vaccines and other diagnostics received huge public funds from several governments and assured pre-purchase contracts for their Corona-related products including vaccines.

The profit or retained earnings of the these pharma companies may go up significantly if the corporate tax rate is cut in the name of garnering incentives to these companies to develop vaccines and like to fight the Pandemic. This is vindicated by Chintan (2021). The world's 20 largest pharma companies reported a global effective tax rate of about 17% compared with about 21% for the world's 20 biggest tech companies (Chintan, 2021).[4] So, on the one hand huge public funding of the largest pharma companies and on the other hand very low effective corporate tax rate for them helped to ensure huge profit at a time when real economy is contracting which we can analytically claim from the complex rate of profit mentioned above.

6.4 In Search of Radical Solutions

In this paper, we have delineated the recurring problems of capitalism (global capitalism in particular). They include (a) recurring crisis every 4–7 years which not only jeopardize the real economy but also devastate the lives and livelihoods of the productive and unproductive labourers as they become the risk-bearing factor of such crisis, (b) widening inequality of income and wealth at the time of crisis (otherwise also) and (c) discretionary increase in wealth of the few billionaire capitalists as the present history of Corona Pandemic indicates to us.

Now, the pertinent question is what is the way out so that the commonplace does not suffer the miseries which they are subject to at the time of this Pandemic-led crisis of global capitalism. New Deal came as a response to the crisis of global capitalism which was the result of Great Depression of the 1930s. This Deal was characterized by some alliances with the labouring class and a change in the state power in favour of welfare state as it happened in the then USA under the leadership of President Roosevelt. Left trade unions played a major role then in fostering such alliance between capital and labour in the name of New Deal.

Will the history repeat itself at the present juncture of the Pandemic-fuelled crisis? The answer probably is no as under neoliberal globalization, a reversal in the nature of state power from a non-interventionist minimalist one to interventionist welfare state may not be plausible. The capital this time will perhaps ignore such transition

[4] The effective tax rate is even much lower than these figures for some pharma companies (for Johnson & Johnson it is 10.8% in 2020 and Pfizer only 5.8% as indicated in Chintan (2021).

as long as surplus and profits accumulation and thereby, wealth generation in favour of the handful few big capitalists is not disturbed. Capitalism or the economic system will be governed or driven by the profit mongering as it is now with all its sickness remaining intact. What is happening now is very few short-lived rescue packages announced by the neoliberal states which may disappear soon once the intensity of the Pandemic and the threat to public health wane out gradually.

The question is whether it is possible to cure the sickness of the economic system which is (global) capitalism keeping the capitalist and other exploitative class processes intact? Once again the answer is perhaps no. Chances to return to Keynesianism to reform the capitalist system by giving some sops to the performers of the surplus labour (value) are bleak and quite unimaginable at this time of neoliberal globalization which will try its best to defend *laissez faire* economic system with state playing the role of facilitator as it is now happening under Corona Pandemic.

To quote Wolff (2020), "The Covid-19 pandemic did more than trigger the third capitalist crash in this new century. It also aggravated the dimensions of the crash. The combined pandemic-plus-crash tore away the veneer that had helped people avoid seeing deep social problems and that had allowed politicians repeatedly to avoid solutions. The unresolved problems now coalesce into a genuinely epic social crisis. Systemic racism, a badly broken education system, a cash-corrupted politics, ecological destruction—the list of problems becomes clearer and more acute daily. Symptoms of a sick society are everywhere and thus, for many overwhelming."

References

Althusser, L. (1962). *Contradiction and overdetermination* (B. Brewster, Trans.). Penguin Press. Retrieved from https://www.marxists.org/reference/archive/althusser/1962/overdetermination.htm.

Chintan, R. (2021, August 23). Big pharma—Maximum earnings, minimum responsibilities. *News Click*. Retrieved August 31, 2021, from https://www.newsclick.in/Big-Pharma%E2%80%93Maximum-Earnings-Minimum-Responsibilities.

Dasgupta, B. (2022). Corona pandemic, sudden visibility of migrant workers, and the Indian economy. In R. Bandyopadhyay, P. Banerjee, & R. Samaddar (Eds.), *India' migrant workers and the pandemic*. Social Science Press.

Oxfam. (2021). *The inequality virus*. Available at https://d1ns4ht6ytuzzo.cloudfront.net/oxfamdata/oxfamdatapublic/2021-01/The%20Inequality%20Virus%20-%20Global%20Report%20%282021%29-3.pdf?N03OMRi1S_PWAiXig7D34AiDJ6ibPSOP

Resnick, S. A., & Wolff, R. D. (1987). *Knowledge and class—A Marxian critique of political economy*. The University of Chicago Press.

Wolff, R. D. (2020). *The sickness is the system—when capitalism fails to save us from pandemic or itself*. Democracy at Work.

World Economic Forum. (2021). *Global risk report*. Available at eb.int/report/world/global-risks-report-2021-16th-edition-insight-report?gclid=Cj0KCQjwuNemBhCBARIsADp74QTv68fcqvvcuf98_iyhC2MZwTp86Z2vHGOnQIGsUxiTS2CYMmT4g6oaAu1mEALw_wcB.

Chapter 7
The Long 2020/21 in India: Models of Pandemic Management and Logistics of Governance

Amit Prakash

Abstract The year 2020 has a peculiar character, full of contradictions. While on the one hand, the country came to a virtual stop owing to restrictions imposed to manage the Covid-19 pandemic, on the other hand, large sections of populations—mostly the poor—were literally on the march to return home. The logistics of governance that unfolded was far more expansive than that dictated by the medical emergency. The legal mechanisms deployed were two: first was the invocation of the colonial era Epidemic Diseases Act, 1897 (popularly called the Plague Act), swiftly amended by an ordinance on 22 April 2020, to ostensibly offer protections for healthcare personnel combatting epidemic diseases. Second was the invocation of the National Disaster Management Act, 2005, under which the National Disaster Management Authority, headed by the Union Home Secretary, can (and did) arrogate to itself powers to issue any direction to anybody, including elected State governments. This chapter will examine these processes across two axes: (a) the logic, mechanisms, and implication of the National Disaster Management Act/Authority and the Epidemic Diseases Act, 1897; and, (b) the political economy of testing and vaccine delivery in terms of its conversion of the process of governance from political to mere management. It is argued that this process which started unfolding during the Long 2020/21 will have a much longer and multidimensional impact on the fundamentals of the governance processes in the country. The chapter will seek to identify, document and analyse this complex process in terms of étatisation of the polity and implications thereof for liberal democracy in India, and the impact of such logistics of governance on the right to life and livelihood, especially that of the poor and marginalised.

Keywords Epidemic diseases act 1897 · National disaster management act 2005 · Governance · Logistics · Right to life and livelihood

A. Prakash (✉)
Centre for the Study of Law and Governance, Jawaharlal Nehru University, New Delhi & MCRG, Kolkata, India
e-mail: amit@jnu.ac.in

S. R. Chakraborty et al. (eds.), *The Long 2020*, India Studies in Business and Economics, https://doi.org/10.1007/978-981-99-4815-4_7

The year 2020 has a peculiar character, full of contradictions. While on the one hand, the country came to a virtual stop owing to the lockdown imposed to manage the Covid-19 pandemic, on the other hand, large sections of populations—mostly the poor migrant workers—were literally on the march to return home from metropolitan towns to their villages. While concerns about filling idle hours with online streaming and exotic cooking occupied the privileged, the rest of the population was left to fend for themselves looking for a non-existent basic meal, basic jobs and livelihood.

Focussing on such contradictions alone glosses over the mechanisms and logistics of governance that were deployed in India to ostensibly manage the exigencies of the pandemic. However, the logistics of governance that unfolded was far more expansive than that dictated by the medical emergency and was not limited to identify, isolate and medicate those infected. The conversion of the health emergency into an issue of order—the curfew model that quickly emerged, creates multiple implications that will cast a long shadow on Indian citizens in times to come. Firstly, the apparatus of the state was geared towards a veritable erasure of right to life and livelihood (Prakash, 2021) and rendering life of a very large section of the population bare (Agamben, 2021). Secondly, the logistics mobilised and deployed to police and enforce the curfew model portends to fundamentally transform the processes of governance—marked by centralisation of powers and funds while decentralisation of responsibilities to lower tiers of governance without concomitant delegation of powers and resources. Thirdly, the logistics of vaccination and failure in procuring and securing the necessary medical infrastructure and supplies contributed another layer to the transformation of governance by prioritisation of logistics.

The legal mechanisms deployed for such logistics of governance were two: first was the invocation of the colonial era Epidemic Diseases Act, 1897 (popularly called the Plague Act), swiftly amended by an ordinance on 22 April 2020, to ostensibly offer protections for healthcare personnel engaged in combatting epidemic diseases. This Act empowers the government to issue any direction it deems fit to manage the epidemic, violation of which invites action under Section 188 of the Indian Penal Code dealing with "Disobedience to order duly promulgated by public servant". This created a degree of impunity in the state that brooks no argument since intention of the accused is no defence under this Act (Prakash, 2021).

The second was the invocation of the Disaster Management Act, 2005, under which the National Disaster Management Authority, headed by the Union Home Secretary, can (and did) arrogate to itself the power to issue any direction to anybody, including elected State governments. While there remains some doubt if the NDMA, 2005, covers health emergency, the state forged ahead without any such concern, including complete violation of some of the Basic Structure of the Constitution such as federalism and powers of the States. Such autocratic legalism (Scheppele, 2018) was upheld by the judiciary through its inaction and credulity in the unfounded claims of the government, until at least the devastation caused by the Second Wave in the months of February/March 2021 to June/July 2021 (Prakash, 2021). The framework of logistics of governance, geared towards ètatisation (Ferguson, 1994) of the polity, leading to state impunity and undermining of a host of citizen's rights was thus complete.

This paper examines such logistics of governance and the corresponding socio-economic and political processes across two axes: (a) the logic, mechanisms and implication of the National Disaster Management Act/Authority and the Epidemic Diseases Act, 1897, and (b) logistics of governance, including medical infrastructure and vaccine delivery, which normalised bare life for a large section of citizenry, even though bare terms of survival could not be ensured for many Indian citizens.

7.1 Conceptualising Governmentality During the Pandemic

Theorisations on pandemic-induced forms of governmentality have a long history, mainly in the Foucauldian tradition, but the ways in which state power has been deployed since the outbreak of the Covid-19 pandemic in 2020 requires a revisit of the main arguments in new ways. It needs to be acknowledged that "… extractive capitalism makes pandemics like COVID-19 more likely, which in turn, translate into massive shifts in biopolitics at the level of the state, economy, society, and subjectivity" (Means, 2021). The biopolitical shifts reflected in the governance of the pandemic needs to be located in Foucault's idea of governmentality which he argued is "[t]he ensemble formed by institutions, procedures, analyses and reflections, the calculations and tactics that allow the exercise of this very specific albeit complex form of power, which has as its target population, as its principal form of knowledge political economy, as its essential technical means apparatuses of security…" This mode of power has "…pre-eminence over all other forms (sovereignty, discipline, etc.) …, resulting on the one hand, in the formation of a whole series of specific governmental apparatuses, and, on the other, in the development of a whole complex of savoirs", owing to which the state "… gradually becomes governmentalised". He further argued that "… what is really important for our modernity—that is, for our present—is not so much the *étatisation* of society, as the governmentalization of the state" (stress in original) (Foucault, 1991). It is these notions of governmentalisation of the state and *étatisation* of society that lends an incisive analytical framework for examining the state during the pandemic.

It is in this vein that Giorgio Agamben stresses on the deployment of techniques of state power to construct exceptions during the pandemic:

> … what is once again manifest is the tendency to use a state of exception as a normal paradigm for government. The legislative decree immediately approved by the government … [which] produces an authentic militarization 'of the municipalities and areas with the presence of at least one person who tests positive and for whom the source of transmission is unknown, ….' [under the guise of health and safety of the population]. [Large scale lockdown that resulted was a result of] the invention of an epidemic [as] .. the ideal pretext for scaling … [up the restrictions without] limitation. [Another] … disturbing factor is the state of fear that in recent years has evidently spread among individual consciences and that translates into an authentic need for situations of collective panic for which the epidemic provides once again the ideal pretext. Therefore, in a perverse vicious circle, the limitations of freedom imposed by governments are accepted in the name of a desire for safety that was created by the same governments that are now intervening to satisfy it(Agamben, 2020a, 2020b).

A combined reading of these analytical insights from Foucault and Agamben enables a critical enquiry into the logistics that have structured the governance of the pandemic in India. Another thread for this analytical framework is Foucault's formulations on biopolitics unleashed under three different episodes of medical emergency: that of the plague, the small pox and the typhoid—each of which lent a different form of governmental rationality—governmentality—by the deployment of the security, territory, population triangle that Foucault stresses as central to the modern state:

> It looks like a biopolitical dream: governments, advised by physicians, impose pandemic dictatorship on entire populations. Getting rid of all democratic obstacles under the pretext of "health," even "survival," they are finally able to govern the population as they have, more or less openly, always done in modernity: as pure "biomass," as "bare life" to be exploited. (Sarasin, 2020)

The process of conversion of people into populations through the techniques and logistics of governance and thereby allowing for production of bare life may be analysed through a series of Foucauldian insights into previous episodes of biopolitics under the modern state. Three different models emerge, mapping to different stages of evolution of the modern state and periods of accumulation. Translating them to serve as a framework to analyse the Covid-19 pandemic, three intertwined but cognitively distinguishable processes emerge; namely, *The Isolation model* derived from the leprosy model (Foucault, 2006)[1]; *The Surveillance model* derived from Foucault's idea of the panopticon (Foucault, 1995)[2] and *the Governmentality of Legibility model*, derived from the Smallpox or inoculation practices (Foucault, 2004).[3]

Deriving from this, it is postulated that there is no exclusivity between these models in the Indian context during the Pandemic; even though Foucault underlined that that the last one—governmentality of legibility—is the characteristic of the real modern state, marked by deployment of detailed knowledge about the population to classify, control and discipline the field of governance. "However, within a liberal governmentality the kind of risk management … must not go so far as to turn into a discipline of individuals, because this would undermine their freedom, which is necessary for the system. A state that is too strong destroys its own goals—it must respect the relative 'impenetrability' of society, even at the cost of a certain risk of infection".[4]

It is this paradox that is embedded in contemporary Indian state's logistical management of the Covid-19 pandemic. Owing to the "unproductivity" of the governmentality of legibility model, ***all three models have been simultaneously deployed through the logistics of management of the pandemic in India***. Since total discipline of the population cannot be a reasonable goal of liberal power even though

---

[1] This model is alluded to in the Michel Foucault's *History of Madness* (2006), when the State power is deployed to isolate those who are ill from the rest of the population.

[2] This model was developed in Michel Foucault, *Discipline and Punish: The Birth of the Prison* (1995), under which emerged the disciplinary power whose subject was the bodies of entire population.

[3] Model developed in Michel Foucault, *Security, Territory, Population: Lectures at the Collège De France, 1977–78* (2004).

[4] Ibid.

state is obliged to pursue it for a variety of political-economy reasons, lapsing to the isolation and Surveillance model is a real possibility—something that has been writ large in the approach of the Indian state. Such a modality of management of the pandemic encourages dependence on the "plague model" under which the state is likely to become authoritarian and even, totalitarian. The impact of such a process is the gradual erasure of citizens' freedoms and rights and an aggrandisement of state impunity. The analysis below of the logistics of governance of the pandemic in the Indian case underlines the *simultaneous operation of the three models of management of the pandemic and resultant lapsing back of the liberal state to sovereignty-derived exercise of impunity and state power*. This is underlined by the mechanics and logistics of governance that has been deployed since March 2020, which further corroded the liberal script already under the onslaught of rising populism.

7.2 Three Models of Pandemic Management: (En)forcement of a New Normal and Normalisation of Violence

A student from Thrissur, Kerala, who returned from Wuhan on 20 January 2020 is reputedly the first recorded case of Coronavirus in India. However, the state did not invoke its impressive array of legal and logistical apparatus for the management of what was soon to be declared a pandemic in India. Only a few *advisories* with respect to surveillance and quarantine of arriving international passengers from select (later all) counties were issued along with steps to disinfect aircrafts and other modes of transport, and, overall general hygiene. A number of such *advisories* were issued from the respective line ministries such as Civil Aviation, Human Resources Development, Health and Family Welfare, Labour and Employment, Home Affairs, and Consumer Affairs, Food and Public Distribution (See Prakash, 2021). Clearly, the model that was in use was that of governmentality of legibility—the state wished to have complete information about the contours of the infection and steps were taken to ensure such legibility. As is always the case, such legibility was to be created under a welfare argument of public health. Simultaneously, an indifferent effort (incapacity?) may be noted towards construction of a Surveillance model, marred by poor logistics of testing kits, their deployment and related data collection and analysis. In any case, the primary policy response to the panopticon surveillance remained that of isolation (See Prakash, 2021).

7.3 Shift from Governmentality of Legibility to the Isolation Model

The evolving pandemic and the logistics of its management shifted suddenly to buttress the isolation model with the proclamation of a "Janata Curfew" on 22 March 2020 from 7 AM to 9 PM by the prime minister. During this period, all citizens were to be isolated by their staying indoors and clapping or ringing bells or banging utensils in appreciation of health workers (Chandra & Basu, 2020). This isolation model emerged as the dominant model with the suspension of all international travels from 22 March 2020 and the invocation of Section 6(2)(i) of the Disaster Management Act, 2005, on 24 March 2020. The order so issued proclaimed that "… the National Disaster Management Authority has decided to direct Ministries/Departments of Government of India, State Governments and State Authorities to take measures for ensuring social distancing …."[5] to enforce a strict lockdown/isolation in accordance with guidelines issued under Section 10(2)(l) of the said Act. Such isolation was to be ensured for a period of 21 days from 25 March 2020 but was repeatedly extended by similar orders for another 19 days, 15 days and another 15 days, to end on 31 May 2020 (See Prakash, 2021, p. 108). The rationale was the same argument that accompanies all such isolations, as Foucault had noted—welfare: to break the "chain" of transmission of the coronavirus and ensure the protection of health of the rest of the population.

In enforcing such isolation, the state combined the isolation model with the Surveillance model as well as the governmentality of legibility model. The NDMA order was accompanied by a detailed set of guidelines, drawing upon its capabilities of deploying logistics of governance to enforce a lockdown. The guidelines so issued to accompany the order have required that "… Offices of the Government of India, its Autonomous/Subordinate Offices and Public Corporations shall remain closed". "Offices of the State/Union Territory Governments, their Autonomous Bodies, Corporations, etc.…"; along with all commercial, private, industrial establishments, transport services, hospitality services, educational institutions, places of worship were to remain closed for public, *without any exception,* while "… all social/political/sports/entertainment/academic/cultural/religious functions/gatherings shall be barred" (emphasis added).[6] Exemptions were granted for police, essential services, banking and financial sector, social welfare functions, etc., to operate with minimal staff or from home (Prakash, 2021). Full might of logistical governmentality of the state was thus deployed to enforce the isolation model. Aside from the deployment of logistics of governmentality to enforce a strict isolation, remission into an older isolation model, marked by centralisation of powers, was also clearly noticeable in the fact that all such orders under the NDMA were issued by the Union Home Secretary in his capacity as chairperson of the National Executive Authority under the NDMA and all orders issued by other ministries and often, State governments too,

[5] NDMA order dated 24 March 2020.

[6] Ibid.

cite these orders as the rationale for their own orders/guidelines. The NDMA order explicitly directed "… all the Ministries/Departments of Government of India, State/ Union Territory Governments and State/Union Territory authorities …." to strictly implement these guidelines.[7]

Aside from the nature and character of the state changing under these models of management of the pandemic, another series of issues also crop up in the way this isolation model as implemented. First, étatisation, pace Ferguson, was clearly visible wherein an unelected bureaucrat could issue directions for strict implementation to elected state governments; second, the distribution of powers under the Constitution was set aside and, without invocation of Article 355, the Union government "required" that such directions of the bureaucrat be strictly implemented; third, the governmentality of legibility was on full display in such orders which provided hyper-details for implementation—the parameters in which the state would make the population legible was clearly laid down. Last, these orders also put in place a state of exception while converting the management of pandemic into that of policing, the tone of which was set by the Janata Curfew of 22 March 2020 (See Prakash, 2021).

One issue that remains unaddressed in this analysis is that the conflation of the three models of pandemic management to operate simultaneously in a context of *étatisation* created conditions for centralisation of powers and finances. However, a peculiar situation also emerged wherein the responsibilities for logistics of implementation of models of pandemic management were devolved to the State governments without the necessary devolution of resources (Sharma, 2020a, 2020b) (their powers to raise resources and supplies already having been circumscribed by the orders of the NDMA—which will also be discussed in the next section). Centralisation and *étatisation* of the state were thus not subject to any countervailing process with the parliament being prorogued, unlike many other countries.[8] Further, the NDMA orders and guidelines also repeatedly stressed prosecution under Section 188 of the Indian Penal Code, 1860, and the Epidemic Diseases Act, 1897, in case of any non-compliance with the order (Prakash, 2021, p. 111). It is apposite that two colonial era laws were cited to enforce an increasingly centralised government. Centralisation of powers and *étatisation* of the state was enabled by an autocratic legalism, which will be discussed below.

The strict isolation model is evidenced by the fact that the Indian state enforced a lockdown that as more stringent than anywhere else in the world—scored at 100 since 22 March 2020 (OxCGRT, 2020). Peculiarly, the combination of isolation, surveillance and governmentality of legibility that characterised the Indian lockdown, in fact, reached an anti-systemic zenith marked by erasure of right to life and livelihood of its citizens. The highly capacious state was unable or unwilling to uphold freedoms, which was a requirement of the liberal script that it purported to uphold, leading to the emergence of a legal-autocratic form.

[7] Ibid. Also see Prakash (2021, p. 108–9).

[8] For instance, the German Bundestag modified its rules of procedure so that parliamentary scrutiny of executive action may continue during the pandemic (Library of Congress, 2020).

The curfew model of isolation that was deployed harked back to the eighteenth-century models of management of disease. Owing to onvertion of the health emergency into a draconian "law and order" matter, police impunity became the main response in initial weeks and months beginning 22 March 2020, as evidenced in more media reportage than one can reasonably peruse. Travel within and across districts and states was barred and any such attempt invited both, police brutality and legal prosecution,even death (Krishnan, 2020), as threatened in the NDMA orders. Requirements of curfew passes (Outlook, 2020, Hindustan Times, 2020a, 2020b) reinforced the isolation model premised on policing the isolation (Sharma, 2020a, 2020b) and not on welfare measures in terms of treatment. It may also be noted that even the Surveillance model, wherein the state makes efforts to locate, identify, map and thereafter implement limited isolation, was marginal.

The most immediate impact of such isolation was the denial and erasure of the rights of a significant section of the citizenry—the poor and migrant workers—who were at the receiving end of both, the police brutality as well as denial of right to livelihood and often, the right to life itself. The simple pursuit of food by the poorest of citizens obliged them break the stringent lockdown, leading to them being converted into a bare life wherein simple biological survival was the only question (see Prakash, 2021).

Critical comments on policing during the pandemic in other parts of the world have underlined the militarisation of policing leading to marginalisation of minorities (Jones, 2020), but in the Indian case, such policing was normalised to enforce the isolation model. The state of exception and recession of rights acquired a new peak in the Uttar Pradesh Special Security Force Bill, 2020, to raise a Special Security Force with powers to search arrest without warrant (Hindustan Times,)—a step reminiscent of the colonial era Anarchical and Revolutionary Crimes Act of 1919 (The Rowlatt Act) (Prakash, 2021). To cite Agamben's reading, which seems to be describing the Indian scenario:

> [T]he epidemic is clearly showing that the state of exception, …, has become an authentically normal condition. There have been more serious epidemics in the past, but no one ever thought of declaring a state of emergency like today, one that forbids us even to move … lives have been reduced to a purely biological condition … A society that lives in a permanent state of emergency cannot be a free one. We effectively live in a society that has sacrificed freedom to so-called "security reasons" and as a consequence has condemned itself to living in a permanent state of fear and insecurity (Agamben, 2020a, 2020b).

While normalisation of violence in India in recent times is not limited to the processes and temporality of management of Coronavirus pandemic,[9] such normalisation reflects an acceptance and condonement (active encouragement?) of rising populism in India. Ably assisted by the progressive decay of institutions, such

---

[9] The infamous 'Romeo squads' of Uttar Pradesh police; 'encounter' killing of alleged rape-accused by a police team in Hyderabad; the condonement of custodial violence and death of prisoners or the brutalisation of dissent witnessed during and after the CAA-NRC-NPR protests since November 2019 until the clamping down of lockdown during the pandemic are some examples of normalization of violence in society, including police violence.

impunity had already laid down a fertile ground for the enforcement of a new normal via the route of logistics of pandemic management.

7.4 Bare Life and Erasure of Rights

The isolation model, backed by police and legal impunity, impacted people in all walks of life and severely truncated their rights and freedoms. However, none was as severely impacted by the implementation of a complete and strict lockdown across the country between 25 March 2020 and 31 May 2020, with a mere four-hour notice, as the poor and migrant labour in the cities. During the lockdown, an "…estimated 40 million internal migrant workers, largely in the informal economy, were severely impacted by the government's COVID-19 lockdown" (Patel, 2020). This isolation model ensured that a significant proportion of the poor and migrant workers was stuck in unsafe and crowded dwellings, with no work or income and therefore, extremely precarious access to food (Pandey, 2020). Such unskilled and semi-skilled daily-waged workers immediately lost source of livelihood in the suddenly implemented lockdown to isolate the whole population from risk of infection. It is also remarkable that the capacious Indian state discarded the possibility of surveillance of the disease as a possible model for managing the pandemic.

Besides, it was also a failure of the logistics of governance whereby no arrangements were made by the state to ward off a looming humanitarian crisis in the form of a huge number of hungry and starving poor with no access to food (Basu, 2020). Physical biological survival was the only concern in these times with the lives of almost all poor and migrant workers rendered bare by the isolation. The much delayed and sporadic efforts by the state to meet this challenge were a case of too little, too late. The civic-minded citizens' groups and civil society organisations who did mobilise swiftly to plug a huge and conspicuous gap left by the state agencies unable or unwilling to protect the right to life of the poorest citizens faced a large number of difficulties owing to the curfew model of lockdown, with its dependence on curfew passes, denial of mobility and strict isolation (See Prakash, 2021 for some details).

An important leaf in the story of such state of exception owing to failed logistics of governance is the denial of the basic necessity for the right to life—food. With some difference in the experience across various states,[10] in most places the narrative was that of the walking migrants being reduced to the meagre charity of citizens and some civil society actors. The efficacy of the much delayed and meagre state support that did materialise was captured in the SWAN survey of April 2020, which found that "96% had not received rations from the government and 70% had not received

---

[10] For instance, Kerala was reported to have been able to set up systems for providing cooked food to migrants in their place of employment fairly early in the lockdown to ensure both, containment of the virus as well as to address emerging destitution amongst them, Philip Shaju (*The Indian Express,* 2020).

any cooked food" (SWAN, 2020a, 2020b). In the next month, the story remained extremely bleak with "[a]bout 82% … had not received rations from the government and 68% … had not received any cooked food" (SWAN, 2020a, 2020b). In fact, the dry rations that comprised the state support were most migrants were unable to access, owing to being away from their registered residences and having no income to purchase the wherewithal to convert dry rations into meals (See also Prakash, 2021).

A logistical tool adopted by the state to enforce its isolation model was to stop all public transports from plying anywhere, save emergency and essential services (later expanded to include delivery of online orders as well). The double whammy of non-accessible food and inability to travel back to their villages hit the poor and migrant workers hard to make their precarious lives even worse. Besides, many were asked to vacate their rented accommodation owing to their inability to pay the rent, their loss of earnings owing to the strict lockdown notwithstanding, leaving them with no option except to walk back home (Prakash, 2021).

Thousands, perhaps millions, therefore literally walked to their homes, often a thousand or more kilometres from their place of employment (Bhowmick, 2020). Media reportage—print, electronic as well as IT-enabled channels—documented hundreds of cases of such workers, irrespective of age, gender, fitness or any other differentiator, literally marching home; sometimes hitching a ride in unsafe modes of transport. In either case, they faced the full brunt of police brutality at the next check point. Loss of lives in this extremely precarious state existence owing to exhaustion or hunger was reported but not acknowledged by the state, whose support was only mostly missing (Chatterjee, 2020; Prakash, 2021). Agamben's camp, where state of exemption was the norm, has arrived into India's main cities and highways. Loss of life had lost any meaning for the state and even bare life was an ambitious target.

The lockdown thus represented the most regressive form of the isolation model for the management of the pandemic. Incapacity and unwillingness of the state to provide food in the place of migrant workers' residence along with loss of earnings owing to strict lockdown, combined with a draconian model of policing, were only bettered by inhuman forms of isolation in makeshift and unsuitable quarantine centres (PTI, 2020). Numerous instances of brutal police action under the curfew model (Munshi, 2020), including a repulsive spraying of poor migrant workers with disinfectants (Rashid, 2020)—have combined to create the state of exception that marked most of state action. Protests against such model of isolation that led to erasure of right to life and livelihood (Bhattacharya, 2020) only invited more police violence—protesters were regularly tear-gassed, lathi charged and sometimes, jailed too (Prakash, 2021, p. 113).

It must be remarked that other two models—that of surveillance or governmentality to render citizens legible to the state, were mostly missing in the first couple of months of the pandemic. Foucault's leprosy model, reinforced by a state of exception, was the dominant mode, which barely fits in with the requirements of a liberal state. It is therefore little wonder that questions of the most basic rights—to life and livelihood—are mostly noticed in its complete erasure.

The first feeble steps towards even acknowledging such rights were visible only after almost 2 months of the lockdown, on 14 May 2020 in a press conference by the Union Finance Minister. A variety of non-measures to create liquidity for small farmers and benefits of provision of "[h]ygienically prepared three meals a day provided for the residents of Shelters for Urban Homeless (SUH)" was asserted. It also underlined the "[w]ork offered to 2.33 Crore wage seekers … [on 13 May 2020] in 1.87 Lac Gram Panchayats", while advising States/UTs to "to provide works to migrant workers as per the provisions of the Act". Assurance was also given that government was "[p]lanning for continuing MNREGA works during Monsoon as well: plantations, horticulture, livestock related sheds", apart from a prospective scheme of "One Nation One Ration Card" as a "[p]art of the PM's Technology Driven System Reforms" which will benefit "67 crore beneficiaries in 23 states covering 83% of PDS population … by August, 2020" (GoI, 2020).[11] If anything, these series of measures complete the state of exception by harping upon a set of prospective measures, which may only be availed by an increasingly destitute set of workers after somehow surviving five months or more without any public support (Prakash, 2021, p. 114).

The MGNREGA alluded to in the government announcement saw a very high demand despite it being able to only provide unskilled manual work at very low wages.[12] This merely attests to the extremely precarious condition of the workers owing to the isolation model in force. Even this avenue of eking out an extremely precarious living faltered since number of jobs provided in April 2020 under MGNREGA was lower than those provided in the same month in 2019 (Economic Outlook, 2020), the much larger threat to life and livelihood notwithstanding. Such precariousness of right to livelihood owing to the lockdown was not limited to the poor, unskilled migrant workers since between April and July 2020, 18.9 per cent of salaried employees lost their jobs (Vyas, 2020), with six million professional jobs lost (India Today Web Desk, 2020). Such erasure of right to life and livelihood was compounded by GDP having contracted by 23.9% during the first quarter of 2020–21—the first economic contraction in four decades (Business Standard Web Team, 2020).

The isolation model, and the stringency of its implementation, thus created a state of exception marked by state's incapacity and normalisation of police violence. The lives of citizens were indeed rendered bare.

The state of exception thus created led to an erasure of the most basic rights of citizens and was ably assisted by deinstitutionalisation, especially in the judiciary,

[11] No detailed documentation of the proposals could be found in the Ministry's documents online.

[12] Mahatma Gandhi National Rural Employment Guarantee Act, 2005, provides for a demand-driven 100 days' employment during the lean season. Work provided under the MGNREGA is manual unskilled earth work at the basic wage rate.

which was unable to uphold the rights of the citizens. While such deinstitutionalisation is a part of a longer-term pattern[13] (Chhibber, 2020), its impact on upholding the isolation model along with the impact on basic rights is of a different order.

An early writ petition in April 2020 under Article 32 seeking protection of right to life guaranteed under Article 21 by ensuring payment of wages to migrant workers was dismissed by the Supreme Court in a virtual hearing by "... call[ing] upon the respondent-Union of India to ... take such steps as it finds fit to resolve the issues raised in the petition".[14] Contrariwise, the Court accepted the Solicitor-General's word that all migrant workers were being cared for, the huge volume of media reportage to the contrary notwithstanding. In a stark example of the judicial apathy to emerging state of exemption, the Court is reported to have observed, "If they are being provided meals, then why do they need money for meals?' (Dixit, 2020; Prakash, 2021).

Almost two months later, in May 2020, Supreme Court took *sou motu* cognisance and issued interim directions for provision of free travel of migrant workers on trains, free food and water on such trains and adequate medical care and monitoring of returning workers[15] (Prakash, 2021). The Surveillance model of managing the pandemic was thus coaxed by the Court. In subsequent hearing on 09 June 2020[16] and 31 July 2020,[17] the focus of the court has moved to logistics of transportation of migrant workers with nary a few words to uphold the right to life and livelihood.

7.5 The Story of Vaccination: Reluctant Emergence of Models of Surveillance and Governmentality of Legibility

While the Indian state was engaged in a deploying a physical isolation model, learnt from the law-and-order mechanisms, for controlling the pandemic, the rest of the world was focussing on a biomedical approach in the form of a quest for a vaccine against the Covid-19 virus. Surveillance and governmental legibility were the primary model for many other countries, which also seeped into India albeit on the back of the vaccine.

---

[13] Deinstitutionalisation of judiciary owing to creeping étatisation was witnessed in many recent instances; most notably in its unwillingness or inability to enforce citizens' basic rights against the state in the series of *habeas corpus* petitions filed in Kashmir in 2019.

[14] Supreme Court Writ Petition (Civil) Diary No(s). 10801/2020, Harsh Mandar v. Union of India, 2020 SCC Online SC 376.

[15] Supreme Court Suo Motu Writ Petition (Civil) No(s). 6/2020 2020 in 'Re: Problems and Miseries of Migrant Labourers', SCC Online SC 490.

[16] Supreme Court Suo Motu Writ Petition (Civil) No(s). 6/2020 2020 in 'Re: Problems and Miseries of Migrant Labourers', SCC Online SC 492.

[17] Supreme Court Suo Motu Writ Petition (Civil) No. 6 of 2020 2020 in 'Re: Problems and Miseries of Migrant Labourers', SCC Online SC 613.

The leader in the pack in creating the conditions for a biomedical approach was indubitably the University of Oxford, which started working on a vaccine in January 2020 and published the results of its Phase I/II trials the Lancet on 20 July 2020 (University of Oxford, 2020). AstraZeneca, the production partner of the University of Oxford secured approval of the UK's Medicines and Healthcare Products Regulatory Agency (MHRA) for "…emergency supply of COVID-19 Vaccine AstraZeneca, …, for the active immunisation of individuals 18 years or older" (AstraZeneca, 2020a, 2020b) on 30 December 2020 after having successfully completing Phase III trials in three countries and published its results in the Lancet on 08 December 2020 (Oxford COVID Vaccine Trial Group, 2021).

Various competing vaccines followed a similar trajectory of which two—the Moderna and Pfizer vaccines—secured necessary regulatory approvals soon after, with many others to follow. The main analytical question that is embedded here is that of the interface of public institutions in making these vaccines speedily available to protect their populations.[18] Foremost in this is the question of public financial support for the development of the vaccine. So far as AstraZeneca vaccine was concerned,

> …public funding sources accounted for 97.1% of the R&D funding towards the ChAdOx technology and its application to SARS-CoV-2, … Direct government funding accounted for 62.5%, … whilst charitable sources accounted for 21.8% … Private industry contributed 1.9% of R&D funding, 1.2% was from other sources. (Cross et al., 2021)

Further, significant public financial support was extended to the various vaccines by the route of advance purchase orders, even before the vaccines had been tested to be safe and efficacious:

> By mid-August [2020], the United States had secured 800 million doses of at least 6 vaccines in development, with an option to purchase around one billion more. The United Kingdom was the world's highest per-capita buyer, with 340 million purchased: around 5 doses for each citizen. The European Union nations—which are buying vaccines as a group—and Japan have locked down hundreds of millions of doses of vaccines for themselves(Callaway, 2020).

This brief summary of the approach of other countries to grapple with the pandemic in terms of securing vaccines for their population is in stark contrast to that of the Indian state. It reflects the smallpox/Surveillance model that quickly emerged as the main approach to manage the pandemic in other countries, many of which had only differing and often only marginal level of adherence to the isolation model.

In the Indian case, the surveillance and other models seeped into the system on the back of logistical requirements of vaccination and not as state policy. No financial support was extended to the development of vaccines to any Indian institution/

[18] This analysis looks at only the University of Oxford-AstraZeneca vaccine on account of factors: (a) this vaccine of the only one that secured direct financial support from public sources since its initial development phase, and (b) it has the largest vaccine coverage in terms of both quantity and number of countries that have approved this vaccine for deployment for general population.

company: "The central government has told the Supreme Court that 'no governmental aid, assistance or grant' was given for the research or development of Covid-19 vaccines Covishield or Covaxin even though the former is manufactured in the country by the Serum Institute of India (SII) and the latter was indigenously developed by Bharat Biotech in the collaboration with the Indian Council of Medical Research (ICMR)" (Anand, 2021). This inexplicable policy was in sharp contrast to the fact that India is the world's largest vaccine producer, not necessarily the prime innovator of vaccines. Besides, it also made India wholly dependent on vaccines being developed elsewhere. It is another matter that the SII was licenced to manufacture the vaccine by AstraZeneca in June 2020 itself (AstraZeneca, 2020a, 2020b), who in turn applied for emergency use authorisation to the Drugs Controller of India on 07 December 2020 to manufacture the said vaccine under the brand name of CoviShield in India.

In light of the fact that most major countries had already placed advance orders for the bulk of the production capacity of all the major vaccine manufacturers across the world, this absence of public support for development of a vaccine in India is puzzling. The already precarious situation was compounded by the absence of any such advance orders by India. The first purchase order was only placed on 11 January 2021—five days before the vaccination drive was to begin—for a mere 11 million doses (Banerjea, 2021)—the impact of pre-booking of bulk of the manufacturing capacity by major countries around the world was beginning to show. Further, it was only in April 2021 that some financial support was extended by the Indian government to vaccine manufacturers to expand their capacity and assure a greater supply of vaccines in the form of "… about ₹ 4,500 crore as advance to vaccine makers like Serum Institute of India (SII) and Bharat Biotech against future supplies …" (PTI, 2021). We shall return to the logistical nightmare that this delayed decision was to cause along with that of pricing and procurement of the two vaccines, not to mention the devastation of the "second wave" leading to India being forced to accept financial aid for funding purchase and delivery of Covid-19 vaccination.

First, however, the Covaxin saga needs to be briefly examined. Covaxin, developed by Bharat Biotech in collaboration with ICMR and NIV (Pune), is a whole virion inactivated Coronavirus vaccine. It was granted approval for immunisation of the general public by the Subject Expert Committee of Central Drugs Standard Control Organisation (CDSCO) on 03 January 2021—the same day as the SII's CoviShield vaccine. The difference cannot be starker: on the one hand was CoviShield, which was peer-reviewed for safety and efficacy on the basis of Phases I-III datasets, even though it was still required to conduct Phase III bridge studies in India (as should be the case). On the other hand, Covaxin was granted approval on the basis of Phase I trials (Press Information Bureau, 2021a, 2021b) "… before the vaccine had completed Phase III trials in humans or published data on Phase II trials" (Parkins, 2021). Phase I safety and immunogenicity data for this vaccine were only published in July 2021 (filed in March 2021) (Ella et al., 2021)—more than six months after approval was granted for it being rolled out for immunisation of the general public, while Phase III data was posted on the pre-print server on 01 July 2021 (COVAXIN Study Group, 2021). As of early October 2021, the WHO had still to approve Covaxin (Som &

Pullanoor, 2021). The implications of exposing large numbers of Indian population to the uncertainties of an untested and unreviewed vaccine are of course a classic case of denial of rights and reducing human beings/citizens to bare life.

The Surveillance model that the vaccination approach reflects comprises of two components, both of which were marked by problems of logistics of governance. Surveillance of the disease required largescale testing, tracing, isolation and medication and was dependent on procurement and supply of testing kits, and ensuring necessary medical follow-up. The supply of dependable testing kits again suffered from the governmental inertia owing to dependence on the Isolation model. Further, effective tracking necessarily requires information systems. However, such information systems in the form of the Aarogya Setu app are a story of both, logistical failures and indifferent state pursual, all at once. The necessary governance logistics required, including clear privacy protocols, that was necessary to implement an effective Surveillance model was clearly marked by its absence. The state was unable to create governance logistics and necessary public trust to ensure its viability.

Turning back to the issue of procurement, allocation, pricing and targeting of vaccine for the Indian population, there is a host of issues that recur with frightening frequency between January 2021 and July 2021, which also was the rough period of the build-up of the "second wave" of Coronavirus infections and its gradual recession, leaving a wasteland of death and devastation. Analysis of three threads may suffice to underline the erasure of right to life and thereby, a kind of biopolitics which reduced human life to a struggle for bare biological survival.

The main thread of this governance logistics revolves around the evolving vaccine policy, which in turn was, largely, determined by the availability of vaccines, as discussed above. Since the "Cabinet Summary for October 2020" (GoI, 2020) delineates a series of committees that were to be appointed for managing diverse aspects of the pandemic and vaccines, there can be no other reason for the haphazard way in which vaccine rollout happened.

The National COVID Vaccination Program, in its first phase from 16 January 2021, covered an estimated 30 million healthcare and frontline workers. From 01 March 2021 began the second phase targeted at those above 60 years of age and those above 45 years with comorbidities. From 01 April 2020, all those above 45 years were to be covered—an estimated population of over 300 million people but only accounting for about 22 per cent of the population (Press Information Bureau,). Expanding vaccination to those 18 years and above on 01 May 2021 added another 600 million to the list of those awaiting vaccines.

The unavailability of vaccines in such large numbers required for a full vaccination of the population was indicated since the start given that the government had barely made adequate arrangements for securing a supply, as discussed. A perusal of Chart 1 indicates that some daily spikes aside, the daily vaccination rates remained in the 30–40 lakh doses per day until at least August 2021. This rate of vaccination remains at about a third of that required to meet the targets of vaccination of most of the adult population by the end of the year (TNN, 2021). It must also be recalled that the data cited are number of doses and each individual requires two doses for the vaccine to be fully effective.

Chart 7.1 also indicates a rough inverse relation between the rate of vaccination and number of new cases diagnosed. So, a conjectural relationship can also be witnessed between the low rate of vaccination and spike in number of diagnosed infections between March 2021 and June 2021—what is generally labelled as the "second wave". The same conjecture can also be extended to argue that behavioural issues aside, had vaccine coverage been sufficiently high, the largescale devastation that was witnessed in the second wave may have been avoided. This line of reasoning is supported by the pattern that as vaccination rates picked up in late August 2021, number of infections diagnosed declined rapidly (Arora & Jamkhandikar, 2021).

One of the factors that link up with the saga of vaccine accessibility is that of procurement and pricing.

The initial tranche of vaccines for inoculating health and frontline workers and those above 45 years of age with comorbidities between January and April 2021 was procured by the Union government and distributed to the states. A new policy was announced on 21 April 2021 (GoI, 2021a), effective from 01 May 2021, under which vaccine manufacturers were permitted to release "… 50% of their monthly … doses to Govt. of India and would be free to supply remaining 50% doses to State Govts. and in the other than Govt. of India channel" (GoI, 2021b). State governments and private hospitals were to negotiate directly with manufacturers for their supply. Consequently, a differential pricing regime emerged in which State governments

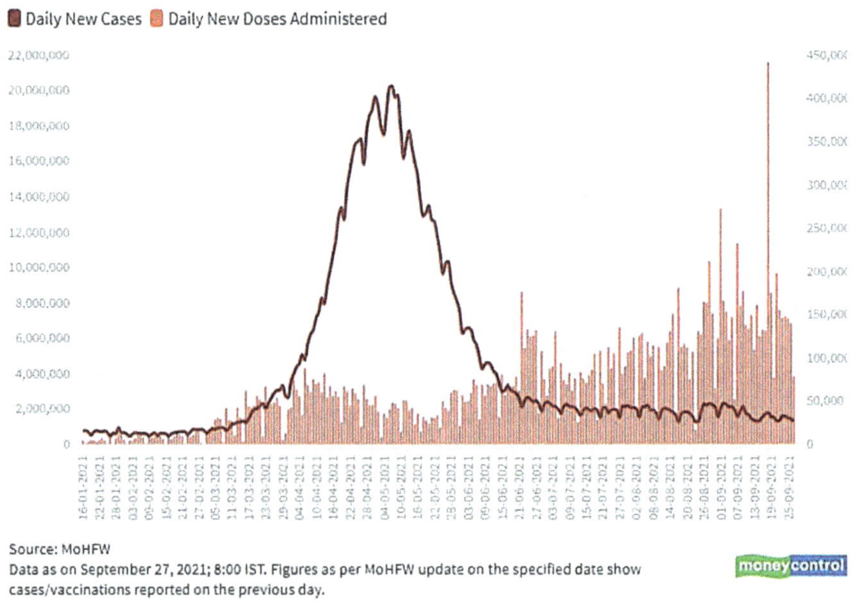

Chart 7.1 New cases and vaccination rate 2021. Collated by Moneycontrol.com from Official Data, https://www.moneycontrol.com/news/india/in-charts-indias-covid-19-case-count-state-wise-trends-vaccination-data-and-other-key-details-70-7511411.html, accessed 21 September 2021

was to pay Rs. 400 and Rs. 600 per dose for CoviShield and Covaxin, respectively, while private hospitals were to be charged Rs. 600 and Rs. 1200, respectively. This differential pricing regime was supposed to be a liberalised approach to vaccine availability. and in a context of acute shortage of vaccines (Indian Express News Service, 2021). In the context of an acute shortage of vaccines and also, given that most of their projected production for many months was already booked, many vaccine manufactures were not willing to deal with State governments.

Given these bottlenecks in making vaccines available to all, the Ministry decided on 19 May 2021 to accept the recommendation of NEGVAC to extend the gap between the two doses of the vaccine to three months (against four weeks being followed by most countries) to tide over acute shortages is being faced in vaccine supply (GoI, 2021b). Such fragmentation of the vaccine market in the context of an acute limitation on production and supply of vaccines was to have a deleterious effect on rapid accessibility of vaccines. While the corporate interests of vaccine manufacturers were protected under this policy, the health interests of the population were another matter.

The vaccine procurement policy was once again revised under the "Revised Guidelines for implementation of National COVID Vaccination Program," and under this policy, from 21 June 2021, the Union government was to procure "… 75% of the vaccines being produced by the manufacturers in the country … to be provided free of cost to States/UTs" and healthcare workers, frontline workers, citizens more than 45 years of age, citizens whose second dose has become due, and citizens above 18 years and above were to be prioritised in that order. The remaining quarter of the production could be sold to the manufacturers of vaccines at predeclared prices to any agency, including private hospitals, who were restricted to charge Rs. 150 for the inoculation. Under this new and "improved" arrangement, the prices for vaccines were fixed at Rs. 780 for CoviShield and Rs. 1410 for Covaxin. This arrangement was again arrived at partly in light of the adverse comments of the Supreme Court in a sou moto petition,[19] including a nudge to consider compulsory licencing, which the government ignored.

The impact of this policy and pricing mechanism may be useful to understand the reluctant operationalisation of the Surveillance model. On a perusal of the Cowin portal through which all vaccines are delivered, one immediately notes that (a) appointments for the free vaccines in government-run medical centres/hospitals are extremely difficult to obtain, which consigns most citizens to pay for the vaccine. This has important implications for a country marked by economic decline, rampantly rising poverty and inequality and a veritable erasure of right to livelihood by the curfew model of lockdown. (b) Given the wide digital divide that the country suffers from, the practical likelihood of most citizens being able to access and book a vaccination slot on the Cowin portal is extremely limited, and (c) limited sampling at government vaccination centres (since walk-in vaccination was allowed to tackle the critique of a digital divide) shows very large queues with limited results. Aside

[19] Supreme Court Sou Moto Writ Petition (Civil) No. 3 of 2021, "In Re: Distribution of Essential Supplies and Services during Pandemic", 2021 SC 228.

from violating the requirements of avoiding crowds to restrict virus transmission, one wonders how many poorer citizens can forego a days' wages to queue up for free vaccination.

It is interesting to note that the same state that was reluctant to fully adopt the Surveillance model was quick to utilise the opportunity offered by the logistics of governance in vaccination to implement an expansive governmentality of legibility model. Each registration under the Cowin portal was allotted a national health identity number that portends to become the basis of a digital health identity card. The combined impact of the panopticon of the Surveillance model and the legibility of the Cowin-collected datasets ensures that disciplinary technologies have entered the very body of the citizens. The logical corollary of severe truncation of citizen' bodily privacy and freedoms is indicated.

7.6 Withering of Healthcare

Amongst the many intertwined issues on the logistics of management of the Coronavirus pandemic, two linked issues of relevance are that of adequate hospital facilities (including for isolation and quarantine) and the aligned issue of availability of medical oxygen.

To briefly recall, the logic of the lockdown from March 2020 that had caused untold miseries to a vast majority of the poorer fellow-citizens, was to limit the spread of the virus and also to buy time to ramp-up the health infrastructure. Besides, it was well known in March 2020 itself that the medical infrastructure is unequal to the task of dealing with the rapidly unfolding coronavirus pandemic. For instance,

> …National Health Profile–2019, [indicates] that there are 7,13,986 total government hospital beds available in India. This amounts to 0.55 beds per 1000 population. The elderly population (aged 60 and above) is especially vulnerable, given more complications which are reported for patients in this age group. The availability of beds for elderly population in India is 5.18 beds per 1000 population. (Chakraborty et al., 2020)

Some effort was made to increase the availability of hospital beds during the first wave with the Annual Report of Ministry of Health and Family Welfare reporting that "as on 11.12.2020, a total of 15,375 dedicated COVID-19 treatment facilities with 15,41,821 dedicated isolation beds (including 2,70,738 oxygen supported beds) have been identified. Also, total of 80,583 ICU beds (including 40,545 ventilator beds) have been earmarked in these facilities" (GoI, 2020–21), which translates into 1 bed per 1000 people of which just 18% were oxygen-supported beds. The additional capacity developed during the First Wave in the form of camp hospitals was dismantled in the misplaced euphoria due to the recession in infection rate. The result was a decrease of 46 per cent in the number of ICU beds by January 2021 while those with oxygen support declined by 36 per cent. Similarly, number of ventilators declined from 33,034 to 23,618—a decline of 28 per cent[20] (Rawat, 2021). It may

[20] Data were collated from Parliamentary documents by Mukesh Rawat from *India Today*.

therefore be no surprise that a very large number of patients were turned away from hospitals, especially in North India (Reuters et al., 2021).

Amidst such declining health infrastructure to grapple with the pandemic, there emerged an acute crisis of medical oxygen for those critically ill with Coronavirus infection. Many states reported oxygen shortage owing to suddenly peaking demand under the Second Wave but the respective governments differ in officially acknowledging the crisis. For instance, in Uttar Pradesh acute shortage was reported, but the State government was in denial, threatening prosecution, under the National Security Act, for reporting the shortage (Ghose, 2021). However, social media feeds were bursting with denizens of the state literally begging for help with both, hospital beds and oxygen supply, not to mention medicines like Remdesivir, which were reputed to be of help. Similarly, local alternate media was reporting both, acute crisis and consequently, large numbers of deaths in the state—something that the State government is still to acknowledge. There are two implications of such denial: (a) official data and details of the true scale of the crisis that resulted from poor health infrastructure, especially the lack of oxygen and other medical supplies, are impossible to estimate and analyse. (b) The process of conversion of citizens into bare biological lifeforms was complete.

A similar situation was reported from a number of states: Maharashtra, Madhya Pradesh, Rajasthan, Punjab, West Bengal, amongst others. However, reading the various reports on oxygen shortage, it is impossible to avoid the conclusion that there was serious shortage of oxygen across the country, but the meeting of clamour for more supply (which was centralised by the Union government[21]) was distinctly along party-political lines.

The main public debate around supply of medical oxygen (with implications for all states) happened around the case of Delhi, perhaps, owing to its visibility being the national capital but also owing to the severe crisis it witnessed. The easiest way to draw the multifarious threads together is to note that matter was the subject of bunch of Writ Petitions before the Delhi High Court. However, the Supreme Court in the Sou Moto Writ Petition (Civil) No. 3 of 2021, "In Re: Distribution of Essential Supplies and Services during Pandemic"[22] also took cognisance of the matter. It is noteworthy that the 64-page order is perhaps, one of the few sources of what the government thinking was on the unavoidably crucial matter of essential supplies, especially, medical supplies during the largescale devastation of human lives during the second wave of the pandemic—something that the Supreme Court order also notes in para 69.

The same Supreme Court order summarises the availability and demand for medical oxygen, reproduced in Table 7.1. Clearly, India has needed to augment

[21] By an order dated 11 September 2020, the Ministry of Home Affairs, in exercise of its powers under Section 10(2)(h) of the DMA had constituted an Empowered Group-II as an inter-ministerial body to ensure availability of essential medical equipment and oxygen management.

[22] Supreme Court Sou Moto Writ Petition (Civil) No. 3 of 2021, "In Re: Distribution of Essential Supplies and Services during Pandemic", 2021 SC 228.

its capacity by a third to meet the projected requirements in less than a week. Consequently, the Union government submitted before the court that various steps such as licencing manufacturers of industrial oxygen to repurpose for medical oxygen, running special trains to supply oxygen all cross the country, requisitioning all kinds of tankers to fulfil the projected demand, setting up of new oxygen plants in major hospitals, and, floating tenders for import of oxygen from abroad, amongst others, was being planned and implemented. However, during the hearing the Solicitor General, who appeared on behalf of the Union government, argued that there was no shortage of oxygen; it was only a logistical matter that it was not available where it was needed! If one was to accept this argument, it boggles the mind as to why additional oxygen was being generated or imported to augment a lack of shortage.

Nonetheless, the complete logistical failure of the Union government is clear. The fact that far more oxygen would be needed than that was available was well understood in light of the experience of other countries. In fact, a tweet put out by the Ministry of Health on 18 April 2021 says:

> One hundred and sixty-two PSA oxygen plants have been sanctioned by Government of India for installation in public health facilities in all states.
>
> Out of 162 PSA plants sanctioned by Govt of India, 33 have already been installed — 5 in MP, 4 in Himachal Pradesh, 3 each in Chandigarh, Gujarat and Uttarakhand, 2 each in Bihar, Karnataka and TL and 1 each in AP, CG, Delhi, Haryana, Kerala, Maharashtra, Puducherry, Punjab and UP.

Table 7.1 Availability and demand for medical oxygen during the Second Wave of the pandemic

S. No	State	Forecast for requirement for medical oxygen (MT) as on		
		Apr-20	Apr-25	Apr-30
1	Maharashtra	1500	1750	2000
2	Uttar Pradesh	400	650	800
3	Chhattisgarh	215	295	382
4	Karnataka	300	155	111
5	Kerala	89	99	104
6	Delhi	300	349	445
7	Tamil Nadu	200	320	465
8	Madhya Pradesh	445	565	700
9	Rajasthan	125	124	124
10	Gujarat	1000	1050	1200
11	Haryana	180	180	180
12	Punjab	126	82	82
Total		4880	5619	6593

Source Supreme Court Sou Moto Writ Petition (Civil) No. 3 of 2021, "In Re: Distribution of Essential Supplies and Services during Pandemic", 2021 SC 228, para 24 (iv)

These will augment medical oxygen capacity by 154.19 MT.[23]

In light to such logistical failure, the Delhi High Court issued a series of orders on 01 May 2021 while dealing with a batch of petitions concerning supply of medicines and oxygen, mainly to ensure implementation of the directions of the Supreme Court. A reading of the Supreme Court order leaves a distinct impression that it is doing the task that Union government should have already performed, especially since it had centralised a large number of powers under the NDMA 2005 for the past year since March 2020.

7.7 In Lieu of Conclusion

The prioritisation of the Isolation model has immeasurably strengthened the law-and-order model with rising impunity of the law enforcement processes, accompanied by social and police violence. The imperative of a surveillance and the governmentality of legibility models, riding on the back of the logistics of vaccination, operates simultaneously with the isolation model. This created a peculiar paradox of high state capacity for the former, which in turn is utilised for a greater degree of governmentalisation of society and étatisation the state. The latter enforced by the sovereign rights of the state (derived from the imperatives of the isolation model) has also buttressed processes of making citizens even more legible. One recent example is the effort to create a digital health identity card[24] for all citizens that will carry their entire health data and history. The governmentality of legibility is therefore no longer restricted to attributes of the population; instead, it now permeates the very body of the citizen.

An implication of this paradoxical process is the undermining of fundamental freedoms of the citizens—a process that is clearly visible today. Further, undermining of such freedoms also undermines the liberal state to create new state forms which may be electorally democratic but illiberal. However, such processes undermine the basis of governmentality of legibility and increases the dependence of the state on its coercion apparatus, undermining its legitimacy.

This process which started unfolding during the Long 2020 will have a much longer and multidimensional impact on the fundamentals of governance processes in the country. The simultaneous operation of the three modes of pandemic management has multiple implication as it has an impact on the nature and character of the state and governance processes.

---

[23] Tweet by Ministry of Health on 18 April 2021.

[24] National Digital Health Mission website claims that the Aadhaar-linked "... Health ID is a *hassle-free* method of accessing your health records digitally ... Presenting this health ID to a participating healthcare provider will allow you to receive your lab reports, prescriptions and diagnosis digitally from verified doctors and health service providers seamlessly" (emphasis added).

References

Agamben, G. (2020a, February 26). The invention of an epidemic [Italian]. *Quodlibet*. Retrieved September 27, 2021, from https://www.quodlibet.it/giorgio-agamben-l-invenzione-di-un-epidemia.

Agamben, G. (2020b, March 17). Coronavirus and philosophers: Giorgio Agamben: Clarifications. *European Journal of Psychoanalysis—New Series*. https://www.journal-psychoanalysis.eu/coronavirus-and-philosophers/.

Agamben, G. (2021). *Where Are We Now? The Epidemic as Politics*. Trans. V. Dani. Lanham, MA: Rowman & Littlefield.

Anand, U. (2021, May 11). No funds granted for vaccine research, development: Govt. *Hindustan Times (New Delhi)*. https://www.hindustantimes.com/india-news/no-funds-granted-for-vaccine-research-development-govt-101620675320843.html.

Arora, N., & Jamkhandikar, S. (2021, August 17). India COVID-19 vaccinations near record, new infections at five-month low. *Reuters*. https://www.reuters.com/world/india/india-reports-25166-new-covid-19-cases-2021-08-17/.

AstraZeneca. (2020a, December 30). *AstraZeneca's COVID-19 vaccine authorised for emergency supply in the UK*. https://www.astrazeneca.com/media-centre/press-releases/2020/astrazenecas-covid-19-vaccine-authorised-in-uk.html.

AstraZeneca. (2020b, June 4). *AstraZeneca takes next steps towards broad and equitable access to Oxford University's potential COVID-19 vaccine*. https://www.astrazeneca.com/media-centre/articles/2020/astrazeneca-takes-next-steps-towards-broad-and-equitable-access-to-oxford-universitys-potential-covid-19-vaccine.html.

Banerjea, A. (2021, January 11). Covid-19 vaccination: India signs purchase order with Serum Covishield vaccine to cost ₹ 200 per dose. *Mint*. https://www.livemint.com/news/india/covid19-vaccination-india-to-buy-1-1-crore-doses-from-serum-dispatches-may-start-today-says-report-11610360963620.html.

Basu, K. (2020, July 8). The way in which it was executed, India's lockdown itself became source of virus's spread. *The Indian Express*. https://indianexpress.com/article/opinion/columns/coronavirus-lockdown-india-covid-19-cases-deaths-6494930/.

Bhattacharya, S. (2020, June 25). India's migrant workers are protesting erasure of their rights amid lockdown: A mapping project documents their resistance. *Firstpost*. https://www.firstpost.com/india/indias-migrant-workers-are-protesting-erasure-of-their-rights-amid-lockdown-a-mapping-project-documents-their-resistance-8463821.html.

Bhowmick, N. (2020, May 27). They treat us like stray dogs: Migrant workers flee India's cities. *National Geographic*. https://www.nationalgeographic.com/history/2020/05/they-treat-us-like-stray-dogs-migrant-workers-flee-india-cities/.

Business Standard Web Team. (2020, August 31). First economic contraction in 4 decades: India's GDP shrinks 23.9% in Q1, FY21. *Business Standard*. https://www.business-standard.com/article/economy-policy/first-economic-contraction-in-4-decades-india-s-gdp-shrinks-x-in-q1-fy21-120083101022_1.html.

Callaway, E. (2020, August 24). The unequal scramble for coronavirus vaccines—by the numbers. *Nature*. https://www.nature.com/articles/d41586-020-02450-x.

Chandra, H., & Basu, M. (2020, March 19). Modi announces 'Janata Curfew' on 22 March, urges for resolve, restraint to fight coronavirus. *The Print*. https://theprint.in/india/modi-announces-janata-curfew-on-22-march-urges-for-resolve-restraint-to-fight-coronavirus/384138/.

Chatterjee, P. (2020, April 12). The pandemic exposes India's apathy toward migrant workers. *The Atlantic*. https://www.theatlantic.com/ideas/archive/2020/04/the-pandemic-exposes-indias-two-worlds/609838/.

Chhibber, M. (2020, September 2). Supreme Court's handling of Kashmir habeas corpus more worrisome than Modi govt's clampdown. *The Print*. https://theprint.in/opinion/supreme-courts-handling-of-kashmir-habeas-corpus-more-worrisome-than-modi-govts-clampdown/286173/.

COVAXIN Study Group. (2021). Efficacy, safety, and lot to lot immunogenicity of an inactivated SARS-CoV-2 vaccine (BBV152): A, double-blind, randomised, controlled phase 3 trial. *The Lancet, 398*(10317), P2173–P2184. https://doi.org/10.1101/2021.06.30.21259439

Cross, S., Rho, Y., Reddy, H., Pepperrell, T., Rodgers, F., Osborne, R., Eni-Olotu, A., Banerjee, R., Wimmer, S., & Keestra, S. (2021). Who funded the research behind the Oxford-AstraZeneca COVID-19 vaccine? Approximating the funding to the University of Oxford for the research and development of the ChAdOx vaccine technology. *BMJ Global Health, 6*, 21255103. https://doi.org/10.1101/2021.04.08.21255103

Dixit, P. (2020, April 9). My lord, migrant labourers need more than just food, just like we all do. *The Print*. https://theprint.in/opinion/pov/my-lord-migrant-labourers-need-more-than-just-food-just-like-we-all-do/398508/.

Economic Outlook. (2020, April 30). Only 30.8 mln provided jobs under MGNREGA in April 2020: 88.8% lower than in previous year. *CMIE*. https://www.cmie.com/kommon/bin/sr.php?kall=warticle&dt=2020-04-30%2016:32:16&msec=126.

Ella, R., Reddy, S., Jogdand, H., Sarangi, V., Ganneru, B., Prasad, S., Das, D., Raju, D., Praturi, U., Sapkal, G., Yadav, P., Reddy, P., Verma, S., Singh, C., Redkar, S. V., Gillurkar, C. S., Kushwaha, J. S., Mohapatra, S., Bhate, A., … Vadrevu, K. M. (2021). Safety and immunogenicity of an inactivated SARS-CoV-2 vaccine, BBV152: Interim results from a double-blind, randomised, multicentre, phase 2 trial, and 3-month follow-up of a double-blind, randomised phase 1 trial. *The Lancet Infectious Diseases, 21*(7), 950–961. https://doi.org/10.1016/S1473-3099(21)00070-0

Ferguson, J. (1994). *The anti-politics machine: Development, depoliticisation, and bureaucratic power in Lesotho*. University of Minnesota Press.

Foucault, M. (1991). Governmentality. In G. Burchell, C. Gordon, & P. Miller (Eds.), *Studies*.

Foucault, M. (1995). *Discipline and punish: The birth of the prison*. In A. Sheridan (Trans.). Vintage.

Foucault, M. (2004). *Security, territory, population: Lectures at the Collège De France, 1977–78*. In G. Burchell (Trans.), M. Senellart (Ed.). Palgrave.

Foucault, M. (2006). *History of madness*. In J. Murphy, & J. Khalfa (Trans.), J. Khafla (Ed.). Routledge.

Ghose, A. (2021, April 27). Fact check: Was Adityanath right in saying that there's no shortage of medical oxygen in UP? *Scroll.in*. https://scroll.in/article/993435/fact-check-was-adityanath-right-in-saying-that-theres-no-shortage-of-medical-oxygen-in-up.

GoI. (2020, May 14). *Aatmanirbhar Bharat Abhiyaan phase-II to support Indian economy in fight against COVID-19*. https://covid19.india.gov.in/document-category/ministry-of-finance/.

Government of India. (2020–21). *Annual report 2020–21* (p. 213). Ministry of Health and Family Welfare.

Government of India. (2020). *Cabinet summary for October 2020*. https://dbtindia.gov.in/sites/default/files/English%20Cab%20summary_Oct20.pdf.

Government of India. (2021a, April 21). *Liberalised pricing and accelerated national covid-19 vaccination strategy*. https://www.mohfw.gov.in/pdf/LiberalisedPricingandAcceleratedNationalCovid19VaccinationStrategy2042021.pdf.

Government of India. (2021b, May 19). *Press release*. https://pib.gov.in/PressReleasePage.aspx?PRID=1719925.

Hindustan Times. (2020a, March 24). From today, curfew passes must for crossing interstate borders to enter Delhi amid coronavirus lockdown. *Hindustan Times*. https://www.hindustantimes.com/delhi-news/curfew-passed-need-too-cross-interstate-borders-in-delhi/story-ETT5Ba7pLGvoq7GACrqPbN.html.

Hindustan Times. (2020b, September 14). Arrest, search without warrant under UP's new special security force rules. *Hindustan Times*. https://www.hindustantimes.com/india-news/arrest-search-without-warrant-under-up-s-new-special-security-force-rules/story-4O9dJ6pAkfikgW2cU5msvJ.html.

in Governmentality. University of Chicago Press, 102–104.

India Today Web Desk (2020, September 18). Unemployment crisis: Over 60 lakh white collar professional jobs lost during May–August. *India Today*. https://www.indiatoday.in/business/story/unemployment-crisis-deepens-over-60-lakh-white-collar-professionals-lost-jobs-during-may-august-1722971-2020-09-18.

Indian Express News Service. (2021, April 29). 1.33 crore sign in as Covid-19 vaccine doors open, states flag stock shortage. *Indian Express*. https://indianexpress.com/article/india/registration-on-cowin-1-33-crore-sign-in-states-flag-vaccine-stock-shortage-7293029/.

Jones, D. J. (2020). The potential impacts of pandemic policing on police legitimacy: Planning past the covid-19 crisis. *Policing: A Journal of Policy and Practice, 14*(3), 579–586.

Krishnan, M. (2020, May 26). Police excesses for lockdown violation led to 12 deaths: Study. *Hindustan Times*. https://www.hindustantimes.com/india-news/police-excesses-for-lockdown-violation-led-to-12-deaths-study/story-qj5dZ68nxPBc3B0HbSBg3L.html.

Library of Congress. (2020, April 15). *Germany: Parliament changes rules of procedure to ensure functioning during COVID-19 pandemic*. https://www.loc.gov/law/foreign-news/article/germany-parliament-changes-rules-of-procedure-to-ensure-functioning-during-covid-19-pandemic/.

Means, A. J. (2021). Foucault, biopolitics, and the critique of state reason. *Educational Philosophy and Theory, 54*(2022), 1968–1969.

Munshi, S. (2020, April 22). Starvation, police beatings and covid-19: For migrant workers stuck in Delhi, the choices are stark. *News18*. https://www.news18.com/news/india/starvation-police-beatings-and-covid-19-for-migrant-workers-stuck-in-delhi-the-choices-are-stark-2588163.html.

Outlook (2020, March 23). Curfew passes to be necessary for travel between Delhi, neighbouring areas. *Outlook*. https://www.outlookindia.com/website/story/india-news-curfew-passes-to-be-necessary-for-travel-between-delhi-neighboring-areas/349309.

OxCGRT. (2020). *Oxford COVID-19 government response tracker*. https://www.bsg.ox.ac.uk/research/research-projects/coronavirus-government-response-racker.

Oxford COVID Vaccine Trial Group. (2021). Safety and efficacy of the ChAdOx1 nCoV-19 vaccine (AZD1222) against SARS-CoV-2: An interim analysis of four randomised controlled trials in Brazil, South Africa, and the UK. *The Lancet, 397*(10269), 99–111.

Pandey, G. (2020, April 21). Coronavirus in India: Desperate migrant workers trapped in lockdown. *BBC News*. https://www.bbc.com/news/world-asia-india-52360757.

Parkins, K. (2021, April 27). Covaxin: India's homegrown Covid-19 vaccine brings hope and controversy. *Clinical Trials Arena*. https://www.clinicaltrialsarena.com/analysis/covaxin-indias-homegrown-covid-19-vaccine-brings-hope-and-controversy/.

Patel, C. (2020, July 13). COVID-19: The hidden majority in India's migration crisis. *Chatham House*. https://www.chathamhouse.org/expert/comment/covid-19-hidden-majority-indias-migration-crisis.

Prakash, A. (2021). Shadow of the pandemic and the beleaguered liberal-democratic script in India'. *India Review, 20*(2), 104–120.

Press Information Bureau. (2021a, January 3). *Press statement by the Drugs Controller General of India (DCGI) on restricted emergency approval of COVID-19 virus vaccine*. https://www.icmr.gov.in/pdf/press_realease_files/HFW_DCGI_energency_use_authorisation_03012021_2.pdf.

Press Information Bureau. (2021, May 13). *Press Briefing on the actions taken, preparedness and updates on COVID-19*. https://www.youtube.com/watch?v=ijLcZ8G84FI.

PTI. (2020, May 22). Quarantine centres in Uttar Pradesh are so bad they have become torture camps: Samajwadi Party. *The Economic Times*. https://economictimes.indiatimes.com/news/politics-and-nation/quarantine-centres-in-uttar-pradesh-are-so-bad-they-have-become-torture-camps-samajwadi-party/articleshow/75894700.cms.

PTI. (2021, April 20). Serum hails financial aid from govt to ramp up Covid-19 vaccine production. *The Hindu*. https://www.thehindu.com/business/Industry/serum-hails-financial-aid-from-govt-to-ramp-up-covid-19-vaccine-production/article34367000.ece.

Rashid, O. (2020, March 30). Coronavirus: In Bareilly, migrants returning home sprayed with disinfectant. *The Hindu*. https://www.thehindu.com/news/national/other-states/coronavirus-in-bareilly-migrants-forced-to-take-bath-in-the-open-with-sanitiser/article31204430.ece.

Rawat, M. (2021, May 3). Just before 2nd Covid wave hit India, ICU beds decreased by 46%, oxygen ones by 36%. *India Today*. https://www.indiatoday.in/coronavirus-outbreak/story/just-before-2nd-covid-wave-hit-india-icu-beds-decreased-by-46-oxygen-ones-by-36-1796830-2021-05-03.

Reuters, Jadhav, R., & Kalra, A. (2021, April 17). India's capital Delhi faces hospital beds shortage as coronavirus cases surge. *Reuters*. https://www.reuters.com/world/india/india-reports-another-record-daily-rise-covid-19-infections-2021-04-17/.

Sarasin, P. (2020, March 31). Understanding the coronavirus pandemic with Foucault? *Genealogy+Critique*. Retrieved September 28, 2021, from https://www.fsw.uzh.ch/foucaultblog/essays/254/understanding-corona-with-foucault.

Scheppele, K. L. (2018). Autocratic legalism. *The University of Chicago Law Review, 85*(2), 545–583.

Shaju, P. (2020, March 30). Kerala: Migrant workers say they want food, ask to be taken back home. *The Indian Express*. https://indianexpress.com/article/india/coronavirus-india-lockdown-kerala-migrant-workers-say-they-want-food-ask-to-be-taken-back-home-6337850/.

Sharma, S. (2020a, April 13). 2020. India cannot fight a pandemic with police lathis. It must ensure people have food—and dignity. *Scroll.in*. https://scroll.in/article/958993/india-cannot-fight-a-pandemic-with-police-lathis-it-must-ensure-people-have-food-and-dignity.

Sharma, S. N. (2020b, September 6). How the recent decision by GST Council has further deepened states' financial woes". *The Economic Times*. https://economictimes.indiatimes.com/news/economy/policy/how-the-recent-decision-by-gst-council-has-further-deepened-states-financial-woes/articleshow/77951570.cms.

Singh, P., Ravi, S., & Chakraborty, S. (2020, March 24). COVID-19: Is India's health infrastructure equipped to handle an epidemic? *Brookings*. https://www.brookings.edu/blog/up-front/2020/03/24/is-indias-health-infrastructure-equipped-to-handle-an-epidemic/.

Som, V., & Pullanoor, H. (2021, September 27). WHO's Covaxin clearance delayed further over technical queries: Sources. *NDTV*. https://www.ndtv.com/india-news/covaxin-faces-more-delay-for-who-clearance-technical-queries-need-to-be-answered-by-bharat-biotech-sources-2555676.

Srivastava, P. (2021, April 27). Uttar Pradesh: Oxygen crisis far from over, kin wait for wait for hours in queues. *Times of India*. https://timesofindia.indiatimes.com/city/lucknow/oxygen-crisis-far-from-over-kin-wait-for-hours-in-queues/articleshow/82265439.cms.

SWAN. (2020a). *21 Days and counting: COVID-19 lockdown, migrant workers, and the inadequacy of welfare measures in India*. http://publications.azimpremjifoundation.org/2272/1/lockdown_and_distress_report_by_stranded_workers_action_network-2.pdf.

SWAN. (2020b). *32 Days and counting: COVID-19 lockdown, migrant workers, and the inadequacy of welfare measures in India*. https://covid19socialsecurity.files.wordpress.com/2020/05/32-days-and-counting_swan.pdf?fbclid=IwAR0-kuFz9pV9drrshn7NLnOUOuVbkv7NbrGzcqMLBMwyel0isEsaoLO-dw0.

TNN. (2021, August 2). Covid-19: To meet its vaccination target, India needs to give 92 lakh shots per day. *Times of India*. https://timesofindia.indiatimes.com/india/covid-19-to-meet-its-vaccination-target-india-needs-to-give-92-lakh-shots-per-day/articleshow/84959504.cms#:~:text=Covid%2D19%3A%20To%20meet%20its,92%20lakh%20shots%20per%20day&text=India%20will%20need%20to%20administer,those%20aged%2018%20or%20more.

University of Oxford. (2020, July 20). *New study reveals Oxford coronavirus vaccine produces strong immune response*. https://www.research.ox.ac.uk/article/2020-07-20-new-study-reveals-oxford-coronavirus-vaccine-produces-strong-immune-response.

Vyas, M. (2020, August 18). An unhealthy recovery. *CMIE*. https://www.cmie.com/kommon/bin/sr.php?kall=warticle&dt=2020-08-18%2011:02:19&msec=596.

Part III
Refugees and Labouring Lives

Chapter 8
Politics of Health in Post-partition Calcutta: The Refugees, the Left Movements and the Question of Life in the City

Priyankar Dey

Abstract This chapter investigates how the presence of the refugees from East Bengal within the city of Calcutta shaped the discourses and the practices of public health of the city in the post-partition decades. The refugees in the city laid bare the fault lines in the 'social' discourse of public health of the time which is reflected in the peculiar pathological figuration of the displaced population in the contemporary municipal debates. Further, focusing on the struggles of the refugee squatters in ensuring healthcare facilities, the chapter shows how the question of public health could produce different forms of alliances and solidarity networks within the colony and beyond its confines. Public health practices in the colonies assembled many different actors, not all of them were residents of the colonies. A close investigation of these networks then problematizes the standard historiographical tradition of casting the history of refugee rehabilitation into a neat binary between charity and self-reliance. Finally, linking the above discussion with the healthcare movement organized by the left in the decades under consideration, this chapter argues that all of these point towards alternative ideals of protection and care. They hinted towards a newly emerging *politics of life* in the city, which would be reflected in the populist rhetoric of the left in the years to follow. This politics of life imagined the citizen as a bio-social entity and the state as the ultimate protector of their bio-social life.

Keywords Partition · Calcutta · Refugee · Left politics · Public health · Colonies

The city has a foundational connection with the question of health. The history of Calcutta bears evidence of the fact that the physical layout of the city grew much in response to the colonial elites' concern to find a sanitized space for healthy living. This paper seeks to revisit the question of the city-space, public health and protection of life by critically looking at the history of Calcutta in the context of the refugee influx in the

P. Dey (✉)
Anandabazar Online, Kolkata, India
e-mail: priyankar08@gmail.com

S. R. Chakraborty et al. (eds.), *The Long 2020*, India Studies in Business and Economics, https://doi.org/10.1007/978-981-99-4815-4_8

three decades following partition of India in 1947. The question of public health, we need to keep in mind, is always a question of spaces—of spatial (re)organization. The refugees from East Bengal, alongside the state and other political actors, are the main protagonists as well as co-founders of the stage which is the city of Calcutta and the urban areas of the Greater Calcutta region. Their presence in the city in huge numbers, I will try to show, complicated the discourse of protection and framed the question of health care in a particular manner. The collective actions the refugee colony residents in ensuring healthcare services for themselves not only helped them to find a place in the city by incorporating them into a larger network of power, but also reflected a notion of protection and care which the state was thought to provide but failed. Through a contentious politics of health that emerged at a historical conjuncture of the post-partition West Bengal, an informal discourse on the right to life could be seen in the horizon of the public debates. The struggle for life, *jiban* in Bengali, along with livelihood (*jibika*) would become the most used catchphrase of radical politics in West Bengal for years to come. This paper hopes to provide a material history of that populist rhetoric and practices that dominated the left-communist politics of Bengal for long.

8.1 A Background: Right to Health, 'Social' Medicine and the Politics of Life

The post-second world war years in many ways marked a shift in the official discourse on health care and the state's role in it in many countries all over the world. As we know from the existing literature on this subject, it was connected with the post-war reconstruction efforts of the recently victorious liberal economies. The Beveridge Report of 1942 in England and the Bhore Committee Report of 1946 in India followed the same trajectory which identified health care for all as a primary responsibility of the state (Mitra, 2021).[1] Both of these documents invoked an imagination of the 'social' in the effective management of diseases and recommended health care as a right of 'all citizens, irrespective of their abilities to pay for it' (Health Survey and Development Committee, 1946: 6). In its conceptualization of health, this discourse of 'social medicine' pointed out environmental as well as social conditions as sources of diseases. Materialities of living conditions, following this, could become an integral part of the understanding of diseases and epidemics. The definition of health provided in Bhore Committee's Report therefore placed the health of an individual right in the physical milieu they live in:

[1] For a critical discussion on the Bhore Committee Report and the transition from a 'social' discourse to the neoliberal discourse of public health.

> The term health implies more than an absence of sickness in the individual and indicates a state of harmonious functioning of the body and mind *in relation to his physical and social environment*,[2] to enable him to enjoy life to the fullest possible extent and reach his maximum level of productive capacity. (Health Survey and Development Committee, 1946: 21)

It is the duty of the state to ensure the suitable physical and social environment' in which a healthy body could thrive in harmony. The state, in other words, is the protector of this biosocial body. In this formulation of health, life itself became the focus of governance. One can argue that it is precisely in this moment, citizenship is imagined as biosocial in nature. The Bhore Committee Report would become a foundational document in the public debates on health care in post-colonial India for decades to come. The principles laid out in this document would serve both as a guideline for the government's actions in matters related to public health as well as a ready reference for criticizing the government failures in this domain. Following the Second Five Years' Plan (1956–61), the government 'revised priorities in health' and,

> focused attention on expansion of basic services, medical personnel, provision of free basic health care, referral facilities for primary health centres, and set priorities for water supply, sanitation, infrastructure growth, and control of communicable diseases. (Qadeer, 2005: 88)

Increasing government expenditure on these matters hinted at an ideal of the state which was expected to provide for the basic protections of life. In the government's intervention in milk distribution in the state, the state's role as a caregiver can be seen expanded. The health department, with the help from Red Cross Society, UNICEF and other aid organizations, opened milk kitchens for children and their mothers. More active intervention from the part of the government and the municipal authorities was called for to stop the adulteration of food stuff. In all these instances, the state was imagined as the ultimate caregiver to the biosocial life and at the centre of the discourse on public health. As the rest of this paper will try to show, the contentious politics of the city would revolve much around the issues outlined in the above quote. A politics of health, in other words, became a part of everyday life in the city in the three decades following partition. What this politics of health did was to bring out the question of life, its vital functions and necessities, to the arena of public debate. The state was put on trial for not caring about human life. The government in 1951 therefore faced stringent criticism in the newspapers and by the opposition leaders and various refugee organizations for a series of child deaths in Cossipore, Daspara, Ghushuri and other refugee camps due to unhygienic conditions. It was the state's failure at caregiving that was highlighted. UCRC, the left and the communist-led refugee organization, questioned why the director of the health department had never cared to pay a visit to these camps. In their criticisms of the government, refugee organizations like the UCRC, or the communist-led newspaper *Swadhinata*, the 'animal life' of the camp residents would present itself as a popular trope (Singha, 1999: 23–25). CPI leader Manikuntala Sen, in her speech at the assembly, accused the government of failing to take care of the refugee children:

---

[2] Emphasis added.

> 10 lakhs refugee children have come. By dying out of starvation and lack of proper housing, they are saving this government. But the government is not satisfied with that. Therefore they are sending them to the hell. ... Around 2 lakhs children have died after the partition. Our honourable Governor's speech had nothing to say about saving the rest 8 lakhs. (Sen, 2011: 332)[3]

In Sen's view, the civilizational progress made by a nation could be measured from its government's attitude towards the development of the children and the women. Upholding the role of the state as a caregiver, the politics of health put an ethical onus on the state to provide care and protection for life.

8.2 Public Health and the Responsibility of Protection

While the state was thought to be the primary agency responsible for protecting life in this dominant discourse of public health, the responsibility was not assigned to it only, rather distributed in a shared relationship of the community and the state, the people and the ruling dispensation. If the dominant discourse of public health in the post-independence West Bengal viewed health care as a social right of the citizens and the state as the protector of this right, it also highlighted the responsibilities of the citizens as the flip side of the coin. If this discourse of public health and 'social medicine' conceptualized health care as a right of every citizen, it also highlighted the collective duties on the part of the citizens in this regard. The Bhore Committee Report, once again, is a perfect example of this:

> the people themselves must take proper share and equal responsibility with the profession in order that they might be able to profit by any measure that the State and the profession might introduce and execute. It was essential that those who purveyed the health services and those for whom they were provided should take equal part in them as otherwise the arrangements would be imperfect and people would not get the full benefit of the treatment.

It is the same understanding which led the Governor of West Bengal, C. Rajagopalachari, to describe small-pox vaccination as a 'social duty' when the epidemic was raging in the city in January 1948:

> It is a duty citizens owe to society. We owe it to our brothers and sisters in the city to go through the very slight inconvenience of vaccination in order that we may not become a possible channel for spreading the dread disease to others. I, therefore, hope that all enlightened men and women will get themselves re-vaccinated at once and enable those responsible for the health of the city to feel confident. Vaccination is a social duty (The Calcutta Municipal Gazette XLVII, 1948).

The appeal to a moral indignation to act cannot be missed in this statement. Here the social is framed as the domain of a shared responsibility. As Foucault reminds us, these 'techniques of responsibilization' of the pastoral power were instrumental in

---

[3] Originally part of 'Shishuswasthya O Narider Somosya', a Speech at the West Bengal Legislative Assembly (5 July 1952). Reprinted in Sen's *Jonojagorone Narijagorone* (2011).

producing the city as a space of security (Foucault 2009). In the above statement, it is the jab of the needle on individual arms that produces the social through the formation of a shared immunity. In other words, the social was already biosocial in nature. In the context of the epidemic management in the city of the post-independence years, the peculiar play of the social produced the figure of the 'outsider' who as a potential source of contagion. While asking the citizens to report cholera cases known to them to the government, the Chief Executive Officer of the CMC in January 1948 appealed, 'If you know of anyone who has not been vaccinated and particularly if he is a new-comer to Calcutta, tell him to get vaccinated' (The Calcutta Municipal Gazette XLVII, 1948). As part of their fight against the epidemic outbreaks, the government would vaccinate and inoculate the refugees coming through various check-points (Bandyopadhyay, 2011: 120). There is a pathological gaze of the state at work here which focused on the bodies of the refugees. It would not be an overstatement to claim that for the decolonized nation-state, the refugees provided a pool of labouring bodies to be mobilized for the development of the nation. Similarly, government selected able bodied persons capable of hard labour for the agricultural settlements like that in the Andaman Islands or elsewhere. This productivist lens of the state's gaze over refugee bodies is evident in B. S. Guha's Anthropological Survey of India report of a comparative socio-economic survey of a refugee camp and a colony in the outskirts of Calcutta. In this report, as well as in numerous other government documents, one can notice an implicit bias against the camp refugees who were thought to be living an idle and unproductive life on government doles. Conducted at a time when the anti-government discontent was rising among the refugees and the left and communists-led refugee movement was rocking the streets of Calcutta, Guha's report on the social tensions among the refugees did not shy away from making a straight connection between the precarity of the biological and social life of the refugees and the rising restlessness and discontent among them:

> In the altered conditions of life with scarcity of food and burden of anxieties the subject often fell prey to various diseases and, for that, proper medical treatment was urgently necessary. But in this respect also their experiences were not favourable. Thus the whole picture presents a state of induced restlessness and tension. Induced, because they were assured of Government help and allowed to aspire for better and secure states of living which in turn was frustrated by the inadequacies, irregularities, and inconsistencies of the Government plan and activities. (Guha, 1954: 31)

8.3 Refugees and Migrants as Subjects of Risk

The framing of the refugees and the migrants as the risky subjects happened in other registers as well. The discourse on public health and techniques of epidemic governance carved out the refugees as a distinctive population group which was not only *at* risk but also *of* risk. Since 1948 at least, the municipal authorities of Calcutta were repeatedly blaming the refugee influx as a threat to the overall public health conditions of the city. The 1951 Annual Report of the Directorate of Health Services of the West Bengal government claimed that the incidence of tuberculosis infection was on the rise since the partition. Newspaper articles hinted that the growing cases of TB in the refugee colonies, if not unchecked, would endanger the public health of the whole Bengal. The Mayor of the city, Triguna Sen, in 1957 announced before the house that 'we can no longer shut our eyes to these *sore spots* of Calcutta—the bustees and the refugee colonies' (*Calcutta Municipal Gazette*, 1957a, 1957b). The *Municipal Gazette* of 18 January 1958 had the following to report:

> Corporation is unable to control T.B. effectively as it desires to do. This is because of the city's existing open T.B. cases which in enormous proportion are still thriving in Bustees and causing infection to others. A good number are refugees. They have become a menace to the Tuberculosis Control Programme in the city being unamenable to Clinics based on Domicilliary treatment. Living in crowded areas such cases of T.B. are spreading disease amongst the mass like wild fire. ... These open T.B. cases unamenable to Clinics based on Domicilliary treatment need segregation.[4] (Calcutta Municipal Gazette, 1958: 294)

A fear of contagion marked this civic discourse of the time. The Corporation, the aforementioned Gazettee report added, was trying to establish a segregation hospital at the outskirts of Calcutta where the infectious TB patients from the refugee colonies and the *bustees* could be removed. This very imagination of the sanitized city-space was also at play when the police in 1952 stopped a refugee procession of the deserters of the Bettiah camp from entering into the city from Howrah on the account that some of them might be suffering from small-pox (West Bengal State Assembly, 1957: 9–10). Similarly, refugees crowding at the Sealdah station caused anxieties about the lives of the citizens among some of the city councillors (*Calcutta Municipal Gazette*, 1957a, 1957b: 520). CMC employed Bustee Cleaning Gangs to sanitize the bustees from time to time. The colonies and the bustees got priority in the mass vaccination or inoculation drives. The overcrowding of the corporation area by the refugee squatters led to efforts of spatial reorganization of the Greater Calcutta or Calcutta Metropolitan District area. When the government started establishing government-sponsored colonies in the 1950s to accommodate refugees stuck inside the transit camps, it tried to place these settlements in such a manner that the refugee population was dispersed throughout the CMD area, and not concentrated in one location. Out of the 53 government-sponsored colonies which came up in between 1950 and 55, only one fell within the Calcutta Corporation area. Most of them were founded in municipal areas close to Calcutta, like Barrackpore, Khardah, Bauria, Bally, Jagacha, Chinsurah, Bhadreswar, Chandannagar, etc. (Chaudhuri, 1983: 22). A fear of contagion marked the discourse of the health in the city of the time and often put the refugee and migrant at the centre of it by marking them as a subject of risk and calling for a spatial management of them.

One needs to take into account the fact that the refugee crisis in West Bengal was unfolding at a time when the fears of a population explosion and subsequent food shortage sweeped both popular and academic narratives as well as policy briefs world-wide. The first all-India meeting of the Family Planning Association of India was held

[4] T.B. Problems in the City: A Memorandum Submitted to Dr. P. V. Benjamin and Read by Dr. B. C. Basu.

in 1951. Jack Loveridge shows how international aid organizations like the Rockfeller or the Ford Foundation invested in projects in population control through family planning and community development for the post-partition refugees in Punjab. In West Bengal too there was a growing interest in such issues and increasing claims on the state to intervene. As the West Bengal Assembly proceedings show, public discontent over the food deficit in the state was rising. On the other hand, there was a growing discussion about the congestion in the city's living quarters and the need for healthy housing arrangements. Overcrowding causing unsanitary living conditions in the refugee households, as one survey by the Indian Statistical Survey claimed, was responsible for the growing infant mortality rate in the city (Mitra et al., 1951: 181). This was also the period of increased *bustee* improvement projects or CIT activities. The problem of congestion due to migration to the city and the need for better community housing captured the imagination of the municipal administrators very early in the post-partition years, even much before the full effect of the refugee influx had to be faced. An article published in the pages of the Calcutta Municipal Gazette in 1947 warned its readers that 'bad housing with consequent overcrowding in small apartments resulted in undernourishment and heavy mortality from diseases like tuberculosis, etc.' While emphasizing that 'extreme care is necessary in designing the community buildings', the article quoted by Winston Churchill, 'We shape our buildings and our buildings shape our lives' (*The Calcutta Municipal Gazette*, 1947, 189).

Municipal documents often described the 'floating population', which included the East Bengali refugees as well as Bihari migrant workers in the city, as burden to the rate-payers as they didn't pay any taxes but laid claims to the civic amenities built with tax-payers' money. A neo-Malthussian sentiment is quite evident here as the right to the basic infrastructures of life—right to the city itself—was denied to the 'unproductive' part of a population. If we can stretch it a little further, this argument hints at a differential value of life. If this corresponds to a neoliberal script of modern biopolitics, one has to realize that the formal inauguration of the neoliberal paradigm in India during the 1990s had long antecedents. To think it through, the argument about the 'righlessness' of the refugees and migrants in the city was not ultimately in contradiction with the understanding of the citizenship in the Bhore Committee Report which conceptualized it as a combination of rights and duties. Citizenship was conceived as a transactional contract which would guarantee social protection. The migrants and the refugees could not have any rightful claims to the city because they failed to satisfy their end of the contract by following the duties expected of a citizen. The figure of the migrant or the refugee as a socially irresponsible person marked a deep fault line which in turn helps one to understand the limits of the protectionist discourse of the liberal city and its assurances of social well-being.

8.4 Health Care and the Squatters Colonies in Calcutta: Materialities of Life

The civic infrastructure of the city, built by the colonial authorities, was already overburdened before the refugee influx from East Bengal began. What this massive migration to the city did was to lay bare the fault lines and the structural inequality in the existing system. It was on these very fronts, the contentious politics of the coming days would be performed. But we will come back to this soon. Before that, a little background will help us to historically situate the story.

In the post-partition years, West Bengal, especially the Greater Calcutta area and its surrounding regions, saw a massive population rise, the refugee influx being a primary contributing factor in that. According to a commentator at the Calcutta Municipal Gazette, Greater Calcutta in 1951 had a population of 36 lakhs with a density of 89,000 people per square mile (*The Calcutta Municipal Gazette*, 1957a, 1957b: 470). In 1971, around 2.87 lakhs refugees were living in the Calcutta district and another 5.74 lakhs in the 24 parganas, 42,000 in Howrah and 93,000 in Hooghly. An estimate of 1975 shows that the Calcutta Metropolitan District accounted for 46.19% of the total number of refugee settlements in West Bengal. While Calcutta Corporation area had 46 refugee colonies, the greater Calcutta Metropolitan District had 258 urban colonies. Adjoining areas of the Calcutta Corporation like municipal areas of Dumdum, Panihati, south-west part of the CMD area—Tollygunje-Jadavpur-Kasba-Behala-Garfa-Santoshpur—witnessed a significant concentration of the refugee colonies (Chaudhuri, 1983: 20, 31). It is no surprise that the colonial infrastructure of the city was abysmally inadequate to cope up with the mounting pressure of the population rise in the years following decolonization and partition migration.

In the three decades following partition, Calcutta was ravaged by frequent outbreaks of cholera, small-pox and plague epidemics, while tuberculosis cases rose unabatedly. The material living conditions of the refugees in West Bengal made them especially vulnerable to the epidemics and other health hazards. While the refugees in the camps were living under the most unsanitary and unhygienic conditions, their counterparts in the squatters' colonies also had to survive poor living standards. Most of the squatters could not afford to build more than a one-room hutment during the first decade of the occupation. Often the single room house would accommodate as many as ten family members. The weak structures of the *kutcha* huts made of split bamboos, *hogla* thatched roof and mud floor were not equipped to offer much protection from the harsh weathers and conducive to many dangers including snakes and vermin. Cooking and bathroom activities had to be done outside. Many of these colonies lying in the southern parts of city was developed after reclaiming land from water bodies, swamps and low-lying marshy areas. The ponds and other water bodies in these colonies would often flood the whole area during the rains. Annemiek Prins's interviews with the old residents of the Chittaranjan and Panchannagram colonies recounted that '[t]he water used to come up to people's knees and formed the main element of a landscape consisting of jungle, swamps and wetlands'. 'Hence, the struggle for settlement was a struggle with both land and water', Prins noted (Prins, 2014: 40). The swamps and the jungles provided breeding grounds for mosquitoes and the squatters would have to spend most of the time inside mosquito nets (Prins, 2014: 40).[5] The recollections of the colony residents indicated 'a constant interaction with the environment' of the refugees squatting in those lands outlying the core area of the city. The insanitary and unhygienic living conditions, coupled with malnutrition due to strained financial resources, led to frequent outbreaks of epidemics, enteric diseases, tuberculosis and high mortality rates among the refugees[6] (Das, 2000: 26).

Until the slow and uneven regularization of the south Calcutta squatters' colonies began after 1951, they did not get much civic amenities like drinking water or sanitary arrangements from the municipal and the state governments. It was only after 1955, the government adopted a policy of developing the roads, sanitary arrangements and drinking water facilities in the colonies and sanctioned Rs. 1.73 crores for the development of 39 squatters' colonies (Government of West Bengal, 1954: 13). The healthcare measures for the refugees, as Samir Kumar Das has noted, was tardy at the best (Das, 2000: 26). The Second Five Years' Plan of the union government allocated Rs. 2.82 lakhs for the healthcare expenses of the refugees of the eastern part of India (Government of West Bengal, 1954: 17). Beds were reserved for tuberculosis patients or pregnant women from the refugee families in the hospitals. The TB patient refugees and their families received monthly cash doles. As the municipal documents point out, the colonies and the bustees were no doubt given special attention when it came to the epidemic control measures of the state including vaccination and inoculation programmes. However, these were never enough. It becomes clear from the state of tuberculosis treatment of the refugees in the state. According to the government sources, there were 3000 refugees suffering from TB in 1955–56 and only 419 government TB beds in West Bengal (Ministry of Rehabilitation, 1955–56: 5). It is not difficult to understand that in a condition of strained civic infrastructures the refugee and the migrant were always in a disadvantageous position because of their lack of socio-economic resources. The following case will perhaps make it clearer. The government had secured free beds for the poor TB patients in different hospitals and sanatoria, but as the legislative assembly proceedings of the state show, in many cases a certificate of recommendation from the local MLAs or the local Congress Committee would be required to avail that. One can assume that it wasn't as easy for a migrant in the city or a refugee squatter living illegally in a new land to navigate the corridors of power as the host population. Both the union and the state government had free beds reserved for the refugee TB patients and gave financial assistance to them. Keeping in mind the overall scarcity of TB beds in hospitals and the high infection rates among the refugees living in cramped quarters, it will not be difficult to understand that a large section of the tuberculosis patients in the refugee settlements were left outside the protection of institutional care. To avail the free

[5] Tejendralal Dutta, one of the respondents of Prins from Panchannagram, said 'We became guests of mosquitoes and flies'.

[6] The average mortality rate among the refugees was higher than the national average.

treatment and other medical benefits provided by the state, the displaced persons from East Bengal had to show documents like border slips or others to confirm their refugee identity. The importance of the border slips can be gleaned from the contemporary account of a thriving black market of these papers in Calcutta. As one of the MLAs from the opposition claimed in the assembly, many refugees, having lost their border slips or being unable to produce any document confirming their refugee identity, were finally unable to access the healthcare facilities reserved for them (WBLA, 1955: 520). Even those who had proper identification certificates, it was complained that a bureaucratic apathy stood in their way of getting timely reliefs. A precarious existence marked the lives of the refugees even when their entitlements to certain rights were recognized.

8.5 Health, Care and the Collective Action of the Refugees

Claims to healthcare facilities constituted a significant part of the contentious politics between the refugees and the state. They demanded water supply and sanitary facilities from the Rehabilitation Department (Weber, 1995: 202) and wrote letters to the editors of the city newspapers. UCRC mobilized the residents in the camps and the colonies in demand of food, better housing, health care and other civic amenities necessary for a dignified, better living[7] (Basu, 2017: 272). The plot holders in the colonies, especially under the banner of Dakshin Kolikata Bastuhara Samiti and the CPI, were demanding evaluation of their plots and fixation of taxes by the Calcutta Corporation, so that the civic amenities could be availed by them. Councillors sympathetic to the refugee cause also supported this demand.[8] Bijoygarh, the model on which the later colonies of south Calcutta were founded, had suffered from a lack of drinking water for many years after its foundation. There were no tubewells in the locality and the residents would have to get their drinking water from the *bhistis* or from a government pump nearby. According to a memoir of the Bijoygarh colony, it was from an urge to develop the colony as a healthy living space that the founders of Bijoygarh lobbied with the Tollygunje Municipality in 1950 to incorporate it under its municipal administration.

Faced with limited access to healthcare facilities, the squatters' colony residents would often come up with their own healthcare centres and maternity clinics. This was a part of their larger self-rehabilitation programme. Take the example of Bijoygarh. A few physicians who were living in the colony founded a charitable dispensary for the colony residents in 1950. In 1952 a maternity home was founded at the vacant military

[7] One of the UCRC's pamphlet from 1950, published on the occasion of a signature campaign for regularization of the colonies, against the discontinuation of the camps, right to housing, etc., criticized the government for sending a medical team to Korea instead of taking care of the health of the refugees.

[8] Originally published as 'Tollygunje-e'jabardakhal 'colonyte pouro odhikar somprosaraner siddhanta udbastuder oikyoboddho andoloner joy' in *Swadhinata* (23 October, 1954). Reprinted in *Udbastu Andolon O Punorbosoti: Somosamayik potro-potrikay*, edited by Arpita Basu.

wireless office of Bijoygarh by the colony residents at the initiative of Aparnacharan Dutta, a local doctor. The first few beds of the home, which would later become the Bijoygarh Hospital, were donated by a colony resident named Sarojini Dutta and Chandpur Sammilani club (Dutta, 2001). In Azadgarh, B. S. Guha's report noted, 'a refugee doctor of Homeopathy treats patients at the club room daily, and in return the refugee members provide him with his daily meal by rotation'. If the foundation of Bijoygarh Maternity Home narrates an act of solidarity which moved beyond the confines of the colony, Azadgarh is an act which could transform the colony into a community through collective action. Much like the example of the refugee bazaar at Bijoygarh, a care economy can be seen to be operational in this case. Tejendralal Dutta's memoir of Vidyasagar colony[9] says that members of the colony committee would spend nights taking care of the diseased residents, arrange for hospitalization of the seriously ill, and also cremate the dead. In instances like these, the colony had the potential to emerge as an affective grid of security. As Rachel Weber has noted, the colonies were imagined as some sort of safe spaces by their residents. As one of her respondents said, 'They [women] can go outside in their nighties or wearing a white sari with a red petticoat or with loose, wet hair. You can't do that in north Calcutta'. The physical layout of the colony itself had a role in producing it as a particular kind of an affective space. The houses were in close proximity and often one had to cross the courtyard of another house to reach the main road. The communal life in the colony was therefore very much indebted to the materialities of the living conditions.

8.6 Health Care, Solidarity and the Production of the Colony Space

Colonies would also organize neighbourhood cleanliness competitions between wards to promote public health and hygiene among its residents[10] (Basu, 2017: 223). Tubewells were set up, swamps were filled in and streets were laid out. Bijoygarh had *kutcha* drains dug up by the military which often overflowed during the heavy rains flooding the whole locality. As Debabrata Dutta recounted in his memoir, the residents had to unclog the drains themselves. In the neighbouring Vidyasagar colony, most of the streets would be flooded during the rainy season. The residents had to fill the low-lying roads with ashes brought from the adjacent Krishna Glass Factory to stop water clogging. The idea of health care in these instances, or care in general,

---

[9] Dutta was one of the founder residents of the colony and one of the frontal refugee organizers of RSP in the area.

[10] 'Recently we saw an overwhelming enthusiasm about the clean locality competition through the construction of roads, street lights, water supply and other hygienic measures in the [Netajinagar] colony. Led by the Netaji Sangha, a total number of 40 streets were laid out. 196 ft^2 area was cleaned. More than two hundred men, women and children have actively participated in this competition'. Originally published as 'Netaji Nagar Colony. Jolabhumite Lokaloy Sristi' in *Anandabazar Patrika* (19 November 1952). Reprinted in *Udbastu Andolon O Punorbosoti*, edited by Arpita Basu.

could not be dissociated from the idea of a collective labour. It is deeply rooted in the very imagination of the community. It is in this very context of achieving self-sufficiency through the application of the collective labour of a community—a distinctively *swadeshi* ethos—which made the act of colony building a part of the larger project of nation-building. The development of the civic infrastructures in the Bijoygarh colony by the colony residents themselves attracted praise from the leaders of the government including Prime Minister of the nation, Jawaharlal Nehru, and the press for being an example of 'self-help' and 'co-operative action'. On an official visit to the colony, the minister in charge of the department dealing with co-operatives, loans and rehabilitation, Nikunjabihari Maiti, was full of admiration:

> There is a lack of drinking water, materials required to repair the houses, latrines, work and education for these refugees. They are trying to overcome that on their own. I am delighted by this. Because it contains the seed of our nation's capacity of protecting its newfound freedom. We need to march forward with a determination, with a proper understanding of this distressful situation which the imperialist British diplomacy has left us in. Getting overwhelmed will be a great mistake. If we wish, we can turn this crisis into a source of national wealth.[11]

For Indubaran Ganguli, CPI activist and a refugee leader, the self-help works in the squatters' colonies provided a 'shining constructive example of our own national life'. In other words, national life found expression in the collective labour of the community. The association of refugee self-rehabilitation and nation-building was complete.

If these collective actions on the part of the squatters were acts of solidarity, one needs to understand what kind of a solidarity practice it was. As the memoirs of the colonies suggest, the solidarity had to be *organized*, whether by the colony committee or the local club. Although the materialities of a shared wretched life and a shared space, and mostly belonged to the upper castes, this solidarity was never organic. Tejendralal Dutta's memoir of Vidyasagar Colony narrates many stories of in-fighting, squabbles over control of the colony committee and social organizations in the colony and caste-based alliances among the colony residents. In building commons (in our case, tubewells, healthcare facilities, etc.) through organized collective labour, the refugees, to borrow from Durkheim, performed acts of 'mechanical solidarity' (Durkheim, 1893). It is these acts of mechanical solidarity, especially those related to public health, which were the 'precondition' for the 'collective type' of the colony to come into being.

While discussing the 'self-help' practices related to public health in the squatters' colonies of Calcutta, it needs to be pointed out that public health also provided a site for conversations between the colony and a range of outside actors, forming larger solidarity networks. Various relief organizations provided medical aids to the refugees living in the colonies and in other places. Residents of the Azadgarh colony arranged with the Dalmia Relief Committee to get periodical medical help. A mobile medical relief van visited the colony twice a week to examine the patients and distribute medicine and other necessary articles to the needy. They got milk powder

---

[11] *Ibid.*

free of cost from the Red Cross Society and 'every morning this milk is distributed among the children below 7 years of age, old men, patients and pregnant women' (Guha, 1954: 54).

In order to ensure access to healthcare facilities and other amenities of civic life, the refugee squatters also had to enter into various kinds of interactions and negotiations with the political power structure of the day. Tejendralal Dutta says that the colony committee of Vidyasagar Colony being dominated by RSP elements, the residents of the colony would find it easy to manage a recommendation for hospitalization from the local councillor of the party, Dr. Arabinda Dasgupta. The colony committees would be dominated by the communist and the left parties, and their self-help actions would thus at times involve assistance from political forces from outside. The presence of a plurality of actors complicates a narrow and simplistic view of the refugee self-rehabilitation and pictures the colony as a strictly insular space.

8.7 Left Parties, the Refugees and the Politics of Health

The left political opposition to the Congress government repeatedly made the connection between the claims of a welfare state and the health security of the people. Hence the leadership of the left parties would repeatedly point out the small share of the public health budget in comparison with other expenses of the state like police. The left and the communist's engagements with the politics of health would begin quite early. The fourth state congress of the Communist Party, held just after independence in October 1947, called for a reconstruction of the public health of the state. It claimed that two hundred years of imperial rule had turned Bengalis into a weak race and left the state to become a depot of diseases and epidemics. It also complained about the bureaucratic apathy about disease prevention and treatments which added to the miseries of the people in distress because of the irresponsible health policies of the government.

By the time of the partition, the left, including the Communists, had a fairly substantial experience of organizing medical relief during the famines and other natural disasters. Communist-led Mahila Atma Raksha Samiti (MARS),[12] formed in the background of the Second World War and the subsequent famine devoted itself in what it called a 'constructive programme'. As Manikuntala Sen's memoir suggests, the refugee colonies and the bustees of Calcutta constituted the core area of Samiti work in its initial days. Samiti's welfare activities in these areas included arrangements of medical help to the residents of these squalors, running milk kitchens, arranging caregivers or helping the women to get admitted into the hospitals if necessary. Many of the communist-influenced mass organizations like the Jana Raksha Samiti, Peoples Flood Relief Committee, Peoples Relief Committee (PRC), MARS who were engaged with medial relief work were born at the time of Bengal famine

[12] Later renamed as Paschim Banga Mahila Samiti in 1952.

in 1942–43. The PRC and the Bengal Provincial Student Federation (student wing of the CPI) organized medical units or 'squads' to be sent to the famine-hit regions (Mukhopadhyay, 2007: 370). The Committee came forward to form a coordination committee of similar relief organizations under the presidentship of Dr. B. C. Roy, called Bengal Medical Relief Coordination Committee. MARS was also a part of this committee. It is important to note here that the CPI and its various mass organizations' campaigns for food security began in the early 1940s, much before the larger, more militant food movements of the 1950s and 1960s engulfed Bengal. Since their early days, these campaigns had been stressing the connection between food security on one hand and the poor health of the people and the recurring epidemic outbreaks in Bengal on the other. The first issue of the bulletin published by the MARS, explaining the tasks ahead, wrote:

> Epidemic outbreaks in villages after villages are a natural consequence of food crisis. In many districts, cholera, dysentery etc. have taken the shape of epidemics, but people will never get the basic treatment or care if we do not form *seva dals* trained in medical aids (Mukhopadhyay, 2007: 322).[13]

It is no surprise that the same relief mechanisms of left parties in the pre-independence Bengal would be mobilized in refugee relief in the post-partition days. In the years following the partition, medical relief would emerge as one of the tactics followed by the left parties to expand their political influence. Snehamoy Chowdhury, an MBBS doctor and a member of RSP since 1940, came to live in Bagha Jatin Colony in sometimes around 1952 following his party's instruction. According to Tejendralal Dutta, who was a resident of the neighbouring Vidyasagar Colony, he was the only MBBS doctor in the locality. Chowdhury, who took a leading part in organizing the refugees under the banner of RSP-led RCRC, held a charitable dispensary at his colony home and treated the locals for free of cost.

If one looks at the CPIs discourse on public health since 1940s a little closely, a productivist imagination of labour power as the foundation of the social appears to be a predominant theme. A party pamphlet from 1943 which called for organizing medical relief squads stated:

> labour power of the Bengal villages, which is the foundation of Bengali society, is being destroyed in epidemics ... industrial production is being affected ... motivate the doctors and medical students to fight against the epidemics. Tell them this is the time to set best examples for medical science and *seva dharma* (the calling of social service).[14]

In this order of things, if unhindered reproduction of labour is a precondition of the social, providing an infrastructure to support disease-free life is an urgent task to facilitate that reproduction cycle and hence protect the social from breakdown. Health

---

[13] Originally published in *Nikhil Banga Atmaraksha Samiti Bulletin*, No. 1 (July 1943). Reprinted in Saroj Mukhopadhyay's *Bharater Communist Party O Amra*.

[14] Originally published in 'Mahamarir Haat Theke Banglake Banchao. Medical Squad Gothon Koro'. Reprinted in *Banglar Communist Andoloner Itihas*, Vol. 1, 256–257.

becomes a resource—the bio-capital of a nation.[15] The question of public health was therefore integrally linked with the theme of governance in this imagination. This is reflected in Communist Party's internal party organization of the initial days itself. The state party's bulletin from 27 May 1947 noted, the party was concerned about the health of its cadres and felt that the works of the Red Aid Committee was urgent in this respect. It urged the district committees to take up the responsibility of forming local red aid units.[16] The state Red Aid Committee took the initiative to set up a nursing home, named Red Aid Cure Home, to treat party workers. The Home was discontinued soon after the party was banned in 1948 March.

The Students Health Home, founded in Calcutta in 1952, was definitely a milestone in the communist campaign for universal access to health care. Established by the young doctors and MBBS students affiliated to BPSF like Arun Sen, Manoranjan Rakshit, Subir Dasgupta and Koustabh Mukherjee and others, Students' Health Home was the first of its kind in Asia. Any student could be a member of this establishment and would get free treatment at the cost of a membership fee of Rs. 1 per annum. Activists of the Home would collect free samples from the pharmaceutical companies and arranged them for distribution among the patients visiting the Home. Students, who were in need of serious medical attention, would be referred to other doctors who would treat them free of cost. 40–45 students suffering from TB were even sent to the sanatorium managed by the International Union of Students at Beijing. An X-ray machine was donated by students from Soviet Russia in 1956 with which the Home started a chest clinic in his rented accommodation at the Creek Row. The establishment received financial assistance from the University of Calcutta, while the students' union of the Jadavpur University obtained a permanent membership.

Although formed at the initiative of the BPSF activists, the Home was quite successful in enlisting support from a large number of eminent doctors and other personalities with very different political affiliations. For example, Triguna Sen, Vice-Chancellor of the Jadavpur University and a long-time Congress mayor of the city, was a chief patron of the foundation and according to the memoirs took a lead in securing the land in Moulali where the Home is now situated. Although it could receive support from the Calcutta Corporation, dominated largely by the Congress politicians, the Students' Health Home failed to get much aid from the state government, which considered it as a communist organization. In 1959, Jyoti Basu, a leader of CPI, accused the Congress government of issuing a secret circular labelling the Home as a communist front and barring them from receiving any grant from the rehabilitation department of the union government. When the members of the Home went to meet Dr. B. C. Roy, the then Chief Minister of West Bengal, he questioned the communist association of the Home and expressed his dissatisfaction about countries like China, Czechoslovakia or USSR assisting it. It was alleged that in order to secure government assistance, the organizers of the Home were told to

---

[15] See for example the note on the 'Reconstruction of Public Health' in the report of Fourth State Conference of the West Bengal State Committee of the Communist Party of India, held in October 1947 at Calcutta.

[16] *Ibid.*, 183.

promise in writing that they wouldn't send any patient to counties behind the 'Iron Curtain' (West Bengal State Assembly, 1949). Student's Health Home constituted a significant moment in the history of the politics of health of the left as well as the practices of solidarity in West Bengal. Keeping in mind the demography of the students in West Bengal in the 1950s and 1960s, it won't be incorrect to assume that a large number of beneficiaries as well as activists of the Students Health Home would come from the refugee families.

However, these *seva* or relief works were thought to be secondary to real political work in the dominant communist discourse on politics. Relief work, often translated as *seva*, was looked down upon as something akin to Ramkrishna Mission's activities, and a deviation from the true revolutionary path (Sen, 2011: 58). These solidarity acts, when not overtly criticized by the ideologues of the party, would be considered as mere instrument for popularizing the party. The debate between the *seva* work and the revolutionary politics marked the history of the Students' Health Home too. Shyamal Chakraborty, a communist leader of the state, a student-organizer at that time who worked at the Home in its formative years, writes that initially there were doubts about an establishment like the Students' Health Home inside the communist-led students' organization itself. Some of the activists were of the opinion that this is a revisionist tendency—without revolution the issues of health, education or employment could never be resolved permanently (Chakraborty, 2011: 56). However, Chakraborty says that they later came to the realization that this kind of 'self-help' endeavours would not contradict revolutionary politics and would in fact enhance the sense of self-dignity in the distressed students and promote students' movement. As one of the student-organizers of the Home, Dr. Gita Sen later noted, the idea behind the formation of the Students' Health Home was to uphold the principle of self-cure through collective action, and not with the help of charities. Manikuntala Sen noted that EMS Nambudiripad, the General Secretary of the CPI, supported the organization of different *seva* (relief) works in the women's front. This however doesn't contradict party's overall attitude towards the inferior status of *seva* vis-a-vis what it thought to be true revolutionary politics. The relief work was thought to be as only a means to an end, and not an end in itself. In fact, there was always an argument inside the party and within the women's wing itself that MARS needed to be politicized. Moreover, one can argue that it indicates the basic gendered ideal of the revolution in this discourse which could sit together perfectly with a feminization of care. Care could be delegated to the women's front, while the men could take care of the revolution.

8.8 Conclusion

However, whether medical relief or *seva* was a means to an end for the communist party, the practices of organizing medical relief by the communists along with their campaigns for food, housing and other civic amenities of life indicated a protectionist politics. Micromovements for universal health care, food security, housing and family planning led by the left and the communist parties—they formed a part of a politics that addressed 'the vital processes of human existence' (Rose, 2001: 1). The populist politics of the left and the communist in the decades following the partition would therefore invoke a politics of life. What connected the claims for food security, better housing and healthcare facilities was an idea of social well-being. Life itself, one can argue, was conceptualized in terms of a biosocial well-being. As Sucharita Sengupta and Paula Banerjee have argued, the refugees' would become citizens through their claims 'claims to land, food, right to politically represent oneself, right to mobility etc.' (Sengupta & Banerjee, 2016: 3). All these claims would be questions of life, especially the biosocial life. The populist politics of the left in the three decades following the partition would take up these questions to the streets and the assembly. This would provide an ideal context for the refugees and the left-communists of the state to come together and devise an engage in a politics of life.

References

Bandyopadhyay, H. (2011). *Udbastu.* Deep Prakashan.

Banglar Communist Andoloner Itihas (Vol. 1), 256–257.

Basu, A. (Ed.). (2017). *Udbastu Andolon O Punorbosoti: Somosamayik potro-potrikay.* Kolkata: Gangchil.

Chakraborty, S. (2011). *60–70 Chhatro Andolon* (Vol. 1). National Book Agency.

Chaudhuri, P. (1983). Refugees in West Bengal: A study of the growth and development of refugee settlements within the CMD. *Occasional Paper No. 55.* Centre for Studies in Social Sciences.

Das, S. K. (2000). Refugee crisis: Responses of the Government of West Bengal. In P. K. Bose (Ed.), *Refugees in West Bengal: Institutional Practices and Contested Identities.* Calcutta Research Group.

Durkheim, E. (1893). *The division of labour in society*. Bloomsbury Publishing.

Dutta, D. (2001). *Bijoygarh Ekti Udbastu Upanibesh.* Progressive Publishers.

Foucault, M. (2009). *Security, territory, population: Lectures at the College De France, 1977–78* (G. Burchell, Trans.). Palgrave Macmillan.

Government of West Bengal. (1954). *They live again. Millions came from East Pakistan.* Director of Publicity.

Guha, B. S. (1954). *Studies in social tensions among the refugees from Eastern Pakistan.* Department of Anthropology, Memoir No. 1. Manager of Publications.

Health Survey and Development Committee. (1946). *Report of the Bhore Committee* (Vol. 1 & 2). Government of India Press.

Mitra, K. N., Bhattacharya, B., Dey, K., Dawn, C. S., Obadiah, M., & Gayen, A. K. (1951). A study of recent trend in infantile mortality rates in Calcutta by longitudinal survey. *Sankhyā: The Indian Journal of Statistics, 11*(2), 181.

Mitra, M. (2021). Public health, migrant workers, and a global pandemic: Towards a new politics of life. *Refugee Watch, 57*, 1–13.

Mukhopadhyay, S. (2007). *Bharater Communist Party O Amra.* National Book Agency.

Prins, A. (2014). The plight of dwelling: East-Bengali refugees and the struggle for land in Kolkata. *Refugee Watch,* 43 & 44.

Qadeer, I. (2005). Continuities and discontinuities in public health: The Indian experience. In A. K. Bagchi, & K. Soman (Eds.), *Maladies, preventives and curatives: Debates in public health in India.* Tulika Books.

Rose, N. (2001). The politics of life itself. *Theory, Society & Culture, 18*(6), 1.

Sen, M. (2011). *Jonojagorone Narijagorone.* Thema.
Sengupta, S., & Banerjee, P. (2016). Refugee movement: Another aspect of popular movements in West Bengal in the 1950s and 1960s. In S. Sengupta, P. Banerjee, & A. Sengupta (Eds.), *People, politics and protests I: Calcutta & West Bengal, 1950s–1960s.* Calcutta Research Group.
Singha, T. (1999). *Maranjoyi Songrame Bastuhara.* Dasgupta's.
The Calcutta Municipal Gazette. (1947). (Vol. XLVI & XLVII, No. 24 & 1–11).
The Calcutta Municipal Gazette. (1948). (Vol. XLVII).
The Calcutta Municipal Gazette. (1957a). Refugees at Sealdah (Vol. LXV, No. 21).
The Calcutta Municipal Gazette. (1957b). (Vol. LXV).
The Calcutta Municipal Gazette. (1958). (Vol. LXVII, No. 12).
The Ministry of Rehabilitation. (1955–56). Assistance to Displaced TB patients (Report on the Working). Government of India.
Weber, R. (1995). Re(creating) the home: Women's role in the development of the refugee colonies in south Calcutta. *Indian Journal of Gender Studies, 2*(2), 202.
West Bengal State Assembly. (1949). (Vol. 22, No. II).
West Bengal State Assembly. (1955).
West Bengal State Assembly. (1957). *Assembly Proceedings Official Report, 17*(3), 9–10.

Chapter 9
Guest Workers in Kerala: Is Welfarism Enough?

Jyothi Krishnan, R. Prasad, and Abey George

Abstract The spread of the Covid-19 pandemic and subsequent lockdown measures in the country revealed the scale of internal migration in the country. While the Long March of 2020 brought to light the arduous and painstaking journey back home, it also revealed the precarious livelihood scenario of the migrants and their families. Kerala has witnessed a steep increase in the migrant worker population over the past decade. The increasing shortage of manual labourers in the state has created a situation wherein migrant workers have become an inevitable component of the state's economy. While it is acknowledged that Kerala provides better working and living conditions to the large migrant workforce in the state, a preliminary review of legislations and policies reveals that all is not well. The ambiguity surrounding the terms and conditions under which migrant workers are hired by contractors enhances the possibility of them being hired against advances, leaving much room for exploitation. While the Kerala government was one of the first to formulate welfare programmes for the migrant workers, the overall approach towards the migrant population in the state has been couched in the language of welfare. However, the articulation of rights and accountability mechanisms to define and enforce the responsibilities of the employers/contractors appears to be weak, which leads to a compromise of labour rights vis-a-vis the accumulation of capital in a state that relies heavily on the availability of migrant labour. The examination of issues related to migrant workers will be contextualised within the existing paradox of combining welfarism with a neoliberal development paradigm in the state.

J. Krishnan (✉) · R. Prasad
Department of MSW Disaster Management, Loyola College of Social Sciences, Trivandrum, India
e-mail: jyothikr07@gmail.com; jyothi@loyolacollegekerala.edu.in

R. Prasad
e-mail: dr_prasad_r@uoc.ac.in

R. Prasad
Department of Sociology, University of Calicut, Calicut, India

A. George
KILA-CHRD, Kerala, India
e-mail: abeygeorge@kila.ac.in

S. R. Chakraborty et al. (eds.), *The Long 2020*, India Studies in Business and Economics, https://doi.org/10.1007/978-981-99-4815-4_9

Keywords Migrant workers · Kerala · Welfare · Labour rights

9.1 Introduction

During the initial decades after independence, the state of Kerala experienced a huge exodus of its labour force, both skilled as well as unskilled. This resulted in the formation of Malayali communities across the globe, especially in Europe and the Middle East. The remittances from abroad soon began to constitute a major part of the state's revenue, which played a prominent role in the unique development experience of the state as well as in enhancing the living standards of the people (Rajan & Zackaria, 2016). Migration also acted as a safety valve for the state by controlling unemployment and increasing revenue (Zachariah et al., 2000). This helped to cover up for the sluggish performance in the production sector. Over a period of time, the increased tendency of the youth to shy away from socially 'demeaning' manual labour and large-scale migration has brought changes to the internal labour market of the state (Remesh, 2003). Since, 1980s the state began to face a serious mismatch between labour supply and labour demand, which resulted in an inflow of migrant labourers, from different parts of India. This was further aggravated by the construction boom in Kerala along with an increase in the wage rate in the construction sector that attracted inter-state migrant workers (Prakash, 1998). Over the span of a few decades, migrant labourers became an indispensable part of Kerala's labour market. An estimated population of 25 lakh migrant labourers from different parts of India is engaged in various employment activities, replacing 2.5 million emigrants of the State (Narayana et al., 2013). The construction sector is found to be absorbing the largest proportion of the migrant workers. In addition, marine fishing, plywood, mining and quarrying, plantation, iron and steel, textile and apparel, furniture, seafood, hospitality, footwear, jewellery making, processing of rice, cashew and several other food products and industrial parks in Kerala, now survive on migrant labour power.

9.2 A Brief History of In-Migration

The migrant labourers in Kerala comprise of people from south (Tamil Nadu, Andhra Pradesh), north (Bihar, Uttar Pradesh and Rajasthan), north-eastern (Assam, Manipur) and eastern (west Bengal, Odisha) parts of India. Tracing the historical pattern of their settlements, Peter and Narendran (2017), observe that the initial settlers were from the states of Tamil Nadu and Karnataka. During the latter half of the twentieth century, workers from these neighbouring states complemented the native workers in filling up the requirement of the blue-collar labour force and were employed in plantations, brick kilns, digging earth for laying telephone cables and so on. This was followed by waves of in-migration from eastern India. While migrants from Odisha were commonly found in the plywood industry of Perumbavoor in

Ernakulam district and timber hubs of Kallayi in Kozhikode, workers from Bihar were found to be settled in Kanjikode of Palakkad district (Peter & Narendran, 2017). The labourers from north-eastern states, especially Assam were recruited in large numbers in the veneer and plywood production units. The construction works undertaken by companies were also found to recruit them in large numbers as they were found to be less expensive, more subservient, hardworking and available throughout the year. This has even resulted in the formation of inter-district migration corridors within Kerala, which has facilitated mobility of male and female migrants as well as children.

9.3 Where Do Migrant Workers Come From?

Irrespective of gender or labour categorisations, the migrant labourers in Kerala are mainly engaged in the labour market as footloose labour. Low wages, limited and irregular employment opportunities, failed crops and droughts, family debts, disasters such as floods and cyclones, political instability, caste oppression and communal violence, encroachment of land and properties by the mining lobbies and so on were some of the major factors that pushed them to leave their homes and lands (Moses & Rajan, 2012; Peter & Narendran, 2017; Prasad-Aleyamma, 2011; Raman, 2012). The factors that pulled migrants to Kerala in large numbers were higher wage rates, political stability, comparatively peaceful social environment, relatively less discriminatory treatment, social networks and relatively better education and health facilities (Moses & Rajan, 2012; Peter & Narendran, 2017; Prasad-Aleyamma, 2011; Raman, 2012).

The small group of migrant workers who were interviewed as a part of this study reveals some of the above-mentioned push and pull factors. The shared story of migrants coming from Assam, West Bengal, Jharkhand and Odisha is a narrative of social and economic vulnerability, especially livelihood vulnerability. The reasons for their migration are triggered by failing agriculture, low wages, the hazards of daily wage work and debts. Abu, a 30-year-old man from 24 Parganas in West Bengal was engaged in farming to make a living. He came to hear about the work opportunities in Kerala from his friends, who had been working in the fishing sector in Kerala. For the past five years, he has been going to fish in the sea, a skill he picked up after coming here.

There are many others who work in seafood export processing units, their work in these units ranging from one to eight years. Bimal from Assam has been working in such a unit for eight years in Kollam. The other two earning members in his family of six went to Goa in search of work, revealing the dire need to migrate. Sanjay who works along with Bimal in the seafood unit also comes from a farming family in Assam. He was earlier working in a plastic bottle company in Tamil Nadu and came to Kerala in search of higher wages. There are those like Bipin from Assam whose family used to work as farm labourers and MGNREGA workers.[1] Bipin used to get Rs. 250 per day for daily wage work which was insufficient. He first moved to work in the construction sector in Nagaland and then to Bangalore and finally reached Kerala. In Kerala, he has worked as an agricultural labourer, also on seasonal agricultural tasks such as plucking jackfruits, and later worked in the construction sector and in installing roadside hoardings.

It was poor wages that drove 28-year-old Ajay out of his village in Assam. He has a widowed mother and brothers in Assam. After having worked for Rs. 80 per day in a garment factory in Rajasthan, he moved to Kerala 12 years ago when he was barely an adult. He was initially working in the plywood industry in Ernakulam in Kerala (a sector that employs a significant section of the migrant population), but later moved on to installing flex hoardings.

Though difficult to establish contact, conversations with women working in seafood export processing units was revealing. Securing access was a challenge, and interviews were conducted in the presence of either managers/supervisors. The women were often tense and hesitated to express their views openly. The women were in the 20–22 age group, having barely completed their primary education. Most of them had been working in the seafood processing units for about a year, having spent the entire lockdown period in Kerala. 22-year-old Mina from Jharkhand came from a poverty-stricken family, her brother working as a driver in Odisha. She was forced to leave home as her mother found it difficult to sustain the family. 22-year-old Sonali comes from a eight-member family in Odisha who sustained on agricultural labour alone. In order to support her family, she now works in the packing section in the unit. The others had similar stories to share. Almost all the women were working for Rs. 300 per day, far below the average daily wage rate in the state. They were however not complaining as this was far better than what they got at home.

9.4 Vulnerability of the Migrant Population

Moses and Rajan (2012) point out the ways in which migrant labourers are isolated from the local community in terms of language and local communication, recruitment channels, accommodation and food provision and political integration. Based on these four measures of integration they find the migrant workers to be isolated from the local population, and poorly positioned to secure information about local working conditions, wage levels and the rights and benefits available to them while living in Kerala. The migrant workers are vulnerable to exploitation as they have little recourse to accurate information about the rights they enjoy or the prevailing wages and regulations in the local labour market. Irudaya Rajan (2012) through the CDS-ISMSK survey also emphasises the isolation of migrant workers from the local population. Migrant workers cope with social exclusion by building and maintaining

[1] The Mahatma Gandhi National Rural Employment Guarantee Act is a critical social protection measure, which guarantees 100 days of work to unskilled labourers across the country.

social networks. Discussions with migrant workers reveal that it is social networks consisting of other migrant workers and certain key contacts with the local population that provide them information regarding work availability or support during times of crises. While there were proposals from the side of the government to set up help desks, they do not appear to have taken off. A migrant worker from West Bengal spoke of how their local networks with other migrant workers helped them to pass on information regarding job availability, as well as about support available during times of crisis (such as health care or treatment in the case of accidents). He also mentioned how the first few years were always tough as the worker would not have built networks. Duration of stay and the presence of friends/relatives define the social networking of a migrant labourer.

9.5 Measures to Protect Rights of the Migrant Workers

While issues regarding low wages and poor working and living conditions have been reported from many parts of the state, Kerala is also considered to be a migrant friendly state, having formulated migrant worker-focused welfare programmes. The reference to migrant workers as 'guest workers' during the pandemic was viewed as an endorsement of the state's commitment to the welfare of the migrant workforce. Before we look into these welfare schemes and programmes, it is important to review existing legal measures that protect the labour rights of the migrant workforce, as they directly address the vulnerabilities that migrants face.

This section therefore undertakes a quick review of the existing legal measures for the protection of the rights of this group. These legislations are a commitment of the state to the redressal of the difficult working conditions of informal sector and inter-state migrant workers (almost all of whom fall in the former category). They are judiciable and provide the opportunity to the worker to exercise a formal legal claim and demand accountability from the state through its functionaries. Equally important, effective implementation of these legislations could enhance the quality of working conditions for the most vulnerable sections of the informal sector. Another reason why these legislations require a closer review is because of the silence about them in the entire narrative about the state of Kerala being migrant friendly. The over emphasis on the welfare measures formulated by the state for the migrant workers and the under emphasis on these legislations and their implementation are a matter that needs careful scrutiny.

Some of the critical legislations that govern the working and living conditions of unorganised sector workers will be discussed here briefly in order to make explicit the protection offered by the law in protecting their working conditions. These include the Inter State Migrant Workmen Act of 1979, the Contract Labour (Regulation and Abolition) Act of 1970, the Minimum Wages Act of 1948 and the Building and Other Construction Workers Act of 1996. The first two legislations specifically address the obligations of the contractor/employer vis-a-vis the worker and are important as two thirds of migrant workers are estimated to be employed by contractors (Peter & Narendran, 2017).

9.5.1 *The Inter State Migrant Workmen (Regulation of Employment and Conditions of Service) Act, 1979*

The Inter State Migrant Workmen (Regulation of Employment and Conditions of Service) Act (ISMWA) 1979 emphasises on the duties and obligations of the contractor, an emphasis that may be viewed as a recognition of the vulnerability of inter-state workers and the possibility of exploitation at the hands of the former. As per the Act, the duties of the contractor include regular payment of wages, equal pay to both sexes, residential accommodation to migrant workers, prescribed medical facilities free of cost and protective clothing at the work site. The contractor is also liable to pay a displacement allowance (amounting to 50% of the monthly wage) and a journey allowance (to and fro and wages during the journey).[2] The provisions that relate to payment of wages in the Act[3] emphasise non-discrimination by stating that migrant workers are to be paid minimum wages and are to receive an equal pay for equal work when compared with non-migrant workers. Men and women are to be paid equal wages as well.

The Act also mandates compulsory registration of establishments[4] and licencing of contractors.[5] It also helps to maintain a database of contractors/employers who hire inter-state workmen as well as a database of all inter-state migrant workmen who are recruited through contractors. This would therefore enable the state to monitor whether the provisions related to working conditions are being fulfilled.

---

[2] The provision related to payment of return fare is important, as the Act stipulates that return fare is to be provided in the event of expiry or termination of employment, incapacitation, cessation of work for no fault of the migrant worker or resignation, owing to non-fulfilment of terms of engagement by the contractor. The non-implementation of this provision was much evident during the lockdown following the pandemic, as there were reports of migrant workers unable to make their way home for want of money. The payment of the displacement allowance is also critical as it could prevent the migrant worker from taking a loan to meet travel expenditure. Moreover, the Act states that if the contractor fails to make payment of wages and other allowances (including displacement allowances and journey fare), the principal employer is liable to pay the same.

[3] The date of recruitment of the migrant worker is considered as the date of commencement of employment in order to claim entitlements under the Workmen's Compensation Act, 1923 (8 of 1923), the Payment of Wages Act, 1936 (4 of 1936), the Industrial Disputes Act, 1947 (14 of 1947), the Employees' State Insurance Act, 1948 (34 of 1948), the Employees' Provident Funds and Miscellaneous Provisions Act, 1952 (19 of 1952) and the Maternity Benefit Act, 1961 (53 of 1961).

[4] All establishments that employ at least five inter-state workmen or more have to go through a process of registration and verification. It also mandates licencing of contractors at the source and destination state.

[5] The licencing of contractors and the details to be furnished by the contractor (including hours of work, fixation of wages and other essential amenities) provide the possibility of holding the contractor (or in his absence, the employer) responsible for violations of the Act.

While the central Act mentions the work site and accommodation facilities to be provided by the contractor, the Kerala state rules detail them further. The Kerala Rules specify the work site and accommodation facilities to be provided to migrant workers, which have a direct bearing on the well-being of migrant households and the children in such households.[6]

While the provisions of ISMWA attempt to protect the migrant worker in a worker-employer relationship that is unequal, the extent to which workers access their entitlements in such relationships depends upon the level of awareness of legal entitlements and recourse to legal action in the event of violations. Grievance redressal is weak as per the Act, as it provides that a complaint can be filed in court only with the written sanction of the inspector. Regular inspections and monitoring are therefore critical to effective implementation of the ISMWA. Studies indicate that migrants find it difficult to realise benefits due to them owing to lack of legal literacy and fear of reprisals (Peter & Narendran, 2017). Weak implementation and casual inspections have been pointed out by the Public Accounts Committee of the Kerala Legislative Assembly (Govt. of Kerala, 2016) as well.

Studies indicate that very few contractors have been issued licences as very few enterprises employing inter-state migrants are registered under the Act. Migrant workers were also found not to possess passbooks prescribed by law, which is a basic record of their identity and their transactions with contractors and employers (Abraham et al., 2014). In Kerala for instance, studies indicate that registration of migrant workers and issuing of ID cards were found to be wanting (John, 2015). The ISMWA also leaves out of its purview the plight of migrant workers who find jobs without a contractor and who are thereby not registered under the Act, but end up working under a contractor. Studies of migration in Kerala indicate that while only about 28% of migrant workers were recruited by contractors, two thirds end up working under contractors, without being recruited by them. The migrant workers would have reached the contractor through social networks and informal channels provided by friends and relatives (John, 2015; Narayana et al., 2013; Peter & Narendran, 2017). This implies that irrespective of how they are sourced, the majority of inter-state workers end up working under contractors. This also implies that the great majority of migrant workers, while employed by contractors do not receive the protection of the ISMWA. Their vulnerable existence coupled with socio-cultural barriers could prevent them from accessing their entitlements, or even gaining an understanding of what their entitlements are.

---

[6] Sec 44 of the Kerala Rules mentions that the contractor is liable to provide suitable accommodation for families (one roomed house with cooking space and 10 ms^2 floor space, with common bathrooms).

9.5.2 Contract Labour (Regulation and Abolition) Act, 1970

Another legislation that aims to regulate the relationship between contractors and workers is the Contract Labour (Regulation and Abolition) Act of 1970, which was a precursor to the Inter State Migrant Workmen Act of 1979.[7,8] As with the case of the ISMWA, the primary objective of the Act was to put an end to the exploitation of contract labourers carried out by contractors and establishments, with the Act stipulating work site and other facilities to be provided by the contractor.[9] Registration of employers and licencing of contractors mandated maintenance of registers containing details of the contract labourers at the work site. Inspections are the only mechanism through which the state ensures that the Act is being implemented in full spirit. As in the case of the ISMWA, grievance redressal is weak as complaints can be filed only upon receiving written sanction from the inspectors.

The existing situation is such that neither the ISMWA nor the Contract Labour Regulation Act is able to hold contractors and employers responsible for transgression of labour rights of the most vulnerable groups in the unorganised sector. This is pertinent given the increasing casualisation of labour since the introduction of neoliberal policies, wherein labour flexibility strategies have created an employment structure in which the share of the non-regular workers has been rising at the cost of regular workers.

9.5.3 Addressing the Rights of Migrant Workers in the Construction Sector

Given the significant presence of migrant workers in the construction sector, one of the legislations that impacts the well-being of construction workers, the Building and Other Construction Workers Welfare Act (henceforth referred to as the BoCW Act) needs closer scrutiny. As of 2001, 30.4% of male construction workers and 60.4% of female construction workers were migrants (Roy et al., 2017).[10] Census data also indicates that inter-state migrant workers constitute the largest portion of all construction workers in urban areas (ibid.). In Kerala, construction was the

---

[7] It aimed at addressing the exploitation of contract labourers at the hands of contractors, a problem that had emerged as a consequence of large-scale employment of labourers in plants, mines and in agriculture during the 50s and 60s (Upadhyay & Pandey, 2020).

[8] The earlier mentioned ISMWA of 1979 that was brought in as the Contract Labour (Regulation and Abolition) Act, 1970 proved to be insufficient in dealing with the plight of the contract workers and failed to curb the transgression of labour rights by the principal employer/contractor. The ISMWA went further and attempted to strengthen the position of inter-state migrant workers by stipulating parity in wages between migrant and domicile workers, and makes the contractor liable to pay a displacement and home journey allowance.

[9] Act applies to establishments that employ 20 or more contract workers.

[10] The total number of construction workers was estimated as 14.6 million construction workers in the country (not including brick kiln workers) (Roy et al., 2017).

dominant sector that absorbed 60% of the migrant workers in the state, followed by manufacturing and hotels (Narayana et al., 2013).

The BOCW Act aims to ensure social welfare of construction workers and prevent their exploitation by contractors and employers.[11] The significant feature of this Act is that each state has to set up a Construction Workers Welfare Board (CWWB), which has to register all construction workers in the state and provide them with a range of welfare measures.[12] These welfare provisions are funded through the collection of cess levied on construction activities.[13] It is important to note that a 'building worker' includes not just anybody employed in building or construction work, but also those in ancillary activities such as stone cutting, brick making and sand mining.

Migrant works can avail of the welfare measures under this scheme only through registration with the Construction Workers Welfare Board.[14] The review of the Parliamentary Standing Committee in 2012 (Roy et al., 2017) mentioned non-registration of brick kiln workers and migrant labourers, non-issue of identity cards and lack of clarity about the manner in which cess funds were to be spent. As of 2015, only 45% of all construction workers in the country as per NSS estimates had been registered with respective state-level CWWBs. Kerala and Tamil Nadu have relatively higher rates of registration (Roy et al., 2017), but the Kerala state rules do not specify whether migrant workers can register with the Construction Workers Welfare Board (Roy et al., 2017). While Kerala is at the forefront in terms of expenditure of the collected cess (Roy et al., 2017), there is a lack of clarity regarding inclusion of migrant workers in the CWWB. In addition to inclusion in the welfare board, the levels of awareness of BOCW-related entitlements determines conditions of access.

Studies recommend that states explore utilisation of cess funds to support the establishment and operations of helplines and legal redress mechanisms.[15] Self-registration of workers along with localised verification processes has been suggested

[11] The Act applies to all individuals or associations employing workers in building or construction work, except individual construction of houses that cost less than Rs. 10 lakhs. The Act does not cover establishments engaging less than ten workers.

[12] This includes immediate assistance in case of accidents, pensions to those who have completed age of sixty years, sanctioning loans and advances for house construction, payment of an amount towards group insurance scheme, financial assistance for education of children of beneficiaries, medical expenses for treatment of major ailment of beneficiaries or dependents and maternity benefits to female beneficiaries.

[13] For constructions that cost more than Rs. 10 lakhs, 1% of the total cost needs to be given as cess in Kerala.

[14] As per the Act, any building/construction worker between the age of 18 and 60, who has been engaged in building or construction work for at least ninety days in the preceding twelve months is eligible for registration. Registered workers have to contribute a specified amount towards the fund on a monthly basis, and each CWWB is to issue identity cards to all registered workers. The norms for registration vary from state to state, and influence the level of inclusion. Kerala and TN are among the states with a record of higher registrations.

[15] Labour dept. in Rajasthan supports a labour helpline and legal cell, which was initiated by the NGO Aajevika Bureau. This labour line offers mediation services between employers/contractors and workers for wage and other disputes (Roy et al., 2017).

as a way to enhance registrations (Roy et al., 2017). Engagement of civil society organisations in the conduct of registration drives at work sites and in settlements where construction workers live, as well as in networking with the local labour department could resolve barriers to registration. Sinha and Sengupta (2019) have discussed the manner in which absence of active trade unions along with inadequate registration and renewal of annual membership with the CWWB pushes women construction workers into greater difficulty.

In Kerala, efforts have been made by civil society organisations to get migrant workers registered under the Awaz health insurance scheme of the state government, but registration with BoCW has not been observed. Migrant workers in the construction sector are largely unaware of the BoCW provisions. The significance of the welfare measures guaranteed by this Act is indicated by the Supreme Court verdict in 2018 that directed the Ministry of Labour and Employment, state governments and union territories to undertake social audits of the BoCW and to thereby examine matters related to registration, inclusion and welfare expenditure by following the CAG guidelines for social audit.

9.5.4 Ensuring Fair Wages—The Minimum Wages Act, 1948

In the absence of effective implementation of the ISWMA that aims to check exploitation of inter-state migrant workers, legislations like the Minimum Wages Act of 1948 assume importance. The list of works listed in Schedule I of the Minimum Wages Act for instance includes a wide range of sectors including plantations, mills, construction sites, stone breaking and crushing, mines, loading and unloading and sweeping and cleaning activities, all of which employ migrant workers in significant numbers.

As with the case of the earlier discussed legislations, lack of adequate inspections in the unorganised sector has weakened implementation of this Act. Middlemen and contractors are known to take advantage of absence of worker organisations and lack of bargaining power. This is something that needs to be explored in the case of migrant workers, and migrant women workers particularly. The absence of effective grievance redressal mechanisms aggravates the situation.

There has been much discussion on the need to widen the scope of minimum wages, as it is well-accepted that minimum wages provides bare subsistence and is at the poverty line level. The need for fair and living wages has been discussed in the context of labour reforms as well. It is vital that such debates are contextualised for migrant workers as well, who are more vulnerable than other unorganised sector workers, manifest in the extremely low wages in sectors such as seafood processing units.

9.5.5 Transition in Labour Legislations

All of the above-mentioned legislations face uncertainty with the proposed introduction of the four labour codes by the central government that aim to codifying the existing 44 central labour laws. The Code of Wages 2019, which is the first of the four labour codes to have been passed as an Act, will replace four labour regulations viz. the Payment of Wages Act, 1936; the Minimum Wages Act, 1948; the Payment of Bonus Act, 1965 and the Equal Remuneration Act, 1976. Similarly, the draft Labour Code on Social Security and Welfare seeks to replace 15 laws on social security, including the Building and Other Construction Workers Act and various other Welfare Cess/Fund Acts. The repealing of the Building and Other Construction Workers (BOCW) Act of 1996 will lead to the closure of all the 36 state BOCW Boards and cancellation of about four crore registrations of construction workers as beneficiaries (Sharma, 2019).[16] Issues pertaining to inter-state migrant workers find mention in the Occupational Safety, Health and Working Conditions Code of 2020, but further implications on the rights of migrant workers are a cause of concern.

9.5.6 The Need for Effective Implementation of Legislations in Kerala

Migrant workers fill in the gaps created by the exodus of the 'indigenous' workforce; they therefore enter through a peripheral dimension of the labour market (et al., 2007). The migrant work force has been employed in a range of unstable posts that are temporary, seasonal, fixed period and task-based: they are also be subject to casual work and agency employment. Studies report migrant workers experiencing exploitative working conditions, discriminatory wages, long working hours, wage-related cheating and lack of safety measures (Prasad-Aleyamma, 2011). This is particularly so during the first few years, when they have not built up social networks that provide them access to regular work and higher wages. Shortage of sufficient local labourers, readiness to work overtime, low wage rates, willingness to work in any situation, etc., are the major reasons that attract the contractors to prefer migrant labourers over local workers. By the same logic, this necessitates a watchful state that prevents exploitation of this vulnerable group. The effective implementation of the above-mentioned legislations could help to arrest much of the exploitation that migrant workers experience.

---

[16] Sharma (2019). Repealing the Construction Workers Act under new Labour Codes will prove disastrous. https://thewire.in/labour/repealing-the-construction-workers-act-under-new-labour-codes-will-prove-disastrous.

9.6 The Welfare Approach

In contrast to the protection offered by legislations that purport to regulate the relationships between the employer/contractor and the migrant workers, the Kerala government has formulated a set of welfare programmes. These welfare measures need to be viewed against the backdrop of the prevailing labour scenario in which the lives of migrant workers are located. Viewing them as stand-alone measures and programmes would prevent a critical overview of the same.

9.6.1 Kerala Migrant Welfare Scheme Act 2010

Kerala was the first state to enact a social security scheme for migrant workers. A special fund called the Kerala Migrant Workers Welfare Fund was constituted, the management of which is vested with the BOCW welfare board. Migrant workers in the 18–60 age group, with a monthly income of less than Rs. 7500 are eligible for enrollment. Annual membership of Rs. 30 has to be renewed annually. The state government and the BOCW Welfare Board contribute three times the membership fee that is contributed by the workers. The fund so collected is used to support welfare activities provided under the scheme.

As per this scheme, each and every employer/contractor who hires inter-state migrant workers is to ensure that their names are registered as per this scheme. The welfare measures included in this scheme are monetary support to the family in the event of death of a migrant worker, assistance to take the body back home, financial support in the case of accidents at the work site, medical assistance, terminal benefits on cessation of employment (minimum of Rs. 5000 and maximum of Rs. 15,000) and educational assistance to children of migrant workers (mostly of a minimal nature). In a nutshell, the core welfare measure offered herein is of a one-time nature, viz. support to the family in the event of death, medical relief in the event of worksite accidents and minimal educational assistance to children (which is far lower than that provided under the BoCW Act).

Studies indicate inadequate registration of migrant workers under this scheme. As per a 2015 study, only 8000 workers had joined the scheme and only about 500 had renewed their membership in Ernakulam district which is home to the largest migrant population in the state (Roy et al., 2017). The Speaker of the Kerala assembly clarified in the assembly in 2016 that only 50,000 odd workers had registered under the migrant workers welfare scheme. The absence of a clear database regarding migrant workers makes it difficult to assess the extent of registration as well, particularly so in the case of circular migrants.

9.6.2 *The Awaz Health Insurance Scheme*

The Awaz Health Insurance is a state government initiative announced in November 2017 to provide health insurance and accidental death coverage for migrant workers living in the state. It is implemented by the labour and skills department. Migrant workers are to be issued Awaz insurance cards by labour department upon completing formalities.

The insurance coverage includes up to Rs. 25,000 towards free treatment for accidents incurred at the work site, Rupees 1 lakh for disability suffered at the work site and Rupees 2 lakhs for death due to accident at the work site. Once again the focus is on one-time relief measures with a predominant focus on accidents and death.

The purpose of Awaz was always under question. Details of the migrants including their biometric data was collected for registration. Registration was viewed as a cover-up for surveillance of the migrant work force in the state (Maheshwari, 2016). Even though this programme was launched to generate health insurance cards, they came to be publicised as labour cards. In fact many migrant workers refer to them as labour cards.

9.6.3 *Housing Rights for the Migrant Workers*

The cramped living/housing conditions of migrant workers have been a matter of much discussion and debate. This is particularly so when they are provided accommodation by contractors and employers. While random inspections are conducted to assess overall hygiene and sanitation, remedial measures are not visible. The Kerala Govt. implemented the Apna Ghar project as part of the Bhavanam Foundation in 2019, wherein rental bachelor accommodation was provided to migrant workers in hostels. The project was completed in Palakkad providing accommodation to 620 workers. Currently, this stands out as a stand-alone mini experiment at providing housing facilities, as the vast majority does not benefit from it.

9.7 Welfare Versus Rights

Migrant-centric welfare measures offered by the Kerala government require a critical review for two reasons. One, inclusion of migrant workers in these schemes is wanting and needs careful scrutiny. Two, while these schemes offer certain social security measures related to health, accident relief, education and so on, they do not address the critical issue of working conditions of migrant workers. The government on its part does not appear to have made efforts to enhance the implementation of provisions of the Inter State Migrant Workmen Act/Contract Labour Act/ Minimum Wages Act or the BOCW which could make a more tangible difference in this regard. Monitoring contractor/employer–worker relations has received little attention. The extent to which the state is making attempts to hold contractors/employers responsible for violation of labour rights needs careful scrutiny.

The Kerala Labour Policy of 2018 envisages setting up of Facilitation Centres across the state to provide information regarding rights of migrant workers, various welfare schemes, details regarding rail/road/transport facilities, government services, etc. (Govt. of Kerala, 2018). Such facilitation centres do not appear to be functional.

9.8 Glimpses into the Work and Life of Migrant Workers in Kerala

As mentioned earlier, the migrant workers in the state can be categorised into two broad categories, viz. those working with a company on a monthly salary basis or on a daily wage rate basis on a contract arrangement and others who work as daily wage labourers, who can be broadly categorised as footloose informal labourers. These two groups have different kinds of experiences with regard to work and wages and therefore exhibit differences in the wage structure and work timings. Their labour experiences are also different. Those working with companies operate within the company space having limited interaction with society at large. The footloose workers have a wider social interaction, for it is their social networks, especially their relationships with various kinds of employers that assure them of daily wage work.

From among the migrant workers interviewed, those working in companies were in the seafood processing sector. Wages in this sector was found to be very low (as low as Rs. 300 per day for women) compared with the prevailing wage rates in Kerala.

Those who were not hired by any company were found to be engaged in a diverse set of jobs, including construction work, agricultural work, plucking jackfruits, making chips, working on fishing boats and flex hoarding work.

A wage difference was observed between those working in companies and those who were footloose in the same sector. Those in the construction sector for example reported a wage rate of Rs. 1000–1200 a day, in comparison with those hired by companies who reported a wage rate of Rs. 950–1000 per day. The wage difference between those working in a company and those on their own is partly due to the fact that when companies hire workers, they provide accommodation, the cost of which is deducted from the wages paid to them. In the construction sector, there is a reduction in wages of about Rs. 100 per day on this account. The accommodation provided by contractors/companies however is often of a poorer quality, with 10–12 workers cramped into a single room.

The cramped and often unhygienic accommodation facilities have come into sharp critique for many years now. Discussions with civil society organisations working with migrant workers also revealed the same. In the seafood processing units, for example accommodation was provided by the company, with 10–15 workers being accommodated in a single room. There was however no way in which these facilities could be examined. It may be noted that wages, working and living conditions (including timing of work and overtime payment) come under the purview of the ISWMA of 1979. Its weak implementation is an issue of concern.

In addition to the nature of employment, the gender of the labourer also influences their migration experience in Kerala. Women across all employment sectors receive comparatively less wages than their counterparts. They work overtime and even the overtime wage is low. This was observed in the differential wage rates in the seafood export processing units. Women were working in the packing section, whereas men were involved in both packing and loading work. The daily wage rate was appallingly low, with women reporting a daily wage rate of Rs. 300 for 12 h of work, from 8 am to 8 pm or from 9 am to 9 pm, with a lunch break in between. The overtime wages ranged from Rs. 25–40 per hour. Men working in the same units reported a slightly higher wage rate (Rs. 400–450 per day, that as paid on a monthly basis). While both men and women were putting in 12 h of work a day with a lunch break in between, the overtime wages was higher for men. Sonali, a 22-year-old girl from Odisha working in a seafood exporting company in Kollam, shared and mentioned getting Rs. 40 per hour as overtime after her normal working hours of twelve from 8 am to 8 pm. Bela, a 20-year-old Odisha girl working in the packing section of a seafood exporting factory in Kollam had this to say: 'I earn Rs. 300 a day for 12 h of working hours. I get wages regularly, but the pay is low and I get only Rs. 25 for overtime work'.

9.9 Welfare During the Lockdown

The experience of migrants in Kerala during the time of Covid-19 lockdown was defined by the nature of their employment. It is found that labourers who were working under companies and who stayed back, primarily depended on their owners, supervisors, managers or contractors for food and shelter. Some labourers received assistance from NGO's and government agencies. These agencies mainly provided food kits during lockdown.

Sonali, working in the seafood processing unit says: 'We got free food and accommodation from the company. We faced only transportation issues. We got some assistance from the labour department/police/NGOs. The health dept. conducted health check-ups. We also received food and groceries from the labour department and NGOs.'

Similarly, Sanjay from Barpeta of Assam, working at a seafood exporting company in Kollam said that he decided to stay back in Kerala because he expected that work would re-start soon. He knew his family was in stress and he did not want to go back empty handed. He got free food and accommodation from the company and hence did not face problems during the lockdown. Some NGOs and govt. agencies provided food kits during that time.

Some of those who worked on a daily wage basis faced challenges during the lockdown as food supply was not regular. They had no savings with them and relied on the rations made available from the panchayat/corporation and from NGOs. Partho from Haldia in Bengal, who has been working here for the past ten years in the construction sector had this to say: 'Initially, a CPM party worker came and gave us cooked food; he gave us three meals a day, but we are not used to the food here. Also the quantity of food was not enough for us, it would not fill our stomachs. The *upma*[17] in the morning or the 4 *chappatis* at night did not fill our stomachs. So after a few days we requested them to give us dry rations and said we would cook on our own. They gave us dry rations for about 10 days and then it stopped. All of this came from the CPM party workers. When this stopped, I contacted a Malayalee friend of mine, who helps me when I am in stress. He gave me the phone number of the city corporation, and soon we started to get groceries such as rice, potato, oil, dal and some vegetables. Additionally, we would buy tea and sugar. We have heard that in some other areas they would give more, but not here. We did not complain, for we had to live, and we did not want to risk that being stopped. So if the government. gave rations worth Rs. 80 a day for a person, we used to put in Rs. 20 a day (assuming food would cost 100 Rs. per day). We would buy eggs once in a while, or some vegetable, they would give potato and onion's.

They would give rations in a limited quantity that would last for about three days. After it got over we would call again. They used to come regularly for about 10–12 days, after which there would be delays. I would then call my Malayalee friend again and he would give me some other number and it would resume again. He gave me 4–5 numbers during that time and we would call on one of these numbers one by one. I shared these numbers with my friends as well. We also used to call police stations and we got rations from there too. We would call a day before it would finish so that we would not run out of rations. So though we had to make many phone calls in order to get our rations refilled, we somehow coped during that time.

Most of the daily wage workers, who did not have the support of a contractor or employer survived the lockdown with support from various agencies such as the local body, NGOs, the police and local contacts.

The government had directed house owners to not collect rent from migrant workers during the lockdown. In cases where there was a middleman in between the house owner and the worker, rent collection continued. In the absence of the middleman, house owners were found to exempt workers from paying rent during the lockdown (some recovered it after the lockdown). There are reports of magnanimous house owners who did not charge rent and who even provided groceries, there are reports to the contrary as well.

In general, supply of food rations was made available albeit with problems in regularity by the local bodies, NGOs, police and the contractors. The return journey back home was also facilitated by the labour department and the police. However, there are reports of migrant workers who did not leave home because they had not been paid their full wages and they feared they would lose it if they left.

[17] Spiced semolina porridge.

9.10 Involvement in Labour Unions

Kerala is known for its higher level of unionisation. However, the involvement of migrant labourers in labour unions is non-existent. While efforts have been made to register labour unions, they are not very active. Initiatives by some popular political parties to register migrant labourers in unions did not achieve much success. So, in the absence of a formal unions migrants seek assistance from employers, supervisors or contractors during times of crisis. For some others the support is drawn from friends, relatives, local contractors and the local people. Some informal collectives are also found to exist among the migrant labourers. As shared by Partha, 'We don't have unions, but we have groups. I coordinate 15 workers and I am also in constant touch with 4–5 contractors, who call me when they need workers. If they need 10 workers, I call 10 workers from his group. If they need 15, I call all 15. If they need more, I call workers from other groups. For this coordination, I don't get a regular commission or anything, but at times I am paid Rs. 100 by the contractor for getting workers. If I mobilise a larger pool of workers, I get about Rs. 250, or some money to have tea and snacks. More than the money, I am assured of regular work by these contractors'.

He says that he does not do this for any significant monetary benefit, but in order to ensure daily work for himself. He need not depend on anyone else for work and he need not be worried about work availability on each day. Informal contacts and social networks therefore play a role in ensuring availability of work.

The absence of unions was also illustrated in the event of unfair dealings between employer and worker. An incident narrated by an NGO representative working with migrant workers was revealing. The NGO was facilitating registration of migrant workers under the Awaz insurance scheme of the government. The concerned NGO representative was also a member of a convent and she narrated an incident that took place during the lockdown in 2020. A group of migrant workers had come to pluck mangoes by walking a distance of 17 km. They were in desperate need of work and walked the distance as buses were not plying. At the end of the day, she paid them Rs. 500 as daily wage directly as the contractor was absent at the time of payment. They were visibly surprised when they received Rs. 500 as their daily wage. She found out that the contractor would normally pay them only Rs. 250 per day. It was then that she realised that they had been given only half their wages on earlier occasions. She took up the issue and threatened to take the contractor to court if he failed to pay them full wages. As a result, the contractor gave her Rs. 40,000 to be given back to the workers, on account of the money he had deducted so far. The NGO representative said that it was just a pure coincidence that she was made aware of this unfair practice and since then, has found out that many contractors resort to this practice.

Similarly, a migrant worker from West Bengal reported instances when they were not paid full wages. He reported an instance when about 20 of them had gone to work on road construction for two days, and all 20 of them were paid just Rs. 100 per day instead of the full wage of Rs. 1000 per day. They filed a complaint at the police station, but no action was taken. The absence of any organised union was evident here.

9.11 Absence of Inspections

The welfare measures of the state have little effect on the daily lives of migrant workers, especially so as they do not address problems faced at the workplace. For example, the migrant workers are not aware about the inspections happening in their company. This may also be due to the lack of enquiries from the labour officials with the workers. As one of the workers mentioned: I don't remember any such inspection. If at all they come, they do not speak to us. Bimal from Assam working in a seafood exporting company for the past eight remarked: 'Government conducted inspections randomly, but they do not ask us for suggestions or opinions regarding working conditions'.

9.12 Experience of Social Discrimination

Much has been written about instances of discrimination that migrant workers face while living and working in the state. Though the reported number of severe instances have been few, there exists an underlying sense of condescension towards migrant workers. Their inevitability in the labour market however prevents overt expressions of discrimination. And yet, longer conversations with migrant workers reveal that many of them have faced such instances during their life here. The possibility of such experiences could be fewer for those who are hired by companies, with accommodation being provided within the company premises, as it reduces their social interaction.

Twenty-year-old Bela says she has not faced any discrimination from the people as she rarely interacts with people outside the company. Even during the lockdown period, much of their requirements were taken care of by the employers.

Partha, who has been working as a construction worker for 10 years in the state spoke of the many small instances of discrimination that he and others like him faced. Having spent a longer time in the state, he was able to reflect upon his early experiences and the changes over the years. He spoke of occasions when migrant workers end up paying more on fish and vegetables than the local population. This is particularly so when they are new to the state and do not follow Malayalam. Once they pick up the language, the cheating comes down. He also reported instances when migrant workers while hiring autos are made to pay a higher amount than the base fare fixed by the government. He also reported instances when the water bills of the houses in which migrant workers were accommodated shot up without reason.

Citing an incident when lockdown restrictions were relaxed in 2020, Partha says:

> Last year, when the lockdown was on, both Malayalee and Hindi workers would get out for work. When the police would spot us on the road, going for work, they would explain patiently to the Malayalee workers, but with us, they would immediately take their lathis. One day, I was returning from back and all on a sudden, a policeman got out from the vehicle and beat me with his lathi. He told me that I was not supposed to get out of home during the lockdown. I told them to first stop the worksites from functioning rather than beating me.

The police at the nearby police station in Sreekaryam know us, but police in other places don't know us. When they see us 'hindi wallahs', they immediately beat us before asking us where we were going. This is common. If there is a problem at the worksite, immediately we are blamed. If a Malayalee worker is at fault, he will put the blame on us and we are scolded. As I know the language, I speak up and say that we are not at fault. Malayalee workers are clever and get away with such tricks'.

9.13 Life After the Lockdown: Migrants, Labour and Capital

Almost all the 'guest' migrant workers have returned back to work. They have returned as they were unable to find regular work opportunities at desired wage rates in their home states after the lifting of the lockdown. After a temporary shortage of labour during the lockdown phase, the current situation is one in which migrants are back in full numbers. In fact, migrant workers report a slight reduction in the number of work days since the lockdown.

Similar to the pre-lockdown days, migrant workers in small towns and large cities acquire visibility during the early mornings and evenings, as they wait at pick-up points or at tea stalls. In the evenings, migrant workers walking back home in groups to their accommodation facilities are a common sight. A newspaper report in November 2021 spoke of surprise checks being conducted by the health wing of the Trivandrum Corporation in camps where migrant workers were residing. It spoke of 30–40 migrant workers living in a room meant for 10, of insufficient toilets and of improper drainage facilities. Such reports make news once in a while (The Hindu, 2021). There is however no regular monitoring of the working and living conditions of migrant workers. The 'guest workers' live life as they did before.

Existing welfare schemes do little to address the asymmetry between the interests of the labouring migrant workforce and that of the owners/employers. As economic activities gain pace after the lockdowns in 2020 and 2021, these welfare schemes can do little to tilt the balance in favour of the one of the weakest sections of the informal sector. While Kerala offers relatively higher wages and better working conditions (two of the critical pull factors as far as migration is concerned), instances of injustice and discrimination prevail, both at the workplace and in larger social interactions. Absence of state monitoring of the implementation of legal provisions that protect the interests of migrant workers at the workplace gives an upper hand to the owners/contractors in the numerous establishments that hire them. The deal is between the contractor/employer and the worker, and the state's presence is weak. The absence of unionisation and the invisibility of migrant lives pushes such issues out of public attention. The fact that labour rights of the largest majority of the workforce is not given its due place in a state that is known for its labour conscientisation is a contradiction that has escaped any serious political and social contemplation. No amount of welfare measures can compensate for the silence in this regard.

References

Abraham, A., Singh, D., & Pal, P. (2014). Critical assessment of labour laws, policies and practices through a gender lens. *National resource centre for women, national mission for empowerment of women, ministry of women and child development, Government of India.*

Government of Kerala. (2016). 13th Kerala legislative assembly-committee on public accounts (2014–16) on action taken by government on recommendations contained in the 120th report of the committee on public accounts (2008–2011), Secretariat of the Kerala Legislature.

Government of Kerala. (2018). Draft labour policy.

John, J. (2015). Inter-regional migration from eastern states to Kerala: A socio economic analysis. Working paper no. 4, Kerala Development Society.

Lucio, M. M., Perrett, R., McBride, J., & Craig, S., (2007). *Migrant workers in the labour market: The role of unions in the recognition of skills and qualifications.* Technical Paper. London: Unionlearn.

Maheshwari, G. (2016). Migrant crisis in Kerala: Need to change the political culture. *Economic and Political Weekly, 51*(48), 23–25.

Moses, J. W., & Rajan, S. I. (2012). Labour migration and integration in Kerala. *Labour and Development, 19*(1), 1–18.

Narayana, D., Venkiteswaran, C. S., Joseph, M. P. (2013). *Domestic migrant labour in Kerala.* SHRAM Research Report.

Peter, B., & Narendran, V. (2017). *God's own workforce: Unravelling labour migration to Kerala.*

Prakash, B. A. (1998). Gulf migration and its economic impacts: The Kerala experience. *Economic and Political Weekly, 33*(50).

Prasad-Aleyamma, M. (2011). A market place for migrants: Mobility, settlement and social protection in Kerala. In R. Sabates Wheeler & R. Feldman (Ed.), *Social protection and migration: Claiming social rights beyond borders* (pp. 164–182). Palgrave Macmillan.

Rajan, S. I., & Zackaria, K. C. (2016). Kerala migration survey 2014. *Economic and Political Weekly, 51*(6).

Raman, K. R. (2012). Currents and eddies': Indian-Middle East migration processes. *Cambridge Journal of Regions, Economy and Society, 5*, 189–205.

Remesh, B. P. (2003). Changing consciousness and image of Kerala labour in the 20th century. *Labour and Development, 9*(1).

Roy, S. N., et al. (2017). *Migrants in construction work: Evaluating their welfare framework.* Centre for Policy Research.

Sharma, H. (2019). Repealing the construction workers act under new labour codes will prove disastrous. https://thewire.in/labour/repealing-the-construction-workers-act-under-new-labour-codes-will-prove-disastrous

Sinha, D., & Sengupta, S. (2019). How maternity benefits can be extended to informal women workers. https://thewire.in/women/how-maternity-benefits-can-be-extended-to-informal-women-workers

The Hindu. (2021). Poor living conditions at migrant worker camps. https://www.thehindu.com/news/national/kerala/poor-living-conditions-at-migrant-worker-camps/article37367787.ece

Upadhyay, A., & Pandey, S. (2020, July 14). Labour laws and migrant workers during COVID-19 | SCC Blog. SCC. Downloaded from https://www.scconline.com/blog/post/2020/04/15/labour-laws-and-migrant-workersduring-covid-19/

Zachariah, K. C., Mathew, E. T., & Rajan, I. S. (2000). *Dynamics of migration in Kerala: Dimensions, differentials and consequences.* CDS.

Chapter 10
Long 2020 and the Informal Care Economy: Case Studies of Select Careworkers

Sabir Ahamed and Madhurilata Basu

Abstract The health system in India consists of a public sector, a private sector and an informal network of care providers. Though for the formal sectors there have been policies, schemes operative for long, in case of the informal network, due to various reasons (limited access, further worsened by the poor functioning of public health system is one among many), the act of 'caring' takes place mostly in an unregulated environment. It is important to realize that the healthcare crisis following COVID19 pandemic in India has been a result of collective economic strategies adopted by various governments which gave primacy to big capital, infrastructure and financial services and comparatively, less importance was attached to social sectors like health and education. COVID19 pandemic would have lasting impacts on public health, caregiving and informal care economy, human demography, etc. The sudden visibility that careworkers including the ones from formal as well as informal sectors, has gained during the pandemic should not be easily forgotten, and for that, discussions on public health, contagion, health security, etc., should keep focus on areas beyond medical, virological and epidemiological concerns. Based on personal interviews, articles and reports published during the pandemic along with other relevant documents, this paper has tried to understand how three categories of informal careworkers, namely ASHA workers, *ayahs* and *safaikarmacharis*, negotiated with the pandemic on one hand and societal expectations on the other.

Keywords Health care · ASHA workers · *Ayahs* · Informal sector · Public health

The health system in India consists of a public sector, a private sector and an informal network of care providers. Though for the formal sectors there have been policies,

---

This chapter is the product of two independent research, and both are co-first authors

S. Ahamed (✉)
Pratichi (India) Trust and MCRG, Kolkata, India
e-mail: sabirahamed@gmail.com

M. Basu
Department of Political Science, Sarojini Naidu College and MCRG, Kolkata, India

S. R. Chakraborty et al. (eds.), *The Long 2020*, India Studies in Business and Economics, https://doi.org/10.1007/978-981-99-4815-4_10

schemes operative for long, in case of the informal network, due to various reasons (limited access, further worsened by the poor functioning of public health system is one among many), the act of 'caring' takes place mostly in an unregulated environment. It is important to realize that the healthcare crisis following COVID19 pandemic in India has been a result of collective economic strategies adopted by various governments which gave primacy to big capital, infrastructure and financial services and comparatively, less importance was attached to social sectors like health and education.

Based on personal interviews, articles and reports published during the pandemic along with other relevant documents, this paper has tried to understand how three categories of informal careworkers, namely ASHA workers, *ayahs* and *safaikarmacharis*, negotiated with the pandemic on one hand and societal expectations on the other. Further, it would also be pertinent to investigate whether there has been a change with regard to how the work of the above three category of workers is perceived by society, government, etc. This paper has also tried probing how intersecting inequities (gender, age, race, caste, citizenship, income, etc.) shaped the social determinants of health, vulnerabilities, access to health services, etc., during the pandemic.

Independent India, keeping in line with the Montgomery-Chelmsford Constitutional Reforms of 1919 (whereby public health, sanitation, etc., was transferred to the provinces), declared health to be a state subject. Though the states enjoy autonomy, when it comes to health, however, the government at the center has been framing policies, providing frameworks, making laws that impact the whole of India. Such a tendency not only continued but intensified during the pandemic, wherein most crucial steps or responses were framed at the central level. When and where to impose a lockdown, travel bans, screening at entry points, testing, etc., all important decisions were taken by the center and the states had to strictly comply.

It is needless to say that, the idea of 'modern medicine' was a popularized in India during colonial days. Even after independence, the state opted for western system of medicine, which is highly selective and not inclusive, institutionalized, centralized and top down, treating people as objects rather than subjects. This has also resulted in the needs of the majority of the rural population being unfulfilled. The successive rounds of National Family Health Survey (NFHS 1–3) revealed huge rural–urban differences in key maternal and child health indicators, specially, in case of neonatal and post neonatal periods, mortality in rural areas is about 50% higher than mortality in urban areas.

Limited access to quality healthcare services is a feature of most states in India. A recent study regarding the availability of ICU beds in low- and lower middle-income countries, highlighted that in India, the recent ICU beds, available per 100,000 is 2.17, a rise from 1.63. The country topping the list was Mongolia with 8.27 beds for 100,000 (UNDP, 2020). Though nowhere near the top, the healthcare infrastructure in rural areas has been developed as a three-tier system and is based on the following population norms (Rural Health Statistics 2018–2019, 2019).

Center	Population norms	
	Plain area	Hilly/tribal/difficult area
Sub-center	5000	3000
Primary health center	30,000	20,000
Community health center	120,000	80,000

During the 50s, 60s and 70s, the focus has been preventing the spread of communicable diseases, family planning, setting up more teaching hospitals (to produce more doctors and nurses). All of it happened with the realization that the primary healthcare system in India was inadequate (Rao, 2016, 13). Further with the economic reforms of the 90s, the goal of Alma Ata Declaration, which was 'health for all by 2020' was sort of reframed as 'health for the underprivileged' under the 8th Five Year Plan and the first Health Policy (1983) gave emphasis to strengthening primary healthcare in India and setting up a network of primary healthcare services using health volunteers. Before this, the National Planning Committee (NPC hereafter) had given importance to the formation of a cadre of social workers who would be 'imbued with a missionary spirit' to transform the health of the society and take villages away from age-old superstitions and prejudices that hinder good health and better living (NPC, 1947, 44).

In order to deal with the existing inequities in healthcare, after fifty-eight years, the National Rural Health Mission (NRHM), was launched in 2005, which reiterated the need for a cadre of women volunteers dubbed as Accredited Social Health Activists (ASHA), for attaining the above-mentioned goal of attaining health equity. Training and enhancing capacity of Panchayati Raj Institutions (PRIs) to own, control and manage public health services and promoting access to improved healthcare at household level through the female health activist (ASHA) were much sought-after solutions. The programme was aimed to help rural and semi-urban communities gain access to health-related services and the ASHA workers were seen as an interface between the community and the public health system.

Over the years, the programme has expanded significantly, in 2011 the government had claimed to have 'one ASHA in each village', expecting to cover 1000 population. In reality, the population they cover is higher in a densely populated state like West Bengal. According to data available on the website of the Ministry of Health and Family Affairs, there are at least 1,022,265 ASHAs in the country. In West Bengal, as our RTI data reveals that there are 53,485 ASHAs in 28 Health Districts. A married widowed/divorced preferably in the age group of 25–45 years' woman with education qualification of class 10 is eligible for ASHA. Our study finds their educational qualification ranges between higher secondary and post-graduation (she had done B.Ed.).

A careful review of the policy documents related to ASHAs, mostly available on the website of the National Health Mission under the aegis Ministry of Health and Family Affairs, reveals that they are largely 'voluntary health workers'. These documents further note their involvement of merely 3–4 h of work in the same village where she lives. They have never been on the payroll of the health department and there are no other social security benefits available except some amount after retirement. On the contrary, ASHA represents the face of the government at the ground level and on behalf of the state, they meticulously implement the projects designed for improving the indicators of health in general, maternal and child health in particular. They also are empowered to collect the personal information of mothers and children, helping the state to determine the policies including the population policy.

In reality, ASHA workers never have the opportunity to see the aggregate forms of these data which they collect every day, feeding the data into the system burning midnight oil. However, within the apparatus of the 'grand' state, the contributions of the ASHA workers have remained 'overlooked', yet these women working at the grassroot level have made the otherwise 'missing' state visible in the eyes of the masses. Their work entails a wide array of activities including building awareness of the government's family planning policies, along with programmes on maternal and child health. Along with their routine work during 'normal times', they are entrusted with a wide range of works including assisting the general administration in awareness building on various issues, correcting the electoral rolls and helping authorities and other volunteers during natural disasters.

A growing body of evidence suggests that there has been a significant development in mother and child health in India, child mortality rate has drastically reduced, coverage and consistency of child immunization has widened, and institutional delivery is more than 80%. To this end, as several studies have suggested that ASHA worker has played a pivotal role in bringing these perceptible changes in the health indicators, yet their contribution remains unsung within the apparatus of the 'grand' state. They are treated as volunteers in the policy documents, hence denied of the social securities as enjoyed by public sector employees. During these challenging times, they are the face of the state, connecting the state with the citizen. However, critics have pointed out as to how the ASHA programme, is a clear instance as to how the Indian state does development through gender. Through the formal creation of informality, gender injustice at the lowest tiers increases instead of decreasing (Swaminathan, 2015). This paper would like to argue along the line of Swaminathan that the very programme of ASHA workers ignores the moral imperative of empowering women to achieve women's human rights and full equal rights with men.

Despite the launching of NRHM in 2005, as per a report, till 31 March 2015, more than 8% of 25,300 PHCs, had no doctors, 38% had no laboratory technicians and 22% had no pharmacists. A huge number of seats for both male and female health assistants also remained vacant. In case of community health centers there was a dearth of specialists like gynaecologists and paediatricians (Sharma, 2015, 2381). Another study (based on secondary level hospitals) looking into hospital efficiency in West Bengal, highlighted a shortage of doctors and other necessary manpower. That coupled with absenteeism, makes things worse for the already vulnerable section of the society (Dutta et al., 2011).

While the role of ASHA workers is detailed out in several policy documents, the work of *safaikarmacharis* is not found in that detail. Similar is the case of *Ayahs.*

They find space in several government orders pertaining to the organization of a medical unit, departments in several medical institutions, etc. Other than this, this category of women careworkers is not mentioned in the policy documents. Hence, all the details pertaining to this category of workers is based on empirical data alone.

It needs to be stated here that the Government of India had shown a lackadaisical attitude in the initial months of 2020. As the caseload, had suddenly increased globally, they made a wake-up call in March 2020. The central and state governments swung into action to prepare the health system and infrastructure for the expected rise in COVID19 cases. All the three categories of workers had to dive into work without any formal training or any idea about what they were dealing with. Interviews revealed that in the initial days when the devastating effect of COVID19 was yet to be experienced, these workers had worked with almost no protection. Their superiors had not prepared them in terms of what they were supposed to expect. The fast spread of the virus along with the spread of rumours, prejudiced opinions, made their work more difficult.

10.1 ASHA Workers and the Pandemic

In the pre-pandemic years, their 'job descriptions' are clearly articulated, even the number of training they need to undergo before joining, some weeks after joining, and yearly refresher course etc., and they need to record every completed activity in several formats. The onset of the pandemic has undoubtedly increased their workload. The moot question arises, which is also echoed by ASHA workers themselves. 'Have you ever seen such detailed job description of volunteers in the world?', they ask. If we look at their contribution to the state, it is enormous. The health statistics confirm the significant reduction of child mortality rate, increased universal coverage of immunization, increased demand for institutional delivery and increased awareness on health and hygiene practice, etc. Yet, the commitment of the state towards these workers is questionable.

In her seminal work titled *State without Honour: Women Workers in India's Anganwadis*, Sreerekha (2017), explores the political economy of women's work in India and its relationship with the Indian state. Besides Anganwadi workers, this pool of ASHA workers, particularly from the lower social strata, are being employed in new social welfare schemes where the form of work is defined as 'voluntary social service'. Is this, the author asks, the state's strategy to keep these workers invisible? Over the years they are 'overlooked' and their demands are routinely denied, yet, during these times of crisis, they are the face of the state.

During the pandemic, among the several measures, the key decision that was taken by the central and subsequently state governments was to utilize the services of frontline health workers including the involvement of more than 10 lakhs ASHAs spread across the states, to raise awareness and containment efforts at the community level. To this end, the National Health Mission under the Ministry of Health and Family Welfare had issued a few notifications and orders in the last week of March, detailing the activities of the ASHAs in the prevention of viruses. About ten lakhs ASHAs were deployed to visit 25 families in a day, and expected to cover the populating she covers in seven days. The role of the ASHA during the household visits was/is as follows: (1) building awareness about COVID and its symptoms, (2) early detection of cases of corona infection and referral to a suitable medical centre for the treatment of a person suspected of corona infection, (3) identify the person with a travel history in the last fourteen days for mandatory quarantine, (4) follow up with the person isolated for home quarantine, and understand their health status. In addition, many states had involved them in managing the makeshift quarantine centre for the migrant workers. In another notification dated 20 April 2020, the Mission Director, National Health Mission, officially acknowledged the significant contribution of the ASHAs in the containment of COVID19. In addition, the notification notes that ASHAs had taken a wide range of activities beyond the roles and responsibilities stipulated on 27 March. The note directed all the state governments to pay Rs. 2000 in full as their remuneration.

Another notification in the same month has expressed deep concern about the attack on ASHA workers while they were on duty, and urged state governments to take appropriate action for the protection and safety of the workers. In the face of sporadic protest by the ASHAs across the state, policymakers have responded including the opposition leaders like Rahul Gandhi had taken note of the situation and tweeted on the plights of the ASHAs during the pandemic.

Though loss of income and unemployment has been a reality across categories, however, women in general, reported more loss of jobs when compared with men. Again, research revealed that Muslims were at higher risk of losing jobs than Hindus—84% against 66% (Kesar et al., 2020). As per a survey (on 12 cities) by WIEGO (WIEGO, UNICEF and ILO, 2021), almost 70% workers surveyed in their study, comprising—home-based workers, domestic workers, street vendors and waste-pickers, reported zero earnings during the first lockdown period. Lakhs of migrant labourers returned to their hometowns and as per a report by the Stranded Workers Action Network, due to lockdown, workers in India's informal sector, daily wage earners, contractual or casual workers, migrant workers had either lost their jobs or had not received their last payments. It is here that the ASHA *didis* as they are popularly known, played important role in checking the spread of the disease by going house to house making people aware of the dos and don'ts, tracking down, COVID-infected patients, monitoring returnee migrants, etc.

Further, the primary health centres could resume functioning to a lot extent, due to the efforts of the ASHA worders or ASHA *didis* as they are popularly known. However, during pandemic, pregnant women were urged to have deliveries in private nursing homes with which government hospital doctors are associated. In such cases these women care workers who get incentives based on every institutional delivery, they suffered (The Wire, 15 October 2020). Though the work of these workers is officially acknowledged in government documents, but it was during the pandemic that they and their work became 'visible'.

Over the past few months, we spoke to at least 25 ASHAs across three districts in West Bengal, one concern they had consistently aired was their 'earnings are paltry and hardly fair compensation for the scope of services they provide'. The remuneration for ASHAs varies from state to state; the central government bears Rs. 2000, and the state government may add to this paltry amount. In West Bengal, ASHAs earn now 4500 as fixed remuneration, an increment of Rs. 1000 during the pandemic. The additional income of ASHAs is contingent upon the execution of incentive-based tasks, about 36 items are stipulated in the list. An ASHA worker in Goocharan said, 'When we started working on family planning programme in ten years ago, there were several cases of childbirth in my working area, how because of our intervention the birth rate has significantly reduced hence our remuneration is linked with such incentive our income dropped'. He quipped 'We are paying price for our own hard work'. Also, some incentive-based health activities were temporarily suspended; owing to COVID protocol, their income dropped. A recent study has indicated (BehnaBOx, 2020) indicated that ASHAs had experienced debt burden and delay in payment amidst job losses in their families'. Among the demands they have raised during the sporadic protest in the country, their demand for the revisions of their remuneration is on the top. Other demands include restrooms at their workplaces, paid maternity leaves, gender sensitization cells to tackle sexual harassment at the workplace, travel allowances and the right to form unions.

10.1.1 Ayahs *and the Pandemic*

Apart from ASHA *didis* in rural areas, in big towns and urban areas, *ayahs* working in both public and private spaces are careworkers who are mostly untrained, yet they have become crucial in providing care. *Ayahs*, mostly provide a broad range of assistance for, a person in need of care. They hail mostly from the informal sector, doing all the 'dirty work' that otherwise nurses would not want to do. From helping family members to take care of old, ailing family members, the demand for their work has increased overtime and their services were highly sought after during the pandemic. During this time getting non-COVID critical care became very difficult as the number of COVID patients increased in both private and government hospitals. Patients suffering due to cancer, kidney problems, cirrhosis of liver, dementia, etc., who needed urgent attention had to settle for home care. A few agencies during the pandemic did come up with arrangements of blood transfusion at home, under a doctor's supervision. Similar agencies had also arranged for regular home visits by doctors, physiotherapists, nurses (mainly who have studied bedside nursing), hospitalization and overall monitoring by health managers (staff in the agencies acting as liaison officer between the patient's party and all other care providers). However, the day-to-day care was undertaken by the *ayahs*, though these agencies prefer using the term attendants instead of *ayah*, perhaps in order to differentiate themselves from other small placement centres.

In order to check the spread of the virus, lockdown was declared and the *ayahs* who commuted by train went out of work. Many of these women are the sole breadwinners in their families. Other households were the male members worked as a migrant worker in some other states, were equally affected. Sampa Mondol (age 39), an ayah, working in a placement centre in Salt Lake Sector 1 area and living in Barrackpore, regretted and said, *Kolkatar ar ektu kachhe thakle manage korte partam* [Had I lived closer to Kolkata, I would have found out a way to go to work].[1] There is a constant demand for the *ayahs*, and where the daily commuters failed to join work, the 'locals' or the ones living in and around the city, benefitted. It somehow seemed to be true.

In a society already plagued by various forms of inequities existing at various levels, COVID19 increased the already existing inequities. Like all pandemics, COVID19 threatened all communities alike, hence collective measures at the societal or community level was crucial during the pandemic. Though the nation-wide lockdown was aimed at containing the spread of the coronavirus, the sudden announcement had triggered a humanitarian crisis for which the governments both at the center and the states were not prepared for. Researches done during this pandemic reveal that COVID19 negatively impacted the SCs, STs, OBCs, Dalits and women and the impact was considerably less for upper caste persons (Deshpande & Ramachandran, 2020; Kesar et al., 2020).

Shipra Majhi (age 43 years), living in Shodpur, close to Kolkata (takes around 30 min to reach Bidhannagar Railway Station), working with one of the oldest placement centers in Salt Lake area learnt to ride a scooty and continued working. She could study till the fifth standard and that she could come to work on a scooty was unthinkable for her, yet she could do it. During the pandemic and due to paucity of women caregivers like her, centers did charge Rs. 380 per shift, depending on the seriousness of the patient.[2] Parul Naskar (age 28), has been caring for an octogenarian patient with dementia for the last five years and the patient's family is so dependent on her, that they got her a bicycle. She lives near Belghoria and carries a letter from the patient's family, requesting for free passage as she is providing 'essential services' to the patient. But luckily for her, till now, she has never been stopped by the police either on her way to work or back home. When asked if the placement center had provided with an identity card identifying her to be a provider of essential service, care, the answer was in the negative.

Similar experiences get reflected in several works done on paid service providers in different parts of the world. Studies suggest that many require care at home in Europe and the situation worsened when critical care patients were released from hospitals to vacate hospital beds. Further, with the lockdown, migrant care workers were forced to return to their home countries and later found it difficult to cross borders as they worked without legal work contracts. The situation of stay-at-home care seekers worsened as less care was available, while what was needed was just the opposite (Bergmann & Wagner, 2021; Leiblfinger et al., 2020). The informal care workers across regions, in most of the cases, did not have adequate knowledge about how to deal with the ongoing pandemic situation and their burden increased when the old, infirm were released from elderly care facilities. Chang et al. (2020) in their work highlighted the amount of stress that care providers in Hong Kong,

---

[1] Interview conducted on 17.10.20.

[2] Telephonic interview held on 09.06.21.

had to deal with in situations where they were caring for multiple recipients. In general, two billion workers belonging to the informal economy and representing 61% of the global labour-force were hit hard due to the pandemic and the informal care workers are no exception, whose insecurities increased during the pandemic (WIEGO, UNICEF and ILO, 2021).

Ayahs working in hospitals and nursing homes also faced the impact of the pandemic. During the pandemic, access to private hospitals and nursing homes got limited for most of them, as the number of infected patients increased rapidly. The patients' party or the family of the patients who normally hire the services of these *ayahs,* were sceptic in hiring them and these institutions in order to prevent contamination of patients during their stay, limited their entry. This reinforced the image of ayahs as care workers who are not clean, hence can be the bearer of the virus. Parul Nashkar's aunt, Maya Sarkar (age 48) works as an *ayah* in a sub-division hospital in Hoogly district, adjacent to Kolkata and with the ongoing pandemic had lost her source of livelihood as they were no longer allowed to work there. As more and more government hospitals were being designated as COVID hospitals, the livelihood of ayahs in government institutions was seriously getting affected. Official response has been that dearth of formal training coupled with no or very limited education were the main reasons why they could no longer work in such institutions during the ongoing pandemic. There were around 100 COVID patients in that particular sub-division hospital, and there was need of more healthcare staff. Nurses were overburdened and the ayahs wanted to work and were ready to give an undertaking that nobody would be held responsible if they got infected or if something happened to them, Maya informed. '*Nursera khayiye debe, bedpan debe? Patient partykei korte hochhe dekho giye noyto omni e pore achhe*' [Do you think nurses would feed these patients, give them bedpans? Go and check it's the patients' family who are doing all of it or else they are lying in a sorry state], she said.[3] Protesting in front of the hospital administration or committing suicide were the only options in front of them, she said.

Ayahs (along with nurses and doctors) had to face discrimination from the *para* (the locality where they lived), following the rise of vigilantism in different parts of the country. Many, living in ghettoes or slums in urban spaces were asked to leave their homes as other residents feared contacting the virus from ayahs serving patients in hospitals or in private homes. Mira Das (age 34), living in a bustee, near Bidhannagar Railway Station reported that during the first lockdown, local level leaders of the ruling political party forbade everyone from leaving the bustee for work. Police check posts were set up and anybody who ventured out was sent back home. Though they received ration from the government, most of the families like hers faced acute financial problems. '*Amra din ani din khayi, kaj na korle khabo ki*' [Our situation is that of daily wage earners, if there is no work, there is no pay], she said. To add to her plight of loss of livelihood, her husband who works in Bangalore and is associated with the real-estate sector there, was stuck without food, savings and was on the verge of losing his rented accommodation.

---

[3] Telephonic interview held on 26.4.21.

When a country-wide lockdown was announced on 24 March 2020, by Prime Minister Narendra Modi, with a four hours' notice, the uncertainties in the lives of the poor, marginalized sections, migrant workers increased manifold. The blanket lockdown implied closing of state borders, schools, colleges, withdrawal of train and bus services which led to disruption in the supply of essential goods, leading to inflation and fear of shortages. On 26 March 2020, Finance Minister of India, Nirmala Sitharaman declared free distribution of food grains and the payment of cash to be made in favour of women, poor senior citizens and others through Pradhan Mantri Garib Kalyan Yojna. Though the government maintained that food grains were distributed across the country in several households, various news reports and reports from various other organizations, set up by citizens pointed out that despite the claim, a huge section of the population was yet to receive food grains. From May onwards local train services were suspended in West Bengal, meaning that those people living far from the city cannot come to work, or have to figure other ways (often more expensive ones) of reaching work.[4]

A few of the interviewed *ayahs* working in government hospitals of Kolkata and adjacent districts, reported sleeping on a bench in the hospital premises as they could not return home from their *duties* (work). Due to the lockdown, temporary food stalls from where they bought their simple meal of *ghugni-ruti* [beans and flat bread] or *bhaat-tarkari* [rice and vegetables], at reasonable prices, were all closed. As they were working double shifts, they had to live on stale food from home or biscuits or puffed rice, which left them half-fed. Lockdown, night curfews and vigilantism forced them to stay in their places of work. Some of the respondents stated that they could continue working for 12 h shifts daily, only because they were hosted by family members, situated in other parts of the city.

It is pertinent to mention here that unlike nurses or doctors, or others working in various health clinics or diagnostic centers, these women were not vaccinated along with other frontline workers. Neither were they given PPE kits or other protective gears while attending to patients just released from the hospitals, some of whom contacted the virus during their stay in the hospitals. Most of the times families of the patients either did not know or withheld the information that the patients they were attending to are affected by the virus. That is why later on, COVID negative report was made mandatory by various placement centers, for patients to be attended by the *ayahs*. Most of the ayahs working through placement centers are partially vaccinated and only a few of them reported to be fully vaccinated. Out of 25 *ayahs* working through placement centers (who were interviewed for this work along with seven others working in government hospitals) only nine reported receiving vaccine shots in government hospitals, the rest got vaccine shots through vaccination drives organized by some NGO or local political leaders. Parul Nashkar and Shipra Majhi got their vaccine shots at private clinics and they were paid by the patient's family.

Ayahs, be it in government institutions or in private spaces, belong to the lowest tier of direct caregiving (here direct caregiving means they have to come in contact

[4] https://www.hindustantimes.com/cities/kolkata-news/local-trains-to-be-suspended-in-bengal-from-tomorrow-in-view-of-covid19-101620206698571.html.

with the patient's body). Doctors are being situated in the topmost tier. Their job requires them to perform menial work and hence is looked down upon by other female caregivers who are in privileged position (nurses, contractual nurses and diploma nurses). This clean-unclean dichotomy is something that nursing profession had to struggle with, since its beginning in India. No amount of inculcations of missionary or Christian values by various female medical missionaries[5] could persuade nurses in today's government hospitals from touching bed pans of patients. Perceived as doing unclean care work, many women work as ayahs as no other way of earning a livelihood is known or available to them. Many are the sole bread winners of the family and also the head of the family. The well-being of their family, for these women, are primarily their responsibility. The already precarious situation got worse during the pandemic. One respondent in particular reported that one of her children, had to drop out of school (he was in class 8) and join a local car repair shop, so that he could bring home some money, as it was difficult for the mother (who was not vaccinated during the time of interview) to find work.

Thus, unlike other categories of care workers, *ayahs* working in various health facilities did not get vaccinated because in most of the cases, they are not in the payroll of those institutions and enjoy no social benefits. Though providing essential services, assisting nurses in various wards, taking individual care of patients in many cases, these women were ignored mostly in various vaccination drives. It also needs to be mentioned that when much later vaccination drives were initiated by various groups, the ayahs found it difficult to register their names in the COWIN app, first because most of them do not own smart phones and second did not know how to register their names. Even for registering their names, two respondents reported paying Rs. 20 and 40, respectively, to their local 'xerox shop' owners.

Various 'home-healthcare service centers' (as the property owners would like to call them, in order to differentiate their establishments with ayah centers) have been in operation in Kolkata for almost a decade and it was during the pandemic, that their services were sought by even middle-class households as there was dearth of ayahs in several ayah centers following the suspension of local trains. As the risk of contamination increased for critical care patients, hospital authorities were discharging them, which created a huge demand for at home care givers. In this situation, these home-healthcare service providers offered the services of male attendants along with nurses. In a telephonic interview[6] with one such owner Mr. A. Banerjee, revealed that his organization prefers offering the services of male attendants, who can read prescriptions written in English, measure pressure level, pulse rate, administer injections, etc. The ayahs, who are mostly uneducated and not trained can do none of the above things. The service of male attendants for a whole day was fixed at Rs. 1800, a lot more than what an ayah center would charge. The successful running of such home-healthcare service providers no doubt possesses threat to the already marginalized category of healthcare workers, the *ayahs*. Most of the clients of such

[5] Please refer to the articles published in the American Journal of Nursing since the first decade of twentieth century, particularly the section titled 'Nursing in Mission Stations'.

[6] Interviewed on 26.11.2020.

centers are non-resident Indians, who cannot be present to personally look after their loved ones and hence, rely on them as they try to provide that personal touch in their job of caregiving. Attendants work under managers who act like a liaison between the family of the patient located outside India and the organization. All the updates are shared regularly with the patient-party.

10.1.1.1 Safaikarmacharis and the Pandemic

Another category of workers, who provided crucial service during the pandemic were the *safaikarmacharis*. Though there are *safaikarmacharis*, working directly under the local administration (municipality/municipal corporations, etc.), increasingly, we find a rise in contractual workers associated with the job of cleaning. When society treated COVID patients as social outcastes or untouchables, these *safaikarmacharis*, didn't fail their duty of collecting everyday trash which included bio-medical waste, from the concerned households. Based on International Standard Classification of Occupations (ISCO 08) list, cleaners and helpers are listed as care workers (point no. 91).[7] Compared with other groups like doctors, nurses and other workers associated directly or indirectly with healthcare, who were at the frontline during the pandemic, the sanitation workers or the *safaikarmacharis* were/are the most vulnerable because they come in direct contact with several kinds of wastes including hazardous waste. They have to clean and dispose of wastes from our places of stay, but they also have to handle medical wastes collected from homes, housing complexes, small health or testing centers.

As per the 'guidelines' issued by the Ministry of Health and Family Welfare (MoHFW),[8] safaikarmacharis or sanitation workers were at 'moderate risk' and needed N95 masks and gloves to fulfil their duties. Even the World Health Organization interim guidance note recommends that sanitation workers be provided with disposable gowns and gloves, eye-protection gears or a face shield, medical masks and sanitizers.[9] However, interviews revealed that till May 2020, *safaikarmacharis* in ward 41 of Salt Lake, Kolkata relied on store-bought cotton masks which cost them something between 15 and 20 rupees. Just like ASHA workers or *ayahs*, they too were forced to work without any protection. They were not given sanitizers and much later they were given very thin disposable plastic gloves. Some of their colleagues had also contacted the virus, while collecting waste from the patients' households, some of whom had hidden about their disease fearing ostracization from the society. Already vulnerable due to their class and caste positions, the pandemic just increased their vulnerabilities and it was not before the early half of 2021 that all of them were completely vaccinated. It needs to be mentioned here that all the *safaikarmacharis*

[7] See https://www.ilo.org/wcmsp5/groups/public/---dgreports/---dcomm/---publ/documents/publication/wcms_172572.pdf.

[8] See, The Guidelines of the Ministry of Health and Family Welfare (MoHFW). Accessed 21.08.21.

[9] See, https://www.who.int/news-room/q-a-detail/coronavirus-disease-covid-19-health-and-safety-in-the-workplace.

interviewed work in ward number 31 and 41 of the Bidhannagar Municipal Corporation and are contractual workers, meaning they are not permanent staff, hence they did not want their identities to be disclosed.

Though mentioned to be at 'moderate risk', Delhi Commission for *Safaikarmacharis*, in its report submitted to the Delhi government in mid-2020, stated that 16 sanitation workers had died while on duty (TOI, 4 August 2020). The second wave was worse in which till May, 94 civic sanitation workers had died in Delhi, out of which 49 were sweepers (India Today, 28 May 2021). Apart from Delhi, deaths of *safaikarmacharis* were reported from Himachal Pradesh and Tamil Nadu and no data was maintained by the union government on *safaikarmacharis*, or their death (The Wire, 31 May 2021).

In an interview, activist Naba Dutta, revealed that the Ministry of Health and Pollution Control Board, Government of West Bengal had set a committee, looking into the aspect of waste management following the outbreak of the pandemic. He was one of the members of that committee, and he had shared his experience, which is important to understand the high amount of risk, the administration society had put them into. The committee discovered that despite dumping sites being earmarked by the administration, most of the times, strict adherence to rules was absent. On visiting dumping sites, the members had discovered that not even the managers, managing the *safaikarmacharis*, wore masks, gloves or took other precautions. Earlier, during normal times, there were designated dumping sites where household wastes were collected. But with the onset of the pandemic, dumping areas for bio-medical waste even in residential areas were set up. The segregation of waste into yellow, green and black bags, wherein bio-medical waste was discarded in only yellow bags, was not followed in most of the cases. Though the committee, reported the severity of the problem, posed by the mismanagement of bio-medical waste during the pandemic, the format of the inquiry was such that, there was no place for addressing the issue of workers or *safaikarmacharis*. The level of mismanagement was such that in most of the places, bio-medical waste, COVID waste and municipal waste were dumped in same sites, making segregation for the *safai* workers even more difficult and more risky.[10]

10.2 Observations

10.2.1 The Burden of Double Work

Several studies have shown that despite the fact women's mobility for work has significantly increased over the years, yet their responsibilities for household work and care work remain unchanged, often forced them to discontinue formal employment. This claim has been true for both the ayahs and ASHA workers, whose work

[10] Interview conducted on 5.10.21.

during pandemic had increased manifold. Of 25 ASHAs interviewed for the study, about 95% responded that the entire responsibility of household chores rested with them. Same sentiment was expressed by the *ayahs*. Though few of them had an elder daughter or a female family member at home, to help them with the daily chores, bulk of the responsibility was still with them. For both Ayahs and ASHA workers, days start really early, at 4 am or 5 am, daily chores (almost compulsory for most of the women interviewed) include preparing the day's meal, washing the previous day's utensils, helping the children with their study, etc. About 10% of respondents shared their husbands or son helped them in domestic work. The COVID time has added another component of washing their clothes every time they return homes, even at odd hours.

Rabia Sultana (name changed to respect anonymity), aged 35, have been working as ASHA in South 24 Parganas for the last ten years, couldn't recollect when she had taken time off, both from her routine works and household chores. Her situation is further complicated because her husband is a person with disabilities, the burden of 'care work' has stressed her both physically and mentally. She can't think of leaving the job as the main bread earner of the family. Like Rabia, many ASHAs have also accepted the tedious household work as their fate. Even during the normal times, their 'care work' continues in the field with a visit to at least 30–40 families.

During the COVID-19 pandemic, they have been tasked with the arduous work of combating the disease through a wide range of interventions. To contain the further spread of the deadly virus, they were deployed to detect any of the symptoms developed among the individual in her intervention area. This entails a mandatory visit to each household every day during the peak of the pandemic, and if she found any potential virus affected person, she will mobilize for timely testing of the person, and necessary support if the person is found positive, etc. In West Bengal, a door-to-door survey by ASHA on the status of co-morbidities in rural areas was conducted across the state, and similar works were conducted in urban areas too by health workers.

Centers providing services of *ayah mashis* had made a rule that an ayah had to work both shifts for three consecutive days, minimum if they were to find work. This was done to avoid contamination, plus the generic lockdown, made the claims of the centers, logical. This meant that these women could not return home for three consecutive days. Many of these women are the only adult member in their households and they had to ask for favour from neighbours or other family members to look after their children at night as many of them did not live in 'bhadra paras' (respectable areas).

10.2.2 Friends Turning Foes/Strangers During Pandemic

ASHA had faced challenges in the initial years especially regarding family planning, immunization and institutional delivery, etc. The opposition to ASHA's work used to come from male, older women and religious leaders. Even some families had threatened with the dire consequences while ASHA tried to convince an underage bride to use contraceptive methods for delaying the pregnancy. Over the years, ASHA has bridged the trust—deficit and earned a respectful position in society. Most of our respondents shared that they had developed a bonding with the women of their intervention area because of their intensive engagement in the field.

However, the onset of the pandemic has unsettled the hard-earned respect and dignity of the ASHA workers. A series of the newspaper reported the sporadic attack on the frontline workers across the country, respondents in our study also confirm the similar experiences. When many of us had locked ourselves up safely in our houses, ASHAs were mandated to visit at least 25 households every day and were viewed as a potential carrier of the deadly virus, ASHA workers found many families shut their doors during the mandatory visits.

The ayahs due to their nature of the work, are perceived to be 'dirty'. However, they are respected in their family and in their locality as they bring food to the table. However, the image of being 'dirty', coupled with the pandemic made it difficult for them to even live in their homes. As mentioned before, they had to live in hospital premises or in their relatives' home if they wanted to continue working. However, *safaikarmacharis* did not report experiencing such levels of ostracization as mainly they lived in ghettoes or areas where the neighbours were also associated with similar type of job.

10.2.3 Dearth of Protective Gears

During the initial days of the first wave, without adequate protective gear, all the three categories of workers studied for this project, continued to work, at times leading from the front (in case of ASHA workers) to tackle the virus. Proper masks were not given to *either ayah mashis* or the *safaikarmacharis.* In the initial days they wore masks that are meant to prevent dust allergy. Even when ayahs were allowed to function in maternity wards of several government hospitals, no PPE kit or face shields, or gloves were given to them. A few of the *safaikarmacharis* interviewed revealed that they were given gloves made of thin plastic and then that was too discontinued. Just as the authority, the ones supervising these workers did not have any idea as to what type of masks were to be worn, etc.

The sudden announcement of a national-wide lockdown spurred an excruciating journey of migrant's workers from cities to their native places in rural areas. To curb the spread of the virus, makeshift quarantine centres were stepped in villages where the migrants' workers put up for a mandatory quarantine period of 14 days. During the peak of the pandemic, ASHAs had received numerous frantic phone calls, asking for immediate intervention. An ASHA worker in Howrah narrated the nightmare at the makeshift quarantine centres. As the number of migrant labours poured in, it was extremely difficult for three ASHA workers to manage over 350 young adults aged between 18 and 45 years. These migrants had already undergone a long and arduous journey, reached close to their homes, but they could not go home because of the government's restriction. As they found ASHA workers as the face of the government, all their accumulated anger was directed to the ASHA workers for insufficient food and other support available at the centre.

The Government of India has acknowledged the increasing hostilities towards ASHA. The notification dated 3rd April 2021 noted 'incidents of misbehaviour, mishandling and violence against ASHAs have been reported in some places. ASHAs being the key and valuable members of our health system need to be protected against any such incident'. As mentioned earlier also, the Ministry of Health and Family Welfare has acknowledged them as important assets in our health system.

10.2.4 Dearth of Any Training

Our study found there was hardly any training on COVID for the frontline health workers. They had either gathered information from their immediate supervisors or the popular media like news channels and newspapers. As part of the research, we have found a couple of information, education and communication materials (IEC) materials on COVID that were uploaded onto the National Health Mission's website for the ASHA workers. A brochure titled 'Role of Frontline workers in prevention and Management of Virus', detailed the following messages: (a) about the COVID, (b) how its spread, (c) how frontline workers can prevent the spread of the corona, (d) measures for the protection of frontline health workers and (e) myth versus reality. We have checked with our respondents whether they were aware of such communication and training materials, they unanimously said "No".

Amader training dewar shomoy kothay? [Who has time to train us?]. This was the reply of a safai karmi when asked if they were given any training as to what was to be done during the pandemic. Interestingly, they reported that though collected COVID waste separately, it all got mixed up at the local dumping stations, implying that whoever was segregating them at the next level was more at risk of contamination. Similarly, the *ayahs*, received no training from their respective placement centers or any non-governmental organizations as to how they should protect themselves while caring for patients, during the pandemic.

10.3 In Lieu of Conclusion

The ongoing COVID19 pandemic suddenly made an otherwise invisible workforce, 'visible'. From looking after the returnee migrants, to taking care of the patients at home to keeping the community clean, these three categories of workers grabbed attention of media, government and common people. Pandemic has got them recognition, but to what extent their social status would change (or not), only time can tell. Second, in pandemic situation, when boundaries were drawn and re-drawn to protect communities from the "other" (infected bodies), the idea of stigma played a dominant role. Needless to say, that due to the nature of work these workers did, specially, for *ayahs* and *safaikarmacharis*, there exists a certain level of stigma. It is difficult to say as of now if after going through a pandemic, the problem of stigma has been overcome for these categories of workers.

References

BehanBox. (2020). ASHA workers criminalised for fighting for their rights. Available at https://behanbox.com/2020/10/21/3-states-wage-war-against-indias-corona-warriors/. Last accessed October 21, 2021.

Bergmann, M., & Wagner, M. (2021). The impact of COVID-19 on informal caregiving and care receiving across Europe during the first phase of the pandemic. *Frontiers in Public Health.* https://doi.org/10.3389/fpubh.2021.673874

Chang, E. Y. Y. (2020). Informal home care providers: The forgotten health-care workers during the COVID-19 pandemic. *The Lancet, 395*(10242), 1957–1959.

Deshpande, A., & Ramachandran, R. (2020). Is COVID-19 "The Great Leveler"? The critical role of social identity in lockdown-induced job losses, discussion series in economics, no. 34. Ashoka University.

Dutta, A., et al. (2011). *Hospital efficiency in West Bengal: A study on secondary level hospitals.* Department of Health and Family Welfare, Government of West Bengal. Available at https://www.wbhealth.gov.in/uploaded_files/notice/summary.pdf. Last accessed August 21, 2023.

Kesar, S., Abraham, R., Lahoti, R., Nath, P., & Basole, A. (2020). Pandemic, informality, and vulnerability: Impact of COVID-19 on livelihoods in India. CSE working paper 2020-01. Azim Premji University, June 2020.

Leiblfinger, M., Prieler, V., Schwiter, K., Steiner, J., Benazha, A., & Lutz, H. (2020). Impact of COVID-19 policy responses on live-in care workers in Austria, Germany, and Switzerland. *Journal of Long-Term Care,* 144–150.https://doi.org/10.31389/jltc.51

Rao, K. S. (2016). *Do we care? India's health system.* Oxford University Press.

Sharma, D. C. (2015). India still struggles with rural doctor shortages. *The Lancet, 386*(10011), 2381–2382.

Sreerekha, M. S. (2017). *State without honour: Women workers in India's Anganwadis.* Oxford University Press.

Swaminathan, P. (2015). The formal creation of informality, and therefore, gender injustice: Illustrations from India's social sector. *Indian Journal of Labour Economics, 58*(1), 23–42.

UNDP. (2020). COVID-19 and health system vulnerabilities in the poorest developing countries. Transition Series, UNDP Global Policy Network Brief—HEALTH. Available at https://www.undp.org/sites/g/files/zskgke326/files/publications/undp-gpn-transitions-series-health-COVID-19_and_Health_System_Vulnerabilities_EN.pdf. Last accessed August 21, 2023.

WEIGO, UNICEF and ILO. (2021). Family-friendly policies for workers in the informal economy: Protecting and ensuring social protection and care systems for all children and families in the context of COVID-19 and beyond. Available at https://www.unicef.org/media/102821/file/Family-Friendly%20Policies%20for%20Workers%20in%20the%20Informal%20Economy%20.pdf. Last accessed July 21, 2023.

Part IV
Literature and the Literary World

Chapter 11
Coronavirus and Other Epidemics in Bengal: A Reckoning Through Literature

Samata Biswas

Abstract This chapter, divided in three sections, attempts an overview of the contemporary literary productions in Bengali, in the wake of the Covid 19 pandemic and the ensuing lockdown. It also attempts to describe late 19th- and early 20th-century Bengali literature's engagement with multiple epidemics that had devastated the Bengali countryside: malaria, cholera, smallpox, etc. The repeated waves of pandemics and their representation in Bengali literature were integral in the construction of the Bengali realist novel, creating a space of ferment which allowed for reconstruction of society, reconsideration of social divisions and consolidation of social work as an extension of nationalist activities. This second section enquires in some detail about these texts, ranging from Bankim Chandra Chattopadhyay's *Anandamath* to Sarat Chandra Chatopadhyay's *Srikanta*, from Bibhuti Bhushan Bandyopadhyay's *Aranyak* to Banaphul's *Jangam*. The third section of the paper analyzes the construction of an alternate society through Tarasankar Bandyopadhyay's social realist novels, written and set in the 1920s and 30s, in rural Bengal and in Calcutta. Most of his novels like *Ganadebata, Dhatridebata,* etc., reckon with a society in flux, dealing on one hand with colonialism, on the other, with the gradual transformation in traditional societies, the destabilization of existing hierarchies and creation of new ones. In each of these moments of epidemiological crisis, the novels also recognize extraordinary characters, individuals who had been pushed to the margins of traditional society. In moments of crisis, they transcend their marginalities through agentive action and empathy. Their action in the course of the novels, become crucial in framing the post-pandemic social relations.

Keywords Bengali literature · Epidemics · Bankim Chandra Chattopadhyay · Sarat Chandra Chattopadhyay · Bibhuti Bhushan Bandyopadhyay · Tarasankar Bandyopadhyay

---

S. Biswas (✉)
Department of English, The Sanskrit College and University & MCRG, Kolkata, India
e-mail: bsamata@gmail.com; samata.eng@sanskritcollegeanduniversity.ac.in

S. R. Chakraborty et al. (eds.), *The Long 2020*, India Studies in Business and Economics, https://doi.org/10.1007/978-981-99-4815-4_11

11.1 Introduction

For many of us, 2020 was a moment of resonances, resonances that went well beyond the formal limits of 2020. In India, and perhaps the world over, the fear and spread of the Covid 19 pandemic could not be separated from the drastic and draconian lockdown and distancing measures. For many of us, these were unprecedented experiences, experiences that needed to be made sense of, through parallels and comparisons, in facts and in fiction. Resonance with partition refugees (Biswas, 2021) and the Bengal famine (Gangopadhyay, 2020), with the walk of the migrant workers and the memories of Plague in Surat, during our[1] lifetimes. Then there were resonances with images that did not come to us through documentation, but had been prolific in popular culture. I remember reading and being told, in childhood, stories of a man, sometimes a stranger, at other times, a son or a son in law returning to the village. A helpful villager, or his mother, or his wife, cooks for him. When he asks for a lemon, or a pepper—this person stretches her arm outside the house and plucks one. In other narrations, they stick their feet inside the hearth to make it burn brighter. The stranger or the son or the son in law escapes this village of the dead, to be told in the next town that they all died in a pestilence, a *morok*. In an article on epidemics in Bangla literature, published in the *Anandabazar Patrika* on April 2020, Anirban Mukhopadhyay mentions this narrative, calling it an 'oral lore' (Mukhopadhyay, 2020a, 2020b). As a child, I of course did not think much about this narrative, but the present moment forces me to note that the narrative may have been written at the time of what Chinmay Tumbe calls, in his quickly written *History of Pandemics*, the 'semi-permanent, male-dominated, remittance-based Great Indian Migration Wave that took off in the nineteenth century' (Tumbe, 2020). The son or the son in law, being absent for a long time, makes sense in the context of this—as it also does when we remember the repeated bouts of malaria, cholera and pox that ravaged the Bengal country side, and parts of India. David Arnold argues that like all epidemics, cholera attacked entire communities, meriting different kinds of collective response (Arnold, 1986: 119). The First Cholera Epidemic of 1817–1821 was followed by periodical bouts (Harrison, 2020), with estimates ranging up to the death of 1.75 out of every 1000 of the population of British India, dying from cholera, 1870s onwards (Arnold, 1986: 122). Much of colonial writing directed at malaria produced an environmental discourse that considered Bengal to be "intimately connected with the diurnal changes of temperature", in short, endemic (Mukherjee, 2008). Arabinda Samanta considers small pox to have all along been 'a general disease in India', with the first historically recorded virulence dating back to Assam in 1574 (Samanta, 2012). Such recurrent and frequent epidemics, have left their marks in popular and folk culture, the ghost tale I remember, is merely one such.

[1] By "our" the author here means herself and people around her own age, she is now 40 years old.

In the same article Mukhopadhyay also furthers the hope that like the Corona time poems[2] already circulating over social media—literature would also record the present pandemic.

> We cannot let the memory of epidemics be lost. It will be required at the time of some other epidemic. Our experiences will have to be matched. Times will change. But literature will remind us of the change of epochs.[3]

Following this invocation of literature that records and reminds the readers of the change of epochs, the first section of this article enquires into existing and ongoing literary creation in Bengali, during the current pandemic and series of lockdowns.

11.2 Early Tracts of Corona-Kal

Among the many different things a student of Literatures in English learns during her undergraduate studies, is the role of the diarists such as Samuel Pepys (1633–1703) in the growth of the everyday English prose in the seventeenth century.[4] For the reader living through the Covid 19 pandemic, Pepys is also important for recording his impressions and experiences of the Great Plague of London (1665). In the diary Pepys records his fear of seeing the red crosses marking the houses under quarantine in London, his obsession with the daily number of deaths (much like us, almost 400 years later), the night curfew, the procession of dead bodies he barely noticed, and eventually, relief when the playhouses finally opened for the public (Bowyer, 2020). Between 1665 and 2020, the nature of media and the modes of circulation of literary content have changed beyond recognition. Pepys's memoirs were published in 1825, although he wrote them between 1660 and 1669 (Pepys, 1825). As soon as the first lockdown was abruptly announced in India on the evening of 24 March 2020 (Press Information Bureau, 2020), many people took to social media platforms (for those writing in Bengali in West Bengal, primarily on Facebook and on Whatsapp) to express their feelings, confusion, but also to record the extraordinary time they were witnessing. The times were also marked by the writers' relative position of privilege and comfort, they could stay indoors and watch on television the gradual and painful walk of returnee migrant workers across the plains of India (Siddiqi,

[2] Mukhopadhyay does not give instances of these poems, but during the first lockdown of 2020, Bengali social media sphere (primarily Facebook and Whatsapp) was filled with parodies and new poems, about the present crisis. Bengali e-zine *Guruchandali*, among others, published some poems as well, here's a couple from Sridarshini Chakkraborty: https://www.guruchandali.com/comment.php?topic=19439&srchtxt=%E0%A6%95%E0%A6%B0%E0%A7%8B%E0%A6%A8%E0%A6%BE.

[3] https://www.anandabazar.com/editorial/coronavirus-epidemics-and-pandemics-in-bengali-literature-dgtlx-1.1133067. Accessed on 27 August 202. Translation by the author, unless otherwise specified.

[4] Samuel Pepys was a 17th-century naval administrator and Member of Parliament, based in London, England. He kept an on and off record of his days between 1660 and 1669. The diaries entries may be read at www.pepysdiary.com.

2020). Not surprisingly, the daily notes, impressions and observations carried names such as "dinolipi" (records of everyday), "rojnamcha" (daily chronicles), etc. They were soon collated and published in the print format, one of the first among them being *Lockdowner Dinolipi*, edited by Abir Mukhopadhyay (Mukhopadhyay, 2020a) . The Bengali word "dinolipi" translates into a diary, a record of day-to-day events, much like the one Pepys kept. In his preface to the edition, titled "Lockdownunlock", the editor considers artistic, literary and musical activity to be connecting people with one another, despite physical distancing measures (10).

This was followed by publications such as *Coronar Korcha: Mahamarir Aloandharite Banglar Mukhochhobi* (Corona Chronicles: The Face of Bengal in the Pandemic Chiaroscuro) (Mukhopadhyay, 2022a) which includes forty-five articles by people from different walks of life, collated by an academic who lost her doctor father during to the pandemic. *Coronar Korcha* is divided in eight sections, dealing, respectively, with health, education, socio-economic considerations, the dispossessed, middle-class luxuries, psychological issues, entertainment and songs of life. *Coronar Jibonsonkot o Chetonar Bish- Ekush (Corona Crisis of Life: The Twenty-Twenty first Sensibility)* is a collection of Facebook posts by Arup Kumar Das, written between 25th March 2020 and 16th October 2021 (Das, 2021). Arka Deb's *Asukhi Somoyer Brittanto: Sashoker Asuyar Birudhhe Likhito Nibondhho* (*Accounts of a Diseased Epoch*) is a collection of his articles published in "alternative mass media (gonomadhyom)"[5] during the pandemic. Deb recognizes the importance of bringing together these chronicles of the time together, written as immediate impressions and responses to deepening political and social crises during the pandemic (Deb, 2022). Renowned physician and public intellectual Sthabir Dasgupta's columns and interviews between April 2020 and August 2021 were collated and published in the volume *Corona Covid Nostoka*l (The Wasted Corona Covid Epoch) (Dasgupta, 2022), where Dasgupta comments on the possible difficulty in creating literature and art during the pandemic—each requiring a sense of stability, unavailable in the uncertain times (64). Anindya Jana's *Lockdown Diary* (Jana, 2022) (the English word diary transcribed in Bengali letters) is literally the printed version of his lockdown diary. The six books discussed above testify that the unprecedented experiences of the current pandemic, needed newer modes of expressions, in keeping with the rapid inroads made by digitized mediascape, enforced physical isolation and the long-term shutting down of publishing houses and printers. Although many of the initial responses to the pandemic and the lockdown bear names like "dinalipi", "rojnamcha". "dinkal" and "akhyan", in the mode of their circulation, even prior to their eventual collation and publication in printed volumes, they were meant for public consumption—being written in and often, for, social media. Journalist Swati Bhattacharjee's Facebook posts titled "Corona-r Songlap" (Corona Conversations) were collated by Guruchandali in one webpage, these short conversations are dispatches from the field, chronicling the layers of marginalization, hunger, poverty and disempowerment at the borders of the epidemic (Bhattacharya, 2020; Bhattacharjee, 2020).

[5] Although not explained by Deb, the articles in the collection had all first appeared on different Bengali language websites and e-zines.

Manjira Saha collated and published the different columns she wrote in newspapers and periodicals, about Bengali migrant workers, in *Labour Train* (Saha, 2020). The perceived need of these chronicles, these tracts of the time seems to have been to place on record, as well as to share, the tumult of the Long 2020.

I actively used social media and my location on College Street (the hub of Bengali booksellers, publishers and printers in Calcutta) to track the volumes mentioned above, as well as the stories and novels about Corona-*kal* I will now discuss (*Kal*, in Bengali, Hindi and Sanskrit, means time, as well as age/epoch. This is a new coinage in both Hindi and Bengali, to signify the intertwining of this time with the pandemic. I find the coinage to be very apt.) In both cases, the 100,000 strong Facebook group "Molat" (the Bengali word molat means a book jacket) has been invaluable. There, I asked for recommendations about fictional and non-fictional work related to Covid 19, as well as about representation of earlier pandemics in Bengali literature, and received numerous suggestions. Some of these suggestions were followed up on.

Krishnendu Mukhopadhyay's short story "Picnic" (Mukhopadhyay, 2022b) (the English word transcribed in Bengali) describes a get together of friends and their spouses, seemingly after the easing of lockdown restrictions. Each have their share of anxiety, with cut backs at work, job losses and feelings of alienation from the rest of society. At the end of the story the readers discover that the picnic was virtual, with friends eating home delivered food in front of their computers, together. This story flags a recurrent concern we can identity in the Bengali literature of Corona-kal, loneliness and isolation. Samaresh Majumdar's novella "Abagunthan" (Veil) (Majumdar, 2021) is written as a chronological exploration of the way the Covid 19 pandemic took over Bengali middle- and upper-class life in Calcutta. The narrative centres around an ageing doctor and his ailing wife, shifting between the lives of other characters connected with them. The initial unconcern makes way for confusion, panic, disease, till the crisis mounts by creating unbreachable boundaries between people, even those who live under the same roof. *Lockdowner Golpo* (Chakraborty & Roy, 2022) (Stories of Lockdown), a collection of sixteen stories by eight authors continue in the same vein—a result of the editors' desire to chronicle the present time from their position of relative privilege, collectively. Facebook rekindled forgotten friendships, and made collaboration possible in separation (8–10). Despite their marked middle-class bias and concentration on (mostly) heterosexual romance, some stories concern themselves with the returnee migrant workers and the poor. In the striking first story of the collection, domestic worker Tumpa waits for her partner, migrant worker Biju. Biju's return is marked by calamity, his eyes start to bleed from the insecticide the police spray on him. Tumpa ties Biju to the cycle rickshaw she had purchased for Biju's return and drives to the hospital, breaking the curfew and multiple taboos. In Abu Taher's story "Porijayi" (Taher, 2021) (Migrant) Snigdha, like Tumpa, defies the lockdown to reunite with her estranged parents. Lockdown and middle-class fear are breached also in Sayantani Putatunda's story "Bheetu Mānush/ (The/A) Scared Human".[6] The central character, Suresh, living in an affluent multi-storeyed building, watches helplessly as one by one his neighbours die from Covid 19, each

[6] Except otherwise mentioned, all translations are mine.

time preceded by heart rending cries from the stray neighbourhood dog. Through this ageing man's hypochondria and fear of contagion, the gradual alienation of the individual, although here that's a result more of the epidemic, and less of modernity—and the final refusal of his son to be cowed down by fear and his determination to help others—Putatunda attempts a threefold commentary: middle-class precarity in neoliberal regimes, the loneliness of age and the loneliness of the epidemic.

Between October 2020 and July 2021, Anirudhha Chakraborti published half a dozen stories in the Bengali e-zines *Guruchandali* and *4 Number Platform*. Each of his stories are narrated by an unnamed narrator, commenting on the isolation and misery of people during the lockdown as well as the regeneration of nature as a result of it. I will discuss four of his stories here. In "Ganganadir Premik" (Ganga Lover) (Chakraborti, 2021b) an aged and ailing grandmother longs to visit the river of her youth. A longtime Bihari migrant brings her water to bathe in, everyday, and stories to survive on. The grandmother was physically isolated even before the pandemic, her condition acting as a metonymy for that of the rest of the society, Bhushankumar's (the migrant from Bihar) stories becoming the stories the readers must create to survive the Corona-kal. "Hemanter Pakhi" (Autumn Bird) (Chakraborti, 2021c) and its sequel "Coronakale" (Chakraborti, 2021a) (During Covid Times) take the unnamed narrator to a Bihari settlement near a highway in search of a masked woman he had met in his daily commute during the pandemic. He never saw her face, since following Covid protocols, it was always masked. While this mysterious woman cannot be located, the narrator gets drawn in the difficult life of the migrants during lockdown, and the crops that grow despite the diseased Earth. "Lockdowner Jytosnay" (Chakraborti, 2020) (Under the Lockdown Moon) contain the full range of Chakraborti's concerns in the corona times: the plight of the migrant workers, the receding of the Anthropocene and the return of natural beings and the solidarity of the marginalized to resolve an imminent crisis. In it, a migrant worker tries to return home to Bihar to cremate her dead husband's body. She had been stranded in the brick kiln where she was employed, forced to leave with her group after the owner stopped paying them their wages. On the way she gets separated from her group. The swineherd and his group of marijuana smokers, find her shelter and food. In the morning she flies away with a group of migratory birds which may or may not have been a figment of the swineherd's imagination.

Basundharar Nabojagaran (Tarafdar Majumdar, 2020) (Earth's Reawakening) by Shipra Tarafdar Majumdar has the same chronological structure we discussed in Samaresh Majumdar's novella (although Tarafdar Majumdar precedes him by a year). But here, the lives the readers follow are marked by their poverty and their marginalization. Ramu loses his wife while trying to walk back from Delhi with her and his young son, while his closest friend Akbar is helped by a childless couple, who shelter them and nurse their daughter back to health. In the introduction to the novella, the author expresses her hope for that new time when people would once again help each other, irrespective of their differences and identities. In the novella, such hope is embodied in the person of Bhola. When Ramu and his son Biswa are refused accommodation in the ancestral village they return to, Bhola takes them home. "This is that same Bhola, who none of the neighbours liked. None of the boys would be friends with him" (Tarafdar Majumdar, 2020). He who was the designated lumpen in the village, sheltered and fed Ramu and Biswa, in between roaming around different villages, helping in aid distribution.

In the following two sections, I take forward the tone set by "Lockdowner Jyotsnay" and *Basundharar Nabajagaran*. Both of these narratives locate the social outcaste as the agent of social change. I will first attempt an overview of epidemics in Bengali literature—which treated epidemics as a part of quotidian life. Similar to the trope identified above, I will explore those figures who emerge as exceptional, in their care and humanity in times of epidemiological crisis. In the final section, I shall enquire closely at the novels of Tarasankar Bandyopadhyay, and his creation of what Pradyumna Bhattacharya calls "koumo" (Bhattacharya, 2014). community, which contain both the enlightened dominant caste male and the village drunkard, the sexually active woman and other figures from the margins.

11.3 Everyday Epidemics in Bengali Fiction

Another resonance, brought home in 2021, when we watched images of pyres burning endlessly, shallow graves around river banks and dead bodies floating down the river—is discussed by Shekhar Bhoumik in his article of 16th March 2021, in the Sunday supplement of Anandabazar Patrika (Bhowmik, 2021). He draws parallels from 19th- and 20th-century newspaper reports, such as *Sanbada Purnochandradwoy* from 1869 or *Upasana* in 1907, of a young girl abandoned by their mother once she starts to show symptoms, or the difficulty pilgrims face when returning from Puri—because of the number of rotting and smelly bodies on the road. He also draws on memoirs of Dineshchandra Sen, Fanny Parks, Nabinchandra Sen, Suniti Chattopadhyay, etc. There are two fictional narratives that he refers to, Trailokyanath's novel *Bhoyanok Angti* (Terrible ring?) and Albert Camus' *The Plague*. But the Camus reference invokes a certain kind of wishful thinking for a happy resolution.

A similar description is present in the third chapter of Sarat Chandra Chattopadhyay's novel *Srikānta*, published in four parts between 1917 and 1933. Child Srikanta, fishing in the middle of the night with his friend Indranath, intermittently smells something foul with every waft of wind, increasing in intensity as they push forward. Indrananth, older, wiser, tells him that these smells are from the dead bodies killed by cholera. Their family members haven't managed to cremate the bodies, they merely touch the dead faces with fire, and leave them behind to rot, for dogs and jackals to eat. Srikanta also spots the body of a healthy, fair boy about 6–7 years old—perhaps interrupted in the process of being pulled away by predators (Dash, 2020: 273–300). However, this is not a source that Bhaumik draws on.

It is crucial to note that Anirban Mukhopadhyay and Shekhar Bhaumik use two different kinds of sources, the first narrative and fictional—the second, documentary, news. But these two different sources are utilized to the same end, to learn about the past, and to learn from the past. This is a distinction I will bypass for the time being, since like any other literary and cultural studies researcher, I do not read fictional texts for information, but for representational politics, textual and intertextual practices and fictional resolutions. For us, texts are both source and discourse, describing as well as constructing the objects and the subjects.

Daniel Defoe's *A Journal of the Plague Year* is perhaps the only full-length account of the year 1665, the Great Plague of London, but published in 1722. Defoe was only 5-year-old when the Great Plague happened, and this is believed to have been based on his uncle Henry Foe's journals. In John Dryden's long poem, *Annus Mirabillis*—Dryden only comments on the year of wonder that saved London from greater calamities—despite a plague and a fire killing one third of its population.

This brings me to a nagging question that seemed to puzzle readers in literature and culture quite a lot: a question about plague and Shakespeare. Shakespeare wrote during the time of repeated plague outbreaks, in 1582, 1592, 1603, 1606, 1608–09. But in his works Plague occurs as a reference—and increasingly, we will witness, in England and in much of the anglophone world the trend continues. Important literary genres of the time do not directly treat the epidemic they are living through, epidemics occur as reference points—as metaphors and other figures of speech. Defoe, not surprisingly, is writing after many years of the Great Plague. Something similar can be seen in the nineteenth and twentieth centuries, in the case of the cholera and influenza epidemics. Although not Anglophone in nature, Camus's *The Plague* does tackle an epidemic front and centre, but the historical reality of its composition was the influenza epidemic, not the Plague. Katharine Ann Porter's *Pale Horse Pale Rider*, a semi-autobiographical narrative about the time the author suffered from influenza, while working as a reporter, is published twenty years afterwards, but is a notable exception.

For Anglophone literature, the reason might be what Amitav Ghosh calls in *The Great Derangement*, the rise of gradualism in Western societies (19–20) (Ghosh, 2016). Although Ghosh is writing in the context of ecological catastrophe and literature, it is by now very well-established that epidemics are part of our ecological world, and the graver the risks to climate, the more frequent they get to be. Gradualism indicates that change happens in slow motion, almost imperceptibly—an attitude in geology that then became more and more prevalent in natural and eventually human sciences. Ghosh claims that in the great realist novels of the nineteenth century (of which Daniel Defoe's *Journal of the Plague Year* was a precursor) are a prey to this gradualism, where catastrophes occur, but only human ones—not natural. In fact, the rise of realism is connected to the overarching umbrella of gradualism. Where do the natural calamities, the infectious diseases, the extinction of species go then? They are shunted into the realm of science fiction (think Stephen King), of horror (think Mary Shelley's *The Last Man*) and magic realism (think Gabriel Garcia Marquez, *Love in the Time of Cholera* and Jose Saramago, *Blindness*).

Ghosh draws upon Bankim Chandra Chattopadhyay to show him to also categorize catastrophism as un-modern, as "banishing the improbable" and instead, insisting on "insert[ing] the everyday" (Ghosh, 2016: 17). Supriya Chaudhury locates the rise of the Bengali novel in the nineteenth century centrally at the intersection of English historical romances and sensational novels (such as those by Walter Scott, Charles Dickens, Benjamin Disraeli and G. W. M. Reynolds) and traditional story telling practices (Chaudhury, 2012). Despite Bankim's disavowal of the improbable, the presence of epidemics in his and in other Bengali novels must be a testimony to the many epidemics and pandemics that Bengal lived through, an everydayness of its existence, despite the horror and misery associated with them. This everydayness ensured that epidemiological catastrophes, epidemics, were frequently present in Bangla prose fiction, sometimes precipitating a change of epochs.

Bankim's own *Anandamath* (1882) is not an exception. In the first chapter of the novel, the readers are informed about the predecessors to the current epidemic: heatwave, famine, crop failure, taxation and famine, followed by diseases. Bankim writes:

> Disease found her time. Fever, cholera, tuberculosis, pox. Especially pox became virulent. In every home, people started dying from pox. Who will give others water, who will touch others. Who's there to offer treatment to the other, to care for the other, to dispose of the dead bodies. The most beautiful bodies rot unto themselves inside mansions. If pox enters a home once, its occupants run away, leaving the patient behind. (Chattopadhyay, 2022: 15)

The epidemic is the immediate cause that leads to rich landlord Mahendra Sinha's displacement from his village, with his wife and young daughter—which in turn leads to his participation in the militant Sanyasi rebellion. In Bangla literature, epidemics range from stray references to direct cause behind social and structural change, provide impetus to action and create a backdrop of misery and suffering.

From Rabindranath Tagore's *Gora* (1910) (Tagore, 1940) where the conservative Hindu Harimohini recounts the death of her husband and son from cholera, only four days apart; to *Chaturanga* (1916) where wealthy householder Harimohan moves himself and his family from Calcutta to Kalna (Tagore, 1905; Ghosh, 2020: 305), having witnessed the onset of cholera in the neighbourhood and the refusal of the residents to call the doctor, in case they will be removed to the hospital (Mukhopadhyay, 2020b), to Banaful's *Jangam* (published in five volumes between 1943 and 1945) where social worker Sankar watches in helplessness the speed with which Dom and Methar neighbourhoods of the village fall to cholera, eventually reaching the dominant caste neighbourhoods as well, Bangla novels travel the entire gamut of epidemics in the British colony: small pox, cholera, malaria, dengue and plague. In Manik Bandyopadhyay's *Putul Nacher Itikotha* (1935–1936) most of the village suffers from malaria. Sukumar ray's comic short story "Petuk", invokes the menace of rats and plague to teach young glutton Haripada a lesson. In Tagore's short story "Malyadan", Kurani, suffering from heartbreak and hunger is admitted to the plague hospital (Tagore, 1991: 428–436). Sarat Chandra Chattopadhyay's novel *Panditmoshai* declares that it doesn't take long for a woman to be widowed in malaria- and cholera-afflicted Bengal. In his *Sesh Proshno*, Abinash Mukherjee's sister-in-law comes to visit him to recover from malaria. Harendra and Rajendra spend their days helping the ailing residents of the cobbler neighbourhood. All these instances lend credence to my initial claim that in colonial Bengal, epidemiological catastrophes had reached an everyday-proportion, in life as well as in literary representation.

Sarat Chandra Chattopadhyay's proto-nationalist novel *Pather Dabi* (1926) describes two Telugu 'coolies', patients of Pox, being forcibly removed to the hospital by the police, in Burma (Chattopadhyay, 2015: 17–203). Tewari, servant to the protagonist Apurba begs to not be sent away to the hospital, as the hospital is sure to kill him. Bharati nurses both Tewari, and later Apurba back to health. Sarat Chandra's *Srikanta*, in the eponymous hero's epical life, witnesses several epidemics. We have already mentioned the child Srikanta's encounter of those dead from cholera, left behind in riverbanks. In chapter X, Srikanta, now the disciple of a mendicant, takes pity of a generous Bengali man, both of whose children are suffering from small pox. After a month or so, the boys recover, while the disease reaches epidemic proportions. When the family discovers that Srikanta has fever, they hastily abandon him. In book II chapter V, Srikanta has to quarantine for ten days upon reaching Rangoon. In chapter XI he nurses the ailing Manohar Chakraborty, who dies of plague. Srikanta reaches Abhaya's home with raging fever, who nurses him back to health. After the small pox fear, Srikanta was rescued by Piyari aka Rajlakshmi, a courtesan. After the plague scare, he is nursed by Abhaya, abandoned by her husband, for her affinity with another man (Chattopadhyay, 2019: 379–730). Like Abhaya, Bharati of *Pather Dabi* also did not fit the role conservative Hindu society bequeathed upon women. In her revolutionary activities and in her dismissal of the caste system, she, like Abhaya, is an outlier in traditional society. This is a trope I hope to examine in greater detail in Tarasankar: what happens when social security nets collapse, caste hierarchies cannot ensure the mythical purity of endogamy, and disease attacks the body, the site of pollution. Which are the characters who go beyond their traditional roles in society, and how does their intervention, constitute a post-pandemic social? The most famous example of the otherwise undesirable/unsuitable element in society performing crucial functions of care and comfort can be found in Sarat Chandar's Lalu stories, where Lalu is the naughty son of rich parents. Nevertheless, along with Gopalkhuro, Lalu and his friends ensure that those dying by cholera in their town get cremated with due respect. In the third part of Lalu's story, Lalu shelters from the rain in the funeral pyre, under the shroud covering the dead body. Brave Lalu does not abandon the body even in the storm but also does not stop from scaring others by pretending to be a ghost (Chattopadhyay, 2015: 747–749).

In Bibhutibhushan Bandyopadhyay there is also the attempt to locate the causes and victims of epidemics, in the light of available scientific information of that time. *Aranyak* of 1939 and *Jangam*, published in the next decade, record the difficulty in keeping water sources uncontaminated, and the abject poverty and ignorance of exceptionally vulnerable populations that hasten multiple deaths. Sarat Chandra's *Panditmoshai* also narrates Brindaban's futile attempts to stop the villagers from washing clothes and utensils used by diseased persons in the pond designated for potable water (Chattopadhyay, 2019: 141–196).

Modern western novels are characterized by the alienation of the protagonist from their immediate social milieu—in the cases of bildungsroman and küntslerroman, the alienation is even more stark—leading to, at times, a reorganization of the social or a compromise with the social. Satyacharan in *Aranyak*, Sankar in *Jangam*, Srikanta in *Srikanta*—are all protagonists of bildungsromans, coming of age narratives. They are both moved by the suffering of those around them, but in times of epidemiological disasters, they, along with medical practitioners—are the voices of reason, the agential subjects.

11.4 Tarasankar and The Epoch of Epidemics

In the final section of this chapter, I enquire in greater detail, into some of the more well-known works of Tarasankar Bandyopadhyay, easily the most prolific writer in the years immediately after Tagore. Through *Ganadebata*, *Dhatridebata* (1939) and *Arogya Niketan* (1953), *Tarasankar* represents rural Bengal, at the cusp of various transformations: transformation of the relationship between the landlord and the tenant, between the castes and religions, between genders and landholdings, and between the traditional ties to the community and new, nationalist ones. Alok Ray terms him "Kālāntarer Kathākār" "chronicler of the epoch's end" (Ray, 2009)—his contemporary, Amulyadhan Mukhopadhyay considers his novels to bear all the distinguishing features and merits of a modern novel (Mukhopadhyay, 1971: 20). Asitkumar Bandyopadhyay reckons Tarasankar to be acutely conscious of his contemporary society and time: to therefore alter both time and form of the Bangla novel (Mukhopadhyay, 1971: 29). At the same time, Dipendu Chakraborty comments on the limitations of Tarasankar's sense of history, "[his] thoughts about history are incoherent and disjointed" (Chakraborty, 1958: 12). In each of these three novels (the first part of *Ganadebatā*: *Chandimandap* 1942), the cholera epidemic is crucial in consolidating the male protagonist's place in the world he inhabits, and his recognition of that place.

The central character of *Dhatridebatā* is Shibnath, the minor son of a dead landlord. His widowed aunt litigates on his behalf as his guardian, while his mother tries to instill in him a sense of responsibility, as an educated leader of his people, and a responsible landlord. Shibnath is married to Gouri from the neighbourhood—of a family whose earnings are from business, and far more than Shibnath's traditional landholdings can fetch. When cholera strikes the Dom, Bauri and Muchi families of the village, Shibnath is assisted by Sushil and Purna, two medical students from Calcutta. They work throughout the day and night, hydrating ailing people, giving them medicines, disinfecting and also ensuring that the water sources are protected from contamination. Shibnath's wife's family and his aunt want to send him off to Benares, away from any possible harm—but Shibnath is filled with nationalistic zeal, in the company of educated young men like himself, his chants Vandemataram in front of the idol that's worshipped to mitigate the fury of the murdering goddess. Remember, Vandemataram is from *Ãnandamath,* another narrative arising from the crucible of famine and epidemics. They arrange for a magic lantern show to dispel misinformation, collect rice from the neighbourhood to feed the needy and cross the traditional caste boundary to feed the ailing Dom woman.

In *Chandimandap*, Debu Ghosh, teacher of the vernacular school, located in the village square, has spent his entire life learning about the people of the village and its customs—the relationships between different groups and his ability to influence those relationships. Debu is at first unwilling to encourage what the villagers consider the audacity of marginalized professionals like the ironsmith, the potter and the barber. Through his recognition of the communal ownership of the village square where resides the authority of the village, and his ever-increasing friendship with the political detinue Jatin, Debu dedicates his life to the service of his people. When the new year in the month of Baisakh, comes with unmitigated heat and cholera, Debu works tirelessly to give water to the ailing, to cremate the dead—but finally his own wife Bilu and son succumb to the disease.

In *Arogyaniketan* (*The House of Convalescence*)[7] cholera is imagined as skeletal woman, with fiery eyes, wearing soiled saree, carrying a palm-leaf mat, the ones dead bodies are caried on—travelling from village to village in the dusk. Whoever she meets first, dies of cholera. Jeeban Moshai, the ayurvedic doctor in the village, now unsure of his position in the face of allopathic and homeopathic medical practitioners, runs from one hamlet to the other, after the wealthy and the other doctors abandon the villagers to the inevitable. Jeeban Moshai learns to administer certain medicines from old Ranglal doctor—himself an outsider to the caste stratified village society. Ranglal doctor has practiced on dead bodies abandoned by the side of the river, in shallow graves—his constant companion Motu, he who was supposed to have cremated these bodies. Jeeban Moshai circles from village to village, singing the praises and chanting the names of Lord Hari—but also, at the same time, the only help the ailing and the destitute could hope for. In "Popular Response to Epidemics in Colonial Bengal" Chittabrata Palit records instances of the local Kaviraj being the only available help in the Bengal, in the time of an epidemic for cholera cases, the rural practice was abandoning the patient (Palit, 2008: 281). Jeeban Moshai, within the frame of the narrative, goes against this established practice—an act that not only cures patients, but also justifies his name: translated to "life" itself.

In both *Dhatridebata* and *Arogya Niketan*—there are detailed descriptions of the worship of fearsome goddesses. Sitala, the goddess of small pox (Nichols, 1981) and Olabibi/Olaichandi, the goddess of olautha/cholera (Bhattacharya, 2020), are replaced in the novels by the fearsome RakshaKali—the Kali who protects, performing a macabre dance, satiated only with meat and alcohol. Almost all the young Hindus males of the villages participate in these—beyond caste and sectarian beliefs. This violent and virulent goddess, protector from a deadly disease—becomes an occasion for the community to come together.

While in *Dhatridebata*, Shibnath is dissociated from his family, his people and at times, his political colleagues, Debu Ghosh and Jeeban Moshai are the most organic representatives of the communities they are a part of. However, their dissociation

[7] I am using Rajakrishnan V.'s translation of the title, although I do not follow his transcription of Jeeban Moshai as Jeevan Masai, in "Beat from the Territory of the Dead". Rajakrishnan reads the novel as "…portrayal of his protagonist's unending quarrels with himself, and his reactions to the people and the events that crowded into the final phase of his life spanning almost six months" (180). This novel is "the epic realization of the autumnal despair" the likes of which Rajakrishnan identifies in epic fictional characters like Shakespeare's King Lear, Herman Broch's Virgil in *The Death of Virgil* or master builder Solnes in Ibsen's *The Master Builder*.

takes place through the change in the community, in the structure of society, in the redrawing of relations between castes, communities, professions and landowners and farmers. Unlike Srikanta, Sankar or Satyacharan, who are perpetual outsiders to the contexts they find themselves in, Shibnath, Jeeban Moshai and Debu Ghosh are parts of their own communities. They might come in contact with other, enlightened urban characters: Sushil and Purna, Pradyot doctor and Ronglal doctor, detinue Jatin, respectively—but their participation in the life of the community, especially in the time of epidemiological crisis, reconfigures the community, with themselves at its centre.

I argue, that this reconfiguration is perhaps a more democratic one. Because, in each of these flashpoints of epidemiological crisis, the reader encounters other figures from the margins, who also carry out crucial functions. In *Dhatridebata*, the village lunatic takes charge of cremating three dead bodies. He asks Shibnath money for marijuana, participates in the RakshaKali worship (organized to defeat the epidemic) and argues that there's no worship without meat and alcohol (79–89). In *Arogya Niketan* when all the wealthy people abandoned the village in search of a safer place, the only people left behind were the poor and the brave. Of the brave, most were drunks and potheads. They would drink, smoke up and sit around in a constant daze. Motu, Ronglal's helper—would ensure that he did not lack dead bodies to practice on. In *Chandimandap*, disgraced drunk drummer, Patu Bayen, whose primary income is working as a pimp to his sister, overcomes his fear to take away the Bauri dead bodies to the river. Durga, shunned by most of the village due to her licentiousness and her independence, to me is the most admirable character in both *Chandimandap* and its second part, *Panchagrām*—helping the helpless and the protagonist, using her wits, her body and her intellect.

If epidemiological catastrophe eventually makes away for a different kind of community—what would be the place of these marginal characters in that new community? At the end of *Panchagram*, full of nationalist zeal and the promise of the civil disobedience movement, there is the imaginative rendering of such a world—a world without hell, without big or small, without the division between the pure and the polluted, the untouchable. Arundhati Roy's popular essay, "Pandemic is a Portal" asserts

> Historically, pandemics have forced humans to break with the past and imagine their world anew. This one is no different. It is a portal, a gateway between one world and the next.
>
> We can choose to walk through it, dragging the carcasses of our prejudice and hatred, our avarice, our data banks and dead ideas, our dead rivers and smoky skies behind us. Or we can walk through lightly, with little luggage, ready to imagine another world. And ready to fight for it.

Each of the three novels under consideration, end with altered lives for their protagonists. Shibnath is jailed, while his estranged wife comes back with their son, ready to stand by him. Debu Pandit comes out of repeated imprisonments, full of promises of new worlds. Jeeban Moshai dies—but on his own terms, with final recognition of his medical skills. The resolutions then come together with reconciliation—but the reconciliation becomes possible because the communities have also altered enough to make multiple ways of belonging viable. This then leaves us with hope for the marginal figures in the novels, who rose to prominence during epidemiological flashpoints, and whose participation can create another world.

References

Arnold, D. (1986). Cholera and colonialism in British India. *Past & Present, 113*, 118–151.

Bhattacharya, B. (2020). The cold ones: India's epidemic goddesses. *Mint Lounge*. Retrieved October 16, 2021, from https://www.livemint.com/mint-lounge/features/the-cold-ones-india-s-epidemic-goddesses-11587104247592.html

Bhattacharya, P. (2014). *Tarasankar: Akhyan o Samaj*. Ababhas.

Bhattacharjee, S. (2020). Corona sanglap—Prothom kisti. *Guruchandali*. Retrieved January 1, 2022, from https://www.guruchandali.com/comment.php?topic=17413&srchtxt=%E0%A6%95%E0%A6%B0%E0%A7%8B%E0%A6%A8%E0%A6%BE

Bhowmik, S. (2021). Eker por ek mrityur dheu hnush tobu fere na. *Anandabazar Patrika*. Retrieved October 16, 2021, from https://www.anandabazar.com/rabibashoriyo/pandemics-and-epidemics-before-covid-19/cid/1281381

Biswas, S. (2021). Bringing the border home: India partition 2020. In R. Bandyopadhyay, P. Banerjee, & R. Samaddar (Eds.), *India's migrant workers and the pandemic*. Routledge.

Bower, S. (2020). Pepys and the plague. https://wellcomecollection.org/articles/Xn4chRIAAK03rFsj

Chakraborti, A. (2020). Lockdowner Jyotsnaay. *4 Number Platform, 4*(6). Retrieved January 11, 2023, from https://www.4numberplatform.com/?p=21410

Chakraborti, A. (2021a). Coronakale. *4 Number Platform, 4*(12). Retrieved October 16, 2021, from https://www.4numberplatform.com/?p=24891&fbclid=IwAR3l9QbkZLh_8H1YQXEVNO69gZHmdTvqOS3okGK2by4K0qUqeALPjs-L0uk

Chakraborti, A. (2021b). Ganganadir premik. *Parabas, 83*. Retrieved October 16, 2021, from https://www.parabaas.com/article.php?id=2483&fbclid=IwAR0B-VPzZb0Wd_FW6K9NC5TqLAc0OIt954rYHlnCF8o74LeK7QOVT8cVr5s

Chakraborti, A. (2021c). Hemanter pakhi. *Parabas, 81*. Retrieved October 16, 2021, from https://www.parabaas.com/article.php?id=2483&fbclid=IwAR0B-VPzZb0Wd_FW6K9NC5TqLAc0OIt954rYHlnCF8o74LeK7QOVT8cVr5s

Chakraborty, D. (1958). Tarasankr-er samaj chetana o tar safolyo. In U. Majumdar (Ed.), *TaraSankar: Desh, Kal, Sahitya*. Modern Book Agency.

Chakraborty, S., & Roy, R. (Eds.). (2022). *Lockdowner Golpo*. Bindu Bisargo Publishers.

Chattopadhyay, B. C. (2022). *Anandamath*. Bisshwo Sahitto Kendro.

Chattopadhyay, S. C. (2015). *Sarat Rachanabli* (Vol. 3). Dey's Publishing.

Chattopadhyay, S. C. (2019). *Sarat Rachanabli* (Vol. 1). Dey's Publishing.

Chaudhury, S. (2012). The Bengali novel. In V. Dalmiya & R. Sadana (Eds.), *The Cambridge companion to modern Indian literature*. Cambridge University Press.

Das, A. K. (2021). *Coronar Jibonsonkot o Chetonar Bish-Ekush*. Karulipi.

Dasgupta, S. (2022). *Corona Covid Nostokal*. Thikthikana.

Dash, U. (2020). Mahamari o Bangla akhyan. *Korak Sahitya Patrika, Saradiya*, 273–300.

Deb, A. (2022). *Asukhi Somoyer Brittanto: Sashoker Asuyar Birudhhe Likhito Nibondhho*. Tobuo Proyas.

Gangopadhyay, H. (2020). Famine of the mind: A comparison of the 1943 Bengal famine and the covid 19 pandemic. Unpublished MA dissertation, St. Xavier's University.

Ghosh, A. (2016). *The great derangement: Climate change and the Unthinkable*. The University of Chicago Press.

Ghosh, N. K. (2020). Mahamarir akhor. *Korak Sahitya Patrika, Saradiya*.

Harrison, M. (2020). A dreadful scourge: Cholera in early nineteenth century India. *Modern Asian Studies, 54*(2), 502–553.
Jana, A. (2022). *Lockdown diary*. Tramline Books.
Majumdar, S. (2021). Abagunthan. *Saraddiya Desh, 1427*, 140–191.
Mukherjee, S. (2008). Environmental thoughts and malaria in colonial Bengal: A study in social response. *Economic and Political Weekly, 43*(12–13), 54–61.
Mukhopadhyay, A. (2020a). *Lockdowner Dinolipi: Corona Bhubon Kotha*. Boiwala Bookcafe.
Mukhopadhyay, A. (2020b). Saratbabur quarantine, Bankim er morok, Bangla sahitye mohmari. *Anandabazar Patrika*. Retrieved 27 August, 2021, from https://www.anandabazar.com/editorial/coronavirus-epidemics-and-pandemics-in-bengali-literature-dgtlx-1.1133067
Mukhopadhyay, A. (Ed.). (2022a). *Coronar Korcha: Mahamarir Aloandharite Banglar Mukhochhobi*. Rupali Publication.
Mukhopadhyay, D. (1971). *Tarasankar Samakal o Uttarkaler Drishtite*. Sahitya Prakash.
Mukhopadhyay, K. (2022b). Picnic. *Desh, 89*(7), 32–35.
Nichols, R. W. (1981). The Goddess Sitala and epidemic small pox in Bengal. *The Journal of Asian Studies, 41*(1), 21–44.
Palit, C. (2008). Popular response to epidemics in colonial Bengal. *Indian Journal of History of Science, 43.2*, 277–283
Pepys, S. (1825). *Memoirs of Samuel Pepys*. British Library. Retrieved May 1, 2021, from https://www.bl.uk/collection-items/memoirs-of-samuel-pepys
Press Information Bureau. (2020). Prime Minister's Office, Government of India. Retrieved January 21, 2022, from https://pib.gov.in/newsite/PrintRelease.aspx?relid=200658
Ray, A. (2009). *Kalantarer Kathakar: Tarasankar*. Akshar Prakashani.
Saha, M. (2020). *Labour train*. Boiwala Bookcafe.
Samanta, A. (2012). Small pox in nineteenth century Bengal. *Indian Journal of History of Science, 47*(2), 211–240.
Siddiqi, D. (2020). In pictures: The long road home for India's migrant workers. Aljazeera. Retrieved December 24, 2021, from https://www.aljazeera.com/gallery/2020/4/22/in-pictures-the-long-road-home-for-indias-migrant-workers
Tagore, R. (1905). *Rabindra Rachanabali* (Vol. 7). Visvabharati.
Tagore, R. (1940). *Rabindra Rachanabali* (Vol. 6). Visvabharati.
Tagore, R. (1991). *Galpaguchho: Visvabratai Akhando*. Visvabharati.
Taher, A. (2021). Porijayi. Sillypoint. Retrieved December 8, 2021, from https://www.sillypoint.co.in/post/%E0%A6%AA%E0%A6%B0%E0%A6%BF%E0%A6%AF%E0%A6%BE%E0%A7%9F%E0%A7%80/id/ud3z6OsM8eSDmJoIa8xQ
Tarafdar Majumdar, S. (2020). *Basundharar Nabojagaran*. Pandulipi.
Tumbe, C. (2020). *The age of pandemics 1817–1920: How they shaped India and the world*. Harper Collins India.

Chapter 12
Books—And the Time-Warp of Long-COVID

Ritu Menon

Abstract Time's axis has shifted. It has become relative. In a mundane, everyday kind of way it is expansive and leisurely, almost indulgent. Nothing is urgent. I am not bound by a routine that is regulated by my watch. I edit mss., read proofs, correspond with authors, discuss projects, in the knowledge that none of these are going anywhere in a hurry—at least for the "foreseeable" future. I'm not rushing to publish a lot of books, to make up for lost time (there's a thought, time that has been lost in lockdown) because there is a serious question mark hovering over sales. Who will buy? Will people rush out to buy books just because they have been confined, or will they have had their fill of reading already, because they could do so little else? Maybe the last thing they will want to do is pick up another book. Let's give book production a bit of a rest, I think. But at an existential level, time has suddenly collapsed into itself. Is no longer measurable, because—will I even be around to see those books published if I don't hurry up and get them out? Shouldn't I be accelerating instead of slowing down? What if I run out of time? And so I manoeuvre myself into that tiny space, that sliver of time between lockdown and post-lockdown, whenever that might be, to think and plan for a week at a time, which seems to me a good compromise between the everyday and the existential. As for normal, it looks like I might be wishing for too much and too little at the same time for, as Grace says, "everywhere vast public suffering rises in reeling waves from around the earth's nation-states".

Keywords Book publishing · Reminiscences · Time · Experience · Lockdown

An earlier, shorter version of this essay was published as newspaper article https://www.hindustantimes.com/india-news/at-an-existential-level-time-has-suddenly-collapsed-into-itself/story-GbdBmgh8ec4dj07bCA8KcK.html.

R. Menon (✉)
Women Unlimited, New Delhi, India
e-mail: ritumenon1@gmail.com

MCRG, Kolkata, India

S. R. Chakraborty et al. (eds.), *The Long 2020*, India Studies in Business and Economics, https://doi.org/10.1007/978-981-99-4815-4_12

1. *wild berries -*
   the bodies floating
   in the Betwa

2. *this year's blossoms...*
   pyres flaming
   in the countryside

3. *oxygen queue...*
   the night's rain
   held on vines

4. *monsoon grasses...*
   all the deaths
   that were never counted

5. *summer starlings*
   another ambulance
   rushes by
   - (Chaturvedi 2021)

Sometimes, words fail one, and you enter what the poet Meena Alexander called "a zone of radical illiteracy". At such times, a haiku can compress and convey meaning with just a handful of words: this year's blossoms…/pyres flaming/ in the countryside.

I was thinking about time when I chanced upon Salil Chaturvedi's haiku. Time, the old gypsy man, time and tide that wait for no man, time to stand and stare, time lost, how time flies…

But over the last 18 months or so, what I have felt most powerfully is that time's axis has shifted.

It has become relative.

In a mundane, everyday kind of way it is expansive and leisurely, almost indulgent. Nothing is urgent. I am not bound by a routine that is regulated by my watch. I edit manuscripts, read proofs, correspond with authors, discuss projects, in the knowledge that none of these are going anywhere in a hurry—at least for the "foreseeable" future. I'm not rushing to publish a lot of books to make up for lost time (there's a thought, time that has been lost in lockdown) because there is a serious question mark hovering over sales. Who will buy? Will people rush out to buy books just because they have been confined, or will they have had their fill of reading already, because they could do so little else? Maybe the last thing they will want to do is pick up another book. Let's give book production a bit of a rest, I think.

But at an existential level, time has suddenly collapsed into itself. Is no longer measurable, because—will I even be around to see those books published if I don't hurry up and get them out? Shouldn't I be accelerating, instead of slowing down? What if I run out of time??

In between the mundane and the existential is yet another impulse, that of pretending that I can, in the short term, exercise some control over the time at hand. I can pretend that, really, nothing much has changed, everything will settle down, so I should carry on regardless, because time will—if I can hold out for long enough—resume its normal rhythm, and life will resume its normal tenor. I can pretend that if I, personally, carry on as if there had never been lockdowns and a pandemic then I will be able to turn the clock back, and no time will have been lost.

But that will be tilting at windmills...

I was talking about books. An impression has gained ground that during the pandemic—now in elongated time—people have returned to reading because they have time on their hands. Many came to books for the first time, even as they continued to surf the Net, binge-watched films or video-called friends and family. Online book sales jumped, because frequent lockdowns and curfews meant no brick and mortar shops were open, but also because children spent long hours being housebound and needed all available forms of diversion. Adults, too. Whiling away time.

I've been reading, too, or rather re-reading. Going back in time. Escaping briefly from the anxiety-inducing reading around COVID that I have been doing compulsively, into a time that was stable and predictable. This reading is immersive, unmarked by the interruptions of a normal routine which sectioned my days into discrete units of time. I give myself up to the pleasure of not having to look at my watch, of taking it off and not putting it back on again. I realise I don't really need it now.

I realise, too, that I have a little time on my hands, I begin to write. My writing has no urgent purpose, I am under no compulsion, I do not even have a specific subject. This writing is contemplative, it ranges over time and space, it is unfettered. It flows easily, like water. As I write, I find I am writing a remembrance of things past, recalling a time that was rich with promise, of possibilities and opportunities within reach, of an unfolding of activity and change in which I, we, a whole generation, were active participants. A time, it seems to me now, that cannot be retrieved.

We are in Long-COVID, looking at an oppressively unpredictable future.

Just as, in the disease, Long-COVID indicates a medico-clinical condition in which the impact of the virus lingers for an indefinite length of time and affects the body in different ways, so too, with the book trade. We don't yet know what its long-term effects will be, and how they will vary, depending on its severity.

A survey conducted in the U.S. in the first month of their first lockdown in 2020 revealed that 80 per cent of independent bookstores there had furloughed or laid off workers. Some Walmart branches roped off paperback racks as "non-essential". Did they do that here with Flipkart, too? By November 2020, bookshops across the world were in deep distress. In Paris, Shakespeare & Company, the legendary bookshop started by Sylvia Beach, reported that it was on the verge of closing because it had lost 80 per cent of its custom to COVID. In New York, the iconic Strand Bookstore near Greenwich Village, was facing imminent closure and put out a fundraising call to patrons. The New Internationalist in England was forced to close down its book publishing division in order to keep the magazine going. Indies everywhere were, and are, struggling to survive, but Jeff Bezos of Amazon increased his wealth by $74 *billion before 2020 came to a close. Not all of it came from book sales, perhaps, but enough to land a body blow to independent bookshops. The pandemic has been a windfall for Amazon.*

"Non-essential". That description haunted me. It haunted me when I told my senior staff that I was forced to cut their salaries during the two-month lockdown in 2020 as we had not been able to sell a single book in all that time. It haunted me when our printers said that many of their workers were migrants and had started walking back to their villages because the presses were closed. It haunted me when the courier service we have been using for over a decade said they wouldn't be able to guarantee deliveries even after the lockdown was lifted, because their delivery boys had taken other jobs in the meantime. It haunts me still, knowing that our revenues have been dangerously eroded, that we are nowhere near recovering from 2020's calamitous drop in income, and that the next lockdown is just around the corner.

When no postal or courier services are available and when no trucks carry goods across the country, even Amazon can only supply what it has in stock. Large consignments of books piled up in Customs warehouses because there was no labour to clear them—all migrant and contract workers had left the cities for their homes in the hinterland.

*Just Books, the innovative lending library in Bangalore with branches in Chennai, Pune, Hyderabad, Gurgaon and other cities, with a membership of several thousand, used to buy books worth Rs. 4 crores every year. During COVID, the bookshop's supplies have dried up, even as people have been confined; demand saw some growth as the first lockdown was lifted and transport and courier services resumed, but subsequent city and state-specific lockdowns have "left the book business reeling" in the words of its owner, Suresh Narasimha (*Ghoshal, 2021*). Contrary to public perception, e-book sales are just a drop in the ocean, worldwide—5–15%, as against 75–80% for physical books.*

With schools and colleges closed and all classes being held online, textbook publishers held back on producing new books and content for the 2020–21 academic year; and some state governments mandated that educational material be made available online, in digital formats, reducing the sales of physical books.

Zero sales for a protracted period is an unprecedented occurrence; interrupted sales due to selective lockdowns and transport curbs in different states halt the steady flow of books across the country and seriously affect revenues. Larger publishers with deeper pockets have tried to recoup losses through digital editions sold online, but this is an illusory gain as individual sales cannot compensate for the huge loss caused by institutional and public purchases drying up.

Innovations such as teaming up with Zomato or Swiggy to deliver books has helped some bookshops, but as with eating out versus takeaway or home delivery, the experience is less than satisfactory. And, as with restaurants, it cannot ever compensate for the drastic loss in revenue. In the UK, for instance, despite greater Internet penetration and online activity, publishers of scholarly books anticipated a drop of 20–40% in library subscription budgets, and declines of between 20 and 60% in print sales over 2020–21. "Scholarly monograph and journal print publishers have *been frustrated by the number of academic libraries that have stopped firm ordering, preferring a direct digital first content order policy" (*Brinton, 2021*).*

A book is a collaboration. It cannot be produced in isolation, or remotely. While writing itself is a solitary activity, interdependence is the essential characteristic of the production and dissemination of a book. A network of services—from editorial to design, typesetting, processing, printing, binding, distribution, wholesaling, retailing, and transporting to marketing and promoting—are the behind-the-scenes nuts and bolts of the book business; they can be supplemented, but not supplanted, by digital technologies. A virtual book launch is like beer without a head.

With a drop of upto 85–90% in their revenue and extended periods of working from home, many publishers rationalised outsourcing certain functions that had been performed in-house. Publicity and promotion were among the most amendable to this downsizing, but even large publishers cut back on editorial staff, usually at junior levels. Many, especially smaller independent publishers, gave up office space in order to save on expensive rents. Unlike in other parts of the world, the Indian government did not consider books an "essential" item, and so offered no support to the publishing industry, despite it being overwhelmingly educational in nature.

A survey conducted by the International Publishers' Association among member countries—the US, UK, Asia, Africa, Europe—found that governments in several countries offered stimulus assistance to publishers in the form of grants, wage subsidies or tax relief. Argentina, Australia, Canada and the UK offered wage subsidies for up to one year; in France this was up to 84% of employee salaries; Canada and Egypt made grants available; Kenya and Turkey offered tax relief. The IPA's report found global publishing markets split between two starkly different outlooks:

> *... significant double-digit, short-term losses which subsequently rebounded (as in the US) or long-term losses in markets that experienced major sales losses and now foresee slow recoveries because of reductions in consumer purchasing power, lower institutional purchasing budgets and less developed digital economies. (*IPA General Assembly, 2020*)*

The report noted that New Zealand had seen a decline of 70%, Jordan of 60 to 95%, Ivory Coast of 40–80%, and Indonesia, 50–80%. Unfortunately, we have no reliable figures for India.

We had always known that there would be no short COVID, and that it would be marked by serious disruptions. We knew that if one person in either our families or our workplaces fell ill, it would entail a shutdown of activity for a minimum of ten to fourteen days. We knew, too, that such interruptions would have a cascading effect, and that we would need to modify plans accordingly. What we didn't anticipate was that Long-COVID would stretch into an indefinite future with time itself being held to ransom. We can pretend that the normal cycles of time will resume and that therefore routines will follow their normal course, but this is wishful thinking. Long-COVID unfolds in its own time, the illness is not finite, and its aftermath cannot be gauged.

I am gripped by a strange anxiety, that I may not be able to meet my authors in person for an indefinite length of time, or travel to conferences, trade fairs and book events, where many ideas are first articulated, current research presented, book projects planned. There is a rich and diverse book ecosystem that supports, nurtures and cultivates what many of us call bibliodiversity—the same kind of diversity in book publishing and the germination of ideas that we find in the natural world's biodiversity. This bibliodiversity has been quite seriously threatened by the virus because it has impacted not only the sustainability of diversity, it has severely affected the conditions in which such diversity flourishes.

What do I mean by this? There is a creative and collaborative internationalism that exists between independent publishers across the world—not all independents, obviously, but certainly among the politically and socially committed ones—that thrives on meeting, interacting and working collectively, in person. These exchanges can, of course, also take place virtually, and some have, but they are nowhere near as productive or as fruitful as meeting physically. Long-term relationships in the book world are a feature not only between authors and editors, but between publishers in different countries and language areas, which grow and develop over years of meetings, and with the expectation that these will continue. Long-COVID has placed a question mark over this, at least for the foreseeable future, as all formal trade events are on hold and the informal encounters that take place when people travel as individuals have more or less come to a complete halt.

In my own experience, I know that I would never have been able to publish the many Palestinians that I have over the last ten years or so if I had not been to Palestine and heard them at the wonderful Palestine Literature Festival, itself a testimony to what international solidarity means to a people under Occupation. **Arabesque**, our series of fiction and non-fiction translated from Arabic, features some of the best writing from West Asia, a region with which we have deep historical and cultural links, but it remains remote, because we do not know their literature.

Exposures like these make for books, yes, but they also forge bonds that endure whether or not more books are made, because they are about a confluence of minds, of cultures and societies.

Closer home, it would be true to say that much of the collaborative cross-border research and investigation that has taken place in South Asia since the 1980s and to date, has been the result of scores of informal discussions, people-to-people meetings, conferences and consultations, indeed, even social, labour and women's and human rights movements, across the region. The scholarship and insights that mark the publications born of these exchanges would not have been possible without them.

A potentially far more serious problem, in my view, arises if we consider the matter of original research. When mobility is severely curtailed and even the limited movement allowed is beset with interruption and uncertainty, the possibility of empirical work for any meaningful length of time begins to recede. Research that requires archival or secondary source material is hampered by the loss of access to libraries, archives and institutional holdings, all of which means that we are looking at a significant reduction in new academic titles being published. The full implications of this will only be clear a few years hence, when the aridity of the extended pandemic period and of Long-COVID begins to make itself felt.

I find myself wondering about what kinds of books we will see published in India, after say, a couple of years. Fiction, yes, possibly more of it; certain kinds of non-fiction, like memoirs or autobiographies; some journalistic writing that draws on reporting and investigating; a rash of celebrity superficials; reprints; and, I fear, a sizeable reduction in scholarly titles, as works in progress are unable to continue or conclude their research. Speaking for myself as an occasional writer of non-fiction, I hesitate to begin a new project without the assurance of either mobility or access to people and resources.

Paradoxically, Long-COVID has altered our relationship to time—mundane as well as existential—such that one can be simultaneously pragmatic and philosophical about one's priorities, both personal and professional.

How so? you might ask.

For some time now, I have been saying that we publish too many books of indifferent quality in India, at least in English. Quite honestly, too many such books are published all over the world, as high volume/high obsolescence has become the hallmark of corporatised publishing. Publish—rather, over-publish—or perish is something that bedevils both writers and publishers, and both are on a treadmill. This crisis that COVID has precipitated has been in the making for some time, as the long-term viability of a high volume/ excess inventory/high returns model is almost impossible to sustain. Sooner or later, the less self-reliant or sustainable publishers will be absorbed by bigger players, the bigger ones taken over by the giants, all in search of economies of scale. Every few months, the news in the book trade concerns recent mergers and acquisitions across all segment, bar university presses (of which we have none in India). Such events happen with the kind of frequency that leaves editors, employees and authors wondering who actually calls the shots—all too often, the person or entity doing so has nothing at all to do with books or with publishing. And all too often, again, an unacceptable majority of authors fall between the cracks in such conglomerations.

Neither books, nor authors, nor ideas, benefit.

Books, too, can be a casualty of time, if there is an overabundance of them; the way the book business is organised, an optimum number of books needs to be published every month in order to achieve the desirable sales volumes. Unfortunately, at least in India, there is only so much limited shelf space, reviewing space and readership available, with the result that books vie with each other for attention.

The time and life-span for a non-academic title is generally six months—if it hasn't sold well within that time it is unlikely to do so later, because it has to make way for the next lot of new books. Vijay Sharma, sales and marketing director at Pan Macmillan says, "Thousands of books are released every month but airport retail stores—normally a good sales point for physical books—only buy about 20 titles". These are likely to be those titles supported by aggressive marketing, leaving the rest of the thousands to their own devices. In volume and sales-driven publishing, then both space and time militate against the slow but steady selling that is the time-cycle of the books that endure.

Not only do we publish too many books of indifferent quality, we publish too many of the same kind, the so-called safe kind (quickies based on mythology or pop psychology or feel-good true stories, even certain kinds of fiction that flood the market, for example), drastically reducing what we call bibliodiversity in the publishing ecosystem. For, "just as an ecosystem is biodiverse when it has 'dynamic balance'… so, too, an eco-social system is in dynamic balance only when a host of varied voices can be heard… In the eco-social system, the lack of media diversity and the concentration of big publishing and big bookselling reduces the possibility for a diversity of voices to be heard or read" (Hawthorne, 2014: 3). Big Publishing, with its Big Marketing, weeds out and flattens anything different, resulting in what Vandana Shiva has called "monocultures of the mind".

As with biodiversity in the natural environment, bibliodiversity in the publishing environment flourishes in a time-cycle that slows down rather than speeds up. Books produced organically—by which we mean those that germinate and are nurtured in keeping with the contexts in which they are written, sold, read and received—follow a process in which time is elastic, where the intent is to produce a work for the long term. An unexpected but very interesting consequence of COVID has been the surge, in online sales, of backlist titles, those books that survived the perishability of quickies produced for the short term. The head of marketing at Penguin India observed in January 2021 that "we are now a backlist market, contributing 85% of total sales" (Scroll Staff, 2021).

By definition, organically produced books cannot be mass produced or produced in bulk, which also means that their numbers are too small for most medium and large publishing houses; and because their gestation is often longer than books produced in volume, they must remain current for longer periods in order to be viable. In my experience as a feminist publisher, I have found that a very large number of books that we published over 20 years ago on a range of issues are still in demand, still relevant, and this is another important characteristic or feature of the long term: the ability to foresee what will become or assume universal significance in future. Inevitably, then, books that anticipate such developments put a very different cast on the notion of "current", and of longevity. In some sense, you could almost say that they defy the passage of time.

Digitisation, and the stunning speed with which it has been widely (albeit unevenly) dispersed across the world, throws up a unique challenge to conceptualising both time and space. The former seems simultaneously instant yet infinite, the latter finite yet boundless. Virtual time and virtual space combine to form a curiously seductive virtual reality, in which anything seems possible. Within reach.

The book trade has welcomed digitisation with open arms. Writers, too. It promises freedom, unlimited access, the elimination of middlemen and women, the promise of huge exposure and independence. Writers can self-publish, publishers can sell directly, booksellers can choose the platform they want to sell through, distributors can "aggregate". And so on. It's a no-holds-barred medium.

In August 2020, with the unprecedented closure of bookstores and retail outlets in the U.S., Moody's Investor Service dropped the credit ratings of McGraw Hill, a major academic and STEM publisher, from B3 to Caa2, close to the lowest possible rating, and did the same for Cengage Learning, Inc. For Pearson PLC, one of the world's largest educational publishers, it dropped to the brink of what Moodys calls "junk bond rating", following a calamitous drop in the demand for printed books. There were predictions that the ongoing pandemic could lead to the permanent closure of 100 higher education institutions that could then "strangle some of the smaller university presses" (Guren et al., 2021).

Through the summer of 2020, the chain bookstore, Barnes & Noble (temporarily), closed more than 400 of its 600 stores in the U.S.

Publishers turned to online platforms and e-commerce with relief, and in fact they became their lifeline. Supply chain problems were greatly reduced, even if not completely resolved, and, in an unexpected development, readership benefitted from being confined and from having to spend long hours in front of a screen. Online learning solutions resulted in a substantial growth for many—32% for Pearson; double-digit increases for McGraw Hill; 40% for Cengage Learning. But this potential for rapidly switching from offline to online, both in terms of product (or content, as it is referred to) and dissemination, is not really available to the majority of Indian publishers.

For those already oriented to digital solutions, it seemed the sky was the limit. Marketing heads relished the thought of being able to accumulate and invest in the kind of data generated by an online presence, a quantum leap from conventional market research that is time and labour intensive. Content producers felt their time had finally come, and even anticipated the withering away of authorship as we know it. The physical book would soon be displaced by its e-version, arguably more eco-friendly as it dispenses with paper, and so on. Some disquiet, it is true, has been expressed. V S Karthika, publishing director of Westland (an Amazon company), fears that:

> Data is going to defeat us. At some point there may be too much data; my biggest worry is that we will end up selling a certain kind of book to a certain kind of reader because that's what the data tell us she's interested in - so, more of the same kind of books and genres and formats in the market. (Scroll Staff, 2021)

The Australian feminist publisher, Susan Hawthorne says,

> Those among us who have been concerned about the increasing control exercised by one or two book e-tailers in digital space have highlighted the need for "digital bibliodiversity" in order to prevent it from being "appropriated, distorted, corporatised and privatised by big publishing." (Hawthorne, 2014: 59)

All this notwithstanding, what is undeniable is that in digital space, books may well become "eternal", retrievable at any time if they have been digitised. There will no longer be anything like "out of print", anyone will be able to print individual, single copies on demand, or download those that allow free access—in this sense, books will indeed be timeless.

This rather long, but necessary, digression brings me back to the second aspect of the paradox that I mentioned earlier: Long-COVID and the enforced repose that it entails offers us the possibility of reflecting on the relationship between books, their role in the production of knowledge, and the space and time in which this take place.

Ancient Greeks had two conceptualisations of time—*kairos*, characterised by a qualitative aura; and *chronos* (hence chronology) assessed by the quantitative measure of seconds, minutes, hours, days, months, years. The French philosopher, Henri Bergson, also differentiated between mechanistic time, exemplified by the clock, a measure he believed to be extremely useful to science, but destructive when applied to lived experience; he therefore proposed the notion of *duration* instead, characterised by a unity of flow, arguing that duration, rather than measurable units of time, "reflects the authenticity of lived experience".

Kairos and *chronos*. The warp speed of a digital realm and the time-warp of Long-COVID. The architect, Prem Chandavarkar's thoughtful reflections on the relationship between *kairos*, *chronos* and his practice as an architect set me thinking about my practice as a publisher, about how, and in what measure of time, I publish the books I do, *now* (Chandavarkar, 2021). At this point of time.

"In publishing we do forecasts," says Udayan Mitra, literary editor at HarperCollins India, "three-year plans, five-year plans, seven-year plans. When you're confronted with a year like 2020 these plans become meaningless. Look at the year—out of twelve months, no publisher was able to put out a single new book for four months" (Scroll Staff, 2021).

The clock, *chronos*, ticked on, but activity came to a stop, that activity which is geared to warp speed, is predicated on volume, high visibility, and, unfortunately, high perishability. Yet what a relief it was to be liberated from that tyranny of the clock, of deadlines, for a while, for those few months then (and, who knows? perhaps again, and again) that we had no choice but to rediscover *kairos*, to pause, and to re-evaluate our priorities with regard to both *chronos* and *kairos*. To think about what we have published and what we should publish henceforth, as part of our contribution to the production of knowledge, the generation of ideas, the scintillation of debate.

Kairos, Chandavarkar elaborates, "is a qualitative phenomenon, resisting concrete intellectual definition, yet indisputably known as tangible reality when consciously experienced… *kairos* faces both inward and outward, simultaneously. *Chronos*, by contrast, being quantitative, rests on abstract external measure… provoking a measure of the self *against* this quantification".

I can acknowledge the tension between *kairos* and *chronos* in daily living, as well as in daily professional practice, can try and reconcile them, even, but what means do I have to deal with Long-COVID's *uncertain* time, with not knowing the duration of this time-warp?

During the first lockdown, I manoeuvred myself into that tiny space, that sliver of time between lockdown and post-lockdown, whenever it might be, to think and plan for a week at a time, which seemed to me to be a reasonable compromise between the everyday and the existential. Now, more than one lockdown and a calamitous resurgence of the virus later, a week or two at a time, at most, a month, still remains the only measure one can rely on, the relatively safe horizon.

I return to the notion of biodiversity and bibliodiversity, both as "complex, self-sustaining systems… that include diversity… within species and within ecosystems"; that, in the case of bibliodiversity in publishing, includes the importance of interdependence. Interdependence versus competition and monopoly. Multi- even hybrid, cultures versus monocultures. Diverse epistemological positions and cultural materials that encourage a kind of "deep publishing" that contributes to enriching both knowledge and bibliodiversity. The time-cycles in biodiversity and bibliodiversity are more akin to *kairos* than *chronos*, to organic rhythms that eschew an artificial or engineered speeding up of process, of maturation and fruition.

Trying to make up for all the time that we have "lost" during the pandemic is a natural and understandable response. Compensate for the time-warp of Long-COVID with the warp speed of the digital realm. But it seems to me that this would, indeed, be like tilting at windmills, that we should instead pause and opt for the long durée by taking our time, pruning our lists and reducing or doing away with the large numbers of redundant books that are currently produced. That quality be preferred over quantity, creativity over "content", and readers and writers over algorithms.

Now would be the time to restore the dynamic balance, to think afresh about book cultures.

References

Brinton, J. (2021). The impact of COVID on the UK publishing industry. *Learned Publishing, 34*(1), 43–48. https://doi.org/10.1002/leap.1363

Chandavarkar, P. (2021, August 25). Ruminations on time. *Medium*. Retrieved August 25, 2021, from https://premckar.medium.com/the-infinitude-within-our-skins-cd65d04c2876.

Chaturvedi, S. (2021, May 25). Corona haiga (haiku+image). *Indian Cultural Forum*. Retrieved June 29, 2021, from https://indianculturalforum.in/2021/05/25/corona-haiga-haikuimage/.

Ghoshal, S. (2021, August 1). Turning a brand new page for the love of books. *MINT*. Retrieved August 1, 2021, from https://lifestyle.livemint.com/news/talking-point/turning-a-brand-new-page-for-the-love-of-books-111627640602297.html.

Guren, C., McIlroy, T., & Sieck, S. (2021). COVID-19 and book publishing: Impacts and insights for 2021. *Publishing Research Quarterly, 37*, 1–14. https://doi.org/10.1007/s12109-021-09791-z

Hawthorne, S. (2014). *Bibliodiversity: A manifesto for independent publishing*. Spinifex Press.

IPA General Assembly. (2020, November 23). From response to recovery. *International Publishers Association*. Retrieved November 23, 2020, from https://www.internationalpublishers.org/copyright-news-blog/1046-from-response-to-recovery.

Scroll Staff. (2021, January 4). Insider predictions: What does the future of publishing look like after the pandemic? *Scroll*. Retrieved January 4, 2021, from https://scroll.in/article/983020/insider-predictions-what-does-the-future-of-publishing-look-like-after-the-pandemic.

References

"A crisis of mounting AIDS hysteria." *Dateline San Francisco*, August 1, 1983, Maclean's archive, https://archive.macleans.ca/article/1983/8/1/a-crisis-of-mounting-aids-hysteria. Accessed on September 15, 2021

"Bat cave solves mystery of deadly SARS virus — and suggests new outbreak could occur." *Nature*, December 1, 2017, https://www.nature.com/articles/d41586-017-07766-9. Accessed on November 7, 2021.

"Black Death," *Encyclopaedia Britannica.* https://www.britannica.com/event/Black-Death. Accessed on June 14, 2021.

"Child migrants: Massive drop in children held by border officials." May 5, 2021, https://www.bbc.com/news/world-us-canada-56405009. Accessed on June 10, 2021.

"Cholera," *The British Medical Journal*, *2*(252), October 28, 1865 (p. 447). https://www.jstor.org/stable/25205066. Accessed on August 16, 2021.

"Covid: South Africa 'punished' for detecting new Omicron variant." November 28, 2021, https://www.bbc.com/news/world-59442129. Accessed on December 12, 2021.

"Global HIV & AIDS statistics—Fact sheet." (2021). *UNAIDS.* https://www.unaids.org/en/resources/fact-sheet. Accessed on November 6, 2021.

"HIV and AIDS an Origin Story." *PublicHealth.org*, A Red Ventures Company, https://www.publichealth.org/public-awareness/hiv-aids/origin-story/. Accessed on October 10, 2021

"Influenza pandemic of 1918–19." *Encyclopedia Britannica*, July 7, 2020, https://www.britannica.com/event/influenza-pandemic-of-1918-1919. Accessed November 2, 2021.

"The rapid journey of a deadly MERS outbreak." *Infectious Disease* (p. 54), December 2019. https://media.nature.com/original/magazine-assets/d42473-019-00422-y/d42473-019-00422-y.pdf. Accessed on November 7, 2021.

"Trump Falls Victim to COVID-19 Misinformation That Study Says He Spread the Most." *The Wire*, October 2, 2020, https://thewire.in/world/donald-trump-coronavirus-misinformation. Accessed November 6, 2021.

Agamben, G. (1998). *Homo Sacer: Sovereign power and bare life* (D. Heller-Roazen, Trans.).

Agamben, G. (2020, February 26). The invention of an epidemic [Italian]. *Quodlibet*. Retrieved September 27, 2021, from https://www.quodlibet.it/giorgio-agamben-l-invenzione-di-un-epidemia.

Agamben, G. (2020, March 17). Coronavirus and philosophers: Giorgio Agamben: Clarifications. *European Journal of Psychoanalysis—New Series*. https://www.journal-psychoanalysis.eu/coronavirus-and-philosophers/.

Agamben, G. (2021). *Where are we now? The epidemics as politics*. Eris.

Agamben, G. (2021). *Where are we now? The epidemic as politics*. Rowman and Littlefield.

Agarwal, A., Gans, J., & Goldfarb, A. (2018). *Prediction machines: The simple economics of artificial intelligence*. Harvard Business Review Press.

S. R. Chakraborty et al. (eds.), *The Long 2020*, India Studies in Business and Economics, https://doi.org/10.1007/978-981-99-4815-4

Ahmed, M. (2021, July 28). *The US is losing the global war against COVID-19—and that is a national security issue*. Retrieved January 10, 2023, from https://www.cgdev.org/blog/us-losing-global-war-against-covid-19-and-national-security-issue.

AIDS. *Moral majority report*, July 1983, https://hivaids.omeka.net/items/show/9. Accessed on November 5, 2021.

Althusser, L. (1962). *Contradiction and overdetermination* (B. Brewster, Trans.). Penguin Press. Retrieved from https://www.marxists.org/reference/archive/althusser/1962/overdetermination.htm.

Anand, U. (2021, May 11). No funds granted for vaccine research, development: Govt. *Hindustan Times (New Delhi)*. https://www.hindustantimes.com/india-news/no-funds-granted-for-vaccine-research-development-govt-101620675320843.html.

Ankersmit, F. R. (1989). Historiography and postmodernism. *History and Theory, 28*(2).

Arendt, H. (1993). *Between past and future: Eight exercises in political thought*. Penguin.

Arnold, D. (1986). Cholera and colonialism in British India. *Past & Present, 113*, 118–151. Harrison, M. (2020). A dreadful scourge: Cholera in early nineteenth century India. *Modern Asian Studies, 54*(2), 502–553.

Arnold, D. (1993). *Colonizing the body: State medicine and epidemic disease in nineteenth-century India*. University of California Press.

Arnold, D. (2020). Pandemic India: Coronavirus and the uses of history. *Journal of Asian Studies, 79*(3), 569–577.

Arora, N., & Jamkhandikar, S. (2021, August 17). India COVID-19 vaccinations near record, new infections at five-month low. *Reuters*. https://www.reuters.com/world/india/india-reports-25166-new-covid-19-cases-2021-08-17/.

Arrighi, G. (1994a). The long twentieth century: Money, power and the origins of our time. Verso.

Arrighi, G. (1994b). The long twentieth century: Money, power and the origins of our times. Verso.

AstraZeneca. (2020, December 30). *AstraZeneca's COVID-19 vaccine authorised for emergency supply in the UK*. https://www.astrazeneca.com/media-centre/press-releases/2020/astrazenecas-covid-19-vaccine-authorised-in-uk.html.

AstraZeneca. (2020, June 4). *AstraZeneca takes next steps towards broad and equitable access to Oxford University's potential COVID-19 vaccine*. https://www.astrazeneca.com/media-centre/articles/2020/astrazeneca-takes-next-steps-towards-broad-and-equitable-access-to-oxford-universitys-potential-covid-19-vaccine.html.

Bandyopadhyay, H. (2011). *Udbastu*. Deep Prakashan.

Bandyopadhyay, R., Banerjee, P., & Samaddar, R. (2021a). *India's migrant workers and the pandemic*. Routledge.

Bandyopadhyay, R., Banerjee, P., & Samaddar, R. (2021b). *India's migrant workers and the pandemic*. Routledge.

Banerjea, A. (2021, January 11). Covid-19 vaccination: India signs purchase order with Serum Covishield vaccine to cost ₹ 200 per dose. *Mint*. https://www.livemint.com/news/india/covid19-vaccination-india-to-buy-1-1-crore-doses-from-serum-dispatches-may-start-today-says-report-11610360963620.html.

Banerjee, P. (2010). *Borders, histories, existences: Gender and beyond*. Sage Publications.

Banerjee, P. (1999). Historic acts: Santal rebellion and the temporality of practice. *Studies in History, 15*, 2.

Banerjee, P. (2004). *Politics of time: 'Primitives' and history-writing in a colonial society*. Oxford University Press.

Banglar Communist Andoloner Itihas (Vol. 1, pp. 256–257).

Barak, O. (2013). *On time: Technology and temporality in modern Egypt*. University of California Press.

Bashford, A., & Hooker, C. (2001). *Contagion*. Taylor and Francis.

Basu, A. (Ed.). (2017). *Udbastu Andolon O Punorbosoti: Somosamayik potro-potrikay*. Gangchil.

Basu, K. (2020, July 8). The way in which it was executed, India's lockdown itself became source of virus's spread. *The Indian Express*. https://indianexpress.com/article/opinion/columns/corona virus-lockdown-india-covid-19-cases-deaths-6494930/.
BehanBox. (2020). *ASHA workers criminalised for fighting for their rights*. Available at https://behanbox.com/2020/10/21/3-states-wage-war-against-indias-corona-warriors/. Last accessed October 4, 2021
Bergmann, M., & Wagner, M. (2021). The impact of COVID-19 on informal caregiving and care receiving across Europe during the first phase of the pandemic. *Frontiers in Public Health*. https://doi.org/10.3389/fpubh.2021.673874
Bernet, B. (2020). The post war marxist milieu of microhistory. In B. Zachariah, L. Raphael, & B. Bernet (Eds.), *What's left of marxism*. Oldenbourg.
Bhattacharya, B. (2020, April 17). The cold ones: India's epidemic goddesses. *Mint Lounge*. Retrieved October 16, 2021, from https://www.livemint.com/mint-lounge/features/the-cold-ones-india-s-epidemic-goddesses-11587104247592.html.
Bhattacharya, P. (2014). *Tarasankar: Akhyan o Samaj*. Ababhas.
Bhattacharya, S. (2020, April 17). Corona sanglap—Prothom kisti. *Guruchandali*. Retrieved January 1, 2022, from https://www.guruchandali.com/comment.php?topic=17413&srchtxt=%E0%A6%95%E0%A6%B0%E0%A7%8B%E0%A6%A8%E0%A6%BE.
Bhattacharya, S. (2020, June 25). India's migrant workers are protesting erasure of their rights amid lockdown: A mapping project documents their resistance. *First-post*. https://www.firstpost.com/india/indias-migrant-workers-are-protesting-erasure-of-their-rights-amid-lockdown-a-mapping-project-documents-their-resistance-8463821.html.
Bhowmick, N. (2020, May 27). They treat us like stray dogs: Migrant workers flee India's cities. *National Geographic*. https://www.nationalgeographic.com/history/2020/05/they-treat-us-like-stray-dogs-migrant-workers-flee-india-cities/.
Bhowmik, S. (2021, May 16). Eker por ek mrityur dheu hnush tobu fere na. *Anandabazar Patrika*. Retrieved October 16, 2021, from https://www.anandabazar.com/rabibashoriyo/pandemics-and-epidemics-before-covid-19/cid/1281381.
Biswas, S. (2021). Bringing the border home: India partition 2020. In R. Bandyopadhyay, P. Banerjee, & R. Samaddar (Eds.), *India's migrant workers and the pandemic*. Routledge.
Blumenthal, M. (2007). Agent of intolerance. *The Nation*, May 16, 2007, https://www.thenation.com/article/archive/agent-intolerance/. Accessed on August 6, 2021.
Bogoch, I., Watts, A., Thomas-Bachli, A., Huber, C., Kraemer, M., & Khan, K. (2020). Pneumonia of unknown aetiology in Wuhan, China: Potential for international spread via commercial air travel. *Journal of Travel Medicine, 27*(2), 1–3.
Borsch, S. J., & Sabraa, T. (2016). Plague mortality in late medieval Cairo: Quantifying the plague outbreaks of 833/1430 and 864/1460. *Mamlūk Studies Review, XIX*(2016), 115–148.
Bower, S. (2020, March 20). Pepys and the plague. *Wellcome Collection*. Retrieved October 5, 2021, from https://wellcomecollection.org/articles/Xn4chRIAAK03rFsj.
Bratton, B. (2006). Logistics of habitable circulation. In P. Virilio (Ed.), *Speed and politics* (pp. 7–25). Semiotext(e)
Bratton, B. (2021). *The revenge of the real: Politics for a post-pandemic world*. Verso.
Braudel, F. (1988). History and the social sciences: The *Longue Durée*. In M. Aymard, & H. Mukhia (Eds.), *French studies in history* (Vol. 1).
Braudel, F. (1995). *Mediterranean and the Mediterranean World in the reign of Philip II* (Vols. 1 & 2). Berkeley.
Braudel, F. (1980). *On history*. University of Chicago Press.
Briggs, A. (1961). Cholera and Society in the Nineteenth Century. *Past & Present* (19).
Brinton, J. (2021). The impact of COVID on the UK publishing industry. *Learned Publishing, 34*(1), 43–48. https://doi.org/10.1002/leap.1363
Bulmus, B. (2012). *Plague, quarantines and geopolitics in the Ottoman empire*. Edinburgh University Press.

Business Standard Web Team. (2020, August 31). First economic contraction in 4 decades: India's GDP shrinks 23.9% in Q1, FY21. *Business Standard*. https://www.business-standard.com/article/economy-policy/first-economic-contraction-in-4-decades-india-s-gdp-shrinks-x-in-q1-fy21-120083101022_1.html.

Callaway, E. (2020, August 24). The unequal scramble for coronavirus vaccines—by the numbers. *Nature*. https://www.nature.com/articles/d41586-020-02450-x.

Carrard, P. (1995). *Poetics of the new history, Fr. historical discourses from Braudel to Chartier*. Baltimore.

Chakrabarti, P. (2021). COVID-19 and the spectres of colonialism. In *India and the pandemic: The first year, essays from* The India Forum. Orient Blackswan.

Chakrabarty, D. (2021a). The Chronopolitics of the anthropocene: The pandemic and our sense of time. *Contributions to Indian Sociology, 55*(3).

Chakrabarty, D. (2021b). *The climate of history in a planetary age*. Primus Books.

Chakrabarty, D. (2021). *The climate of history in a planetary age*. Primus Books.

Chakraborti, A. (2021). Coronakale. *4 Number Platform, 4*(12). Retrieved October 16, 2021, from https://www.4numberplatform.com/?p=24891&fbclid=IwAR3l9QbkZLh_8H1YQXEVNO69gZHmdTvqOS3okGK2by4K0qUqeALPjs-L0uk.

Chakraborti, A. (2021). Ganganadir premik. *Parabas, 83*. Retrieved October 16, 2021, from https://www.parabaas.com/article.php?id=2483&fbclid=IwAR0B-VPzZb0Wd_FW6K9NC5TqLAc0OIt954rYHlnCF8o74LeK7QOVT8cVr5s.

Chakraborti, A. (2021). Hemanter pakhi. *Parabas, 81*. Retrieved October 16, 2021, from https://www.parabaas.com/article.php?id=2483&fbclid=IwAR0B-VPzZb0Wd_FW6K9NC5TqLAc0OIt954rYHlnCF8o74LeK7QOVT8cVr5s.

Chakraborty, D. (1958). Tarasankr-er samaj chetana o tar safolyo. In U. Majumdar (Ed.), *TaraSankar: Desh, Kal, Sahitya*. Modern Book Agency.

Chakraborty, S. (2011). *60–70 Chhatro Andolon* (Vol. 1). National Book Agency.

Chakraborty, S., & Roy, R. (Eds.). (2022). *Lockdowner Golpo*. Bindu Bisargo Publishers.

Chandavarkar, P. (2021, August 25). Ruminations on time. *Medium*. Retrieved August 25, 2021, from https://premckar.medium.com/the-infinitude-within-our-skins-cd65d04c2876.

Chandavarkar, Rajnarayan (1998). Plague Panic and Epidemic Politics in India, 1896–1914. In R. Chandavarkar, *Imperial power and popular politics: Class, resistance and the state in India, c. 1850–1950*. Cambridge University Press.

Chandra, H., & Basu, M. (2020, March 19). Modi announces 'Janata Curfew' on 22 March, urges for resolve, restraint to fight coronavirus. *The Print*. https://theprint.in/india/modi-announces-janata-curfew-on-22-march-urges-for-resolve-restraint-to-fight-coronavirus/384138/.

Chang, E. Y. Y. (2020). Informal home care providers: the forgotten health-care workers during the COVID-19 pandemic. *The Lancet*, 395(10242), 1957–1959.

Chatterjee, P. (2020, April 12). The pandemic exposes India's apathy toward migrant workers. *The Atlantic*. https://www.theatlantic.com/ideas/archive/2020/04/the-pandemic-exposes-indias-two-worlds/609838/.

Chattopadhyay, B. C. (2022). *Anandamath*. Bisshwo Sahitto Kendro.

Chattopadhyay, S. C. (2015). *Sarat Rachanabli* (Vol. 3). Dey's Publishing.

Chattopadhyay, S. C. (2019). *Sarat Rachanabli* (Vol. 1). Dey's Publishing.

Chaturvedi, S. (2021, May 25). Corona haiga (haiku+image). *Indian Cultural Forum*. Retrieved June 29, 2021, from https://indianculturalforum.in/2021/05/25/corona-haiga-haikuimage/.

Chaudhuri, P. (1983). Refugees in West Bengal: A study of the growth and development of refugee settlements within the CMD. *Occasional Paper No. 55*. Centre for Studies in Social Sciences.

Chaudhury, S. (2012). The Bengali novel. In V. Dalmiya, & R. Sadana (Eds.), *The Cambridge companion to modern Indian Literature*. Cambridge University Press.

Chhabria, S. (2021). Manufacturing epidemics: Pathogens, poverty and public health crises in India. In *India and the pandemic: The first year, essays from* The India Forum. Orient Blackswan.

Chhabria, S. (2020). Manufacturing epidemics: Pathogens, poverty, and public health crises in India. *The India Forum*, Issue: June 5, 2020 [Manufacturing Epidemics | The India Forum].

Chhibber, M. (2020, September 2). Supreme Court's handling of Kashmir habeas corpus more worrisome than Modi govt's clampdown. *The Print*. https://theprint.in/opinion/supreme-courts-handling-of-kashmir-habeas-corpus-more-worrisome-than-modi-govts-clampdown/286173/.

Chintan, R. (2021, August 23). Big pharma—maximum earnings, minimum responsibilities. *News Click*. Retrieved August 31, 2021, from https://www.newsclick.in/Big-Pharma%E2%80%93Maximum-Earnings-Minimum-Responsibilities.

Choudhury, Soumyabrata (2020). *Now it's come to distances: notes on Shaheen Bagh and Coronavirus, Association and Isolation*. Navayana.

Chowell, G., & Viboud, C. (2016). Pandemic influenza and socioeconomic disparities: Lessons from 1918 Chicago. *Proceedings of the National Academy of Sciences of the United States of America, 113*(48).

Cipolla, C. M. (1979). *Faith, reason and plague in seventeenth century Tuscany*. W.W. Norton and Company.

Cipolla, C. M. (1981). *Fontana economic history of Europe, The middle ages*. Collins/Fontana.

COVAXIN Study Group. (2021). Efficacy, safety, and lot to lot immunogenicity of an inactivated SARS-CoV-2 vaccine (BBV152): A, double-blind, randomised, controlled phase 3 trial. *The Lancet, 398*(10317), P2173–P2184. https://doi.org/10.1101/2021.06.30.21259439

Crary, J. (2013). *24/7. Late capitalism and the ends of sleep.*

Crosby, A. W. (1986). *Ecological imperialism: The biological expansion of Europe, 900–1900*. Cambridge University Press.

Crosby, A. W. (2003). *The Columbian exchange. Biological and cultural consequences of 1492*. Praeger.

Cross, S., Rho, Y., Reddy, H., Pepperrell, T., Rodgers, F., Osborne, R., Eni-Olotu, A., Banerjee, R., Wimmer, S., & Keestra, S. (2021). Who funded the research behind the Oxford-AstraZeneca COVID-19 vaccine? Approximating the funding to the University of Oxford for the research and development of the ChAdOx vaccine technology. *BMJ Global Health, 6*, 21255103. https://doi.org/10.1101/2021.04.08.21255103

Das, A. K. (2021). *Coronar Jibonsonkot o Chetonar Bish- Ekush*. Karulipi.

Das, S. K. (2000). Refugee crisis: Responses of the government of West Bengal. In P. K. Bose (Ed.), *Refugees in West Bengal: Institutional practices and contested identities*. Calcutta Research Group.

Dasgupta, S. (2022). *Corona Covid Nostokal*. Thikthikana.

Dash, U. (2020). Mahamari o Bangla akhyan. *Korak Sahitya Patrika, Saradiya* (pp. 273–300).

Davis, M. (2002). *Late Victorian holocausts: El Nino famines and the making of the third world*. Verso.

de Vries, J. (2019). Playing with scales: The global and the micro, the macro and the nano. *Past and Present, 242*(Sppl.14), 23–36.

Deb, A. (2022). *Asukhi Somoyer Brittanto: Sashoker Asuyar Birudhhe Likhito Nibondhho*. Tobuo Proyas.

Deshpande, A., & Ramachandran, R. (2020). Is COVID-19 "The Great Leveler"? The critical role of social identity in lockdown—induced job losses. In *Discussion Series in Economics* (No. 34). Ashoka University.

Dixit, P. (2020, April 9). My lord, migrant labourers need more than just food, just like we all do. *The Print*. https://theprint.in/opinion/pov/my-lord-migrant-labourers-need-more-than-just-food-just-like-we-all-do/398508/.

Durkheim, E. (1893). *The division of labour in society*. Bloomsbury Publishing.

Dutta A. et.al. (2011). Hospital efficiency in West Bengal: A study on secondary level hospitals. Department of Health and Family Welfare, Government of West Bengal. Available at https://www.wbhealth.gov.in/uploaded_files/notice/summary.pdf. Last accessed August 23, 2021.

Dutta, D. (2001). *Bijoygarh Ekti Udbastu Upanibesh*. Progressive Publishers.

Economic Outlook (2020, April 30). Only 30.8 mln provided jobs under MGNREGA in April 2020: 88.8% lower than in previous year. *CMIE*. https://www.cmie.com/kommon/bin/sr.php?kall=warticle&dt=2020-04-30%2016:32:16&msec=126.

Eliot, T. S. (2004). Four quartets—burnt Norton. In *Complete plays and poems* (p. 171). Faber and Faber.

Ella, R., Reddy, S., Jogdand, H., Sarangi, V., Ganneru, B., Prasad, S., Das, D., Raju, D., Praturi, U., Sapkal, G., Yadav, P., Reddy, P., Verma, S., Singh, C., Redkar, S. V., Gillurkar, C. S., Kushwaha, J. S., Mohapatra, S., Bhate, A., … Vadrevu, K. M. (2021). Safety and immunogenicity of an inactivated SARS-CoV-2 vaccine, BBV152: Interim results from a double-blind, randomised, multicentre, phase 2 trial, and 3-month follow-up of a double-blind, randomised phase 1 trial. *The Lancet Infectious Diseases, 21*(7), 950–961. https://doi.org/10.1016/S1473-3099(21)00070-0

Engelmann, L. (2020, March 6). *#COVID19: The spectacle of real-time surveillance.* Retrieved January 10, 2023, from http://somatosphere.net/forumpost/covid19-spectacle-surveillance

Ferguson, J. (1994). *The anti-politics machine: Development, depoliticisation, and bureaucratic power in Lesotho.* University of Minnesota Press.

Fesbach, M. (2006). The early days of the HIV/AIDS epidemic in the former soviet union. In J. L. Twigg (Ed.) *HIV/AIDS in Russia and Eurasia* (Vol. 1). Palgrave Macmillan.

Foucault, M. (1991). Governmentality. In G. Burchell, C. Gordon, & P. Miller (Eds.), *Studies.*

Foucault, M. (1995). *Discipline and punish: The Birth of the prison* (A. Sheridan, Trans.). Vintage.

Foucault, M. (2004). *Security, territory, population: Lectures at the Collège De France, 1977–78* (G. Burchell, Trans.; M. Senellart, Ed.). Palgrave.

Foucault, M. (2006). *History of madness* (J. Murphy & J. Khalfa, Trans.; J. Khafla, Ed.). Routledge.

Foucault, M. (2009). *Security, territory, population: Lectures at the College De France, 1977–78* (G. Burchell, Trans.). Palgrave Macmillan.

Foucault, M. (2019). *Security, territory, population: Lectures at the College de France, 1977–78.* Palgrave-Macmillan.

Friedman, M., & Milton, R. (1980). *Free to choose: A personal statement.* Harcourt Brace Jovanovich.

Fryxell, A. R. P. (2019). Time and modern: Current trends in the history of modern temporalities. *Past and Present, 243,* 285–298.

Fukuda, K., Harmanci, H., Park, K., & Chamberland, M. (2009). *Pandemic Influenza preparedness and response: A WHO guidance document.* Nonserial Publication.

Gandhi, G. K. (2021, May 23). Identical horror. *The Telegraph* (Kolkata).

Gangopadhyay, H. (2020). *Famine of the mind: A comparison of the 1943 Bengal famine and the covid 19 pandemic.* Unpublished MA dissertation, St. Xavier's University, Kolkata.

Ghose, A. (2021, April 27). Fact check: Was Adityanath right in saying that there's no shortage of medical oxygen in UP? *Scroll.in.* https://scroll.in/article/993435/fact-check-was-adityanath-right-in-saying-that-theres-no-shortage-of-medical-oxygen-in-up.

Ghosh, A. (2016). *The great derangement: Climate change and the unthinkable.* The University of Chicago Press.

Ghosh, A. (2021, June 26). Amitav Ghosh on Priya Setia's books: 'History has given us tools for upending dominant narratives'. *Scroll.in.* https://scroll.in/article/998495/amitav-ghosh-on-priya-satias-books-history-has-given-us-tools-for-upending-dominant-narratives.

Ghosh, N. K. (2020). Mahamarir akhor. *Korak Sahitya Patrika, Saradiya.*

Ghoshal, S. (2021, August 1). Turning a brand new page for the love of books. *MINT.* Retrieved August 1, 2021, from https://lifestyle.livemint.com/news/talking-point/turning-a-brand-new-page-for-the-love-of-books-111627640602297.html.

Ginzburg, C. (2013 [1976]). The cheese and the worms: The cosmos of a sixteenth-century miller. Johns Hopkins University Press.

Ginzburg, C., Tedeschi, J., & Tedeschi, A. C. (1993). Microhistory: One or two things i know about it. *Critical Inquiry, 20*(1).

GoI. (2020, May 14). *Aatmanirbhar Bharat Abhiyaan Phase-II to support Indian economy in fight against COVID-19.* https://covid19.india.gov.in/document-category/ministry-of-finance/.

Government of India, (2020–21). *Annual report 2020–21* (p. 213). Ministry of Health and Family Welfare.

Government of India. (2020). *Cabinet summary for October 2020*. https://dbtindia.gov.in/sites/default/files/English%20Cab%20summary_Oct20.pdf.

Government of India. (2021, April 21). *Liberalised pricing and accelerated national covid-19 vaccination strategy*. https://www.mohfw.gov.in/pdf/LiberalisedPricingandAcceleratedNationalCovid19VaccinationStrategy2042021.pdf.

Government of India. (2021, May 19). *Press release*. https://pib.gov.in/PressReleasePage.aspx?PRID=1719925.

Government of Kerala. (2016). 13th Kerala legislative assembly-committee on public accounts (2014–16) on action taken by government on recommendations contained in the 120th report of the committee on public accounts (2008–11), Secretariat of the Kerala Legislature.

Government of Kerala. (2018). *Draft labour policy*.

Government of West Bengal. (1954). *They live again. Millions came from East Pakistan*. Director of Publicity.

Guha, B. S. (1954). *Studies in social tensions among the refugees from Eastern Pakistan*. Department of Anthropology, Memoir No. 1. Manager of Publications.

Guldi, J., & Armitage, D. (2014). *The history manifesto*. Cambridge University Press.

Guren, C., McIlroy, T., & Sieck, S. (2021). COVID-19 and book publishing: Impacts and insights for 2021. *Publishing Research Quarterly, 37*, 1–14. https://doi.org/10.1007/s12109-021-09791-z

Hanss, S. (2019). The fetish of accuracy: Perspectives on early modern time(s). *Past and Present, 243*, 277.

Hartog, F. (2015). *Regimes of historicity: Presentism and experiences of time*. Columbia University Press.

Hawthorne, S. (2014). *Bibliodiversity: A manifesto for independent publishing*. Spinifex Press.

Health Survey and Development Committee. (1946). *Report of the Bhore committee* (Vols. 1 & 2). Government of India Press.

Hindustan Times. (2020, March 24). From today, curfew passes must for crossing interstate borders to enter Delhi amid coronavirus lockdown. *Hindustan Times*. https://www.hindustantimes.com/delhi-news/curfew-passed-need-too-cross-interstate-borders-in-delhi/story-ETT5Ba7pLGvoq7GACrqPbN.html.

Hindustan Times. (2020, September 14). Arrest, search without warrant under UP's new special security force rules. *Hindustan Times*. https://www.hindustantimes.com/india-news/arrest-search-without-warrant-under-up-s-new-special-security-force-rules/story-4O9dJ6pAkfikgW2cU5msvJ.html.

Hobsbawm, E. (1959). *Primitive rebels*. Free Press.

Holmes, G. (Ed.). (1990). *The Oxford illustrated history of medieval Europe*. Oxford University Press.

Horowitz, A. (2022). Pandemics as history. In T. J. Sugrue, & C. Zaloom (Eds.), *The long year: A 2020 reader*. Columbia University Press.

hours in queues. *Times of India*. https://timesofindia.indiatimes.com/city/lucknow/oxygen-crisis-far-from-over-kin-wait-for-hours-in-queues/articleshow/82265439.cms.

https://unfccc.int/news/cop27-reaches-breakthrough-agreement-on-new-loss-and-damage-fund-for-vulnerable-countries

Hung, H. (2004). The politics of SARS: Containing the perils of globalization by more globalization. *Asian Perspective, 28*(1).

India Today Web Desk. (2020, September 18). Unemployment crisis: Over 60 lakh white collar professional jobs lost during May–August. *India Today*. https://www.indiatoday.in/business/story/unemployment-crisis-deepens-over-60-lakh-white-collar-professionals-lost-jobs-during-may-august-1722971-2020-09-18.

Indian Express News Service. (2021, April 29). 1.33 crore sign in as Covid-19 vaccine doors open, states flag stock shortage. *Indian Express*. https://indianexpress.com/article/india/registration-on-cowin-1-33-crore-sign-in-states-flag-vaccine-stock-shortage-7293029/.

IPA General Assembly. (2020, November 23). From response to recovery. *International Publishers Association*. Retrieved November 23, 2020, from https://www.internationalpublishers.org/copyright-news-blog/1046-from-response-to-recovery.

Jana, A. (2022). *Lockdown diary*. Tramline Books.

John, J. (2015). Inter-regional migration from eastern states to Kerala: A socio economic analysis. *Working Paper No. 4*, Kerala Development Society.

Johnson, B. D. (2019, April 17). How a typo created a scapegoat for the AIDS epidemic. *Macleans*, April 17, 2019, https://www.macleans.ca/culture/movies/how-a-typo-created-a-scapegoat-for-the-aids-epidemic/. Accessed on August 8, 2021.

Jones, D. J. (2020). The potential impacts of pandemic policing on police legitimacy: Planning past the covid-19 crisis. *Policing: A Journal of Policy and Practice, 14*(3), 579–586.

Kai, J. (8 June 2021). How trump fueled anti-Asian violence in America: Trump's encouragement of white supremacy and his strident anti-China rhetoric proved a toxic combination for Asian Americans. *The Diplomat*. https://thediplomat.com/2021/06/how-trump-fueled-anti-asian-violence-in-america/. Accessed on August 7, 2021.

Kamala Harris tells migrants "do not come" during talks in Guatemala. June 8, 2021, https://www.youtube.com/watch?v=bpGitFIzamQ. Accessed on August 3, 2021.

Katinis, T. (2010). A humanist confronts the plague: Ficino's Consilio contro la Pestilentia. *MLN*, *125*(1).

Kesar, S., Abraham, R., Lahoti, R., Nath, P., & Basole, A. (2020). Pandemic, informality, and vulnerability: Impact of COVID-19 on livelihoods in India. *CSE Working Paper 2020–01*, Azim Premji University, June 2020

Kessler, G. (2021). DeSantis's effort to blame Biden for the covid surge in Florida. *The Washington Post*, August 6, 2021, https://www.washingtonpost.com/politics/2021/08/06/desantiss-effort-blame-biden-covid-surge-florida/. Accessed on August 12, 2021.

Kidambi, P. (2020). A tale of two epidemics: Mumbai, Bubonic Plague and COVID-19. https://www.indiachinainstitute.org/2020/10/22/a-tale-of-two-epidemics-mumbai-bubonic-plague-and-covid-19/.

Koselleck, R. (2004). *Futures past: On the semantics of historical time*. Columbia University Press.

Kosselleck, R. (2000). *Zeitschichten: Studien zur Historic*. Franfurt am Main.

Kosselleck, R. (2004). *Futures past: On the semantics of historical time* (K. Tribe, Trans.). Columbia University Press.

Krishnan, M. (2020, May 26). Police excesses for lockdown violation led to 12 deaths: Study. *Hindustan Times*. https://www.hindustantimes.com/india-news/police-excesses-for-lockdown-violation-led-to-12-deaths-study/story-qj5dZ68nxPBc3B0HbSBg3L.html.

Ladurie, E. L. R. (1979). *The territory of the historian*. Brighton.

Lauritsen, J. (1993). *The AIDS war: Propaganda, profiteering and genocide from the medical-industrial complex*. Asklepios

Lefebvre, H. (1991). *The production of space*. Basil Blackwell.

Leiblfinger, M., Prieler, V., Schwiter, K., Steiner, J., Benazha, A., & Lutz, H. (2020). Impact of COVID-19 policy responses on live-in care workers in Austria, Germany, and Switzerland. *Journal of Long-Term Care*, 144–150. https://doi.org/10.31389/jltc.51

Levi, G. (2019). Fall frontiers? *Past and Present, 242*(Sppl.14), 37–49.

Library of Congress. (2020, April 15). *Germany: Parliament changes rules of procedure to ensure functioning during COVID-19 pandemic*. https://www.loc.gov/law/foreign-news/article/germany-parliament-changes-rules-of-procedure-to-ensure-functioning-during-covid-19-pandemic/.

Lovelace, B., Jr. (2020). Trump claims the worsening U.S. coronavirus outbreak is a 'Fake News Media Conspiracy' even as hospitalizations rise. *Health and Science, CNBC*, October 26, 2020, https://www.cnbc.com/2020/10/26/coronavirus-trump-claims-the-worsening-us-outbreak-is-a-fake-news-media-conspiracy-even-as-hospitalizations-rise.html. Accessed on October 10, 2021.

Ludtke, A. (1995). *A history of everyday life: Reconstructing historical experience and ways of life.* Princeton University Press.

Maheshwari, G. (2016). Migrant crisis in Kerala: Need to change the political culture. *Economic and Political Weekly, 51*(48), 23–25.

Maheshwari, G. (2016). Migrant crisis in Kerala: Need to change the political culture. *Economic and Political Weekly, 51*(48), 23–25.

Majumdar, S. (2021). Abagunthan. *Saraddiya Desh, 1427*(2021), 140–191.

Mander, H. (2021). *Locking down the poor: The pandemic and India's moral centre.* Speaking Tiger.

Martin, R. (2007). *An empire of indifference: American War and the financial logic of risk management.* Duke University Press.

McKay, R. A. (2017). *Patient zero and the making of the AIDS epidemic.* Chicago University Press.

Means, A. J. (2021). Foucault, biopolitics, and the critique of state reason. *Educational Philosophy and Theory, 54*(2022), 1968–1969.

Middle East Respiratory Syndrome (MERS). *Centre for Disease Control and Prevention.* https://www.cdc.gov/coronavirus/mers/index.html. Accessed on November 6, 2021.

Mirowski, P. (2009). Postface: Defining neoliberalism. In P. Mirowski & D. Plewhe (Eds.), *The road from Mont Pelerin: The making of the neoliberal thought collective* (pp. 417–455). Harvard University Press.

Mitra, K. N., Bhattacharya, B., Dey, K., Dawn, C. S., Obadiah, M., & Gayen, A. K. (1951). A study of recent trend in infantile mortality rates in Calcutta by longitudinal survey. *Sankhyā: The Indian Journal of Statistics, 11*(2), 181.

Mitra, M. (2021). Public health, migrant workers, and a global pandemic: Towards a new politics of life. *Refugee Watch, 57*, 1–13.

Moore, J. W. (2016). The rise of cheap nature. In J. W. Moore (Ed.), *Anthropocene or Capitalocene: Nature, history, and the crisis of capitalism.* PM Press.

Moore, M., Gelfeld, B., Okunogbe, A., & Paul, C. (2017). Identifying future disease hot spots: Infectious disease vulnerability index. *Rand Health Quarterly, 6*(3), 5.

Morelli, G., et al. (2010). Phylogenetic diversity and historical patterns of pandemic spread of Yersinia pestis. *Nature Genetics, 42*(12), 1140–1143. https://doi.org/10.1038/ng.705

Morens, D. M., & Fauci, A. S. (2007). The 1918 influenza pandemic: Insights for the 21st century. *Journal of Infectious Diseases, 195*(7).

Morton, A. L. (1984). *A people's history of England.* Lawrence and Wishart.

Moses, J. W., & Rajan, S. I. (2012). Labour migration and integration in Kerala. *Labour and Development, 19*(1), 1–18.

Mukharji, P. B. (2021, June 13). Mahamarir bhut (The ghost of the epidemic). *Anandabazar Patrika (Robibasariyo).*

Mukherjee, J. (2015). *Hungry Bengal: War, famine and the end of empire.* Harper Collins.

Mukherjee, S. (2008). Environmental thoughts and malaria in colonial Bengal: A study in social response. *Economic and Political Weekly, 43*(12–13), 54–61.

Mukhopadhyay, A. (2020). *Lockdowner Dinolipi: Corona Bhubon Kotha.* Boiwala Bookcafe.

Mukhopadhyay, A. (2020, April 7). Saratbabur quarantine, Bankim er morok, Bangla sahitye mohmari. *Anandabazar Patrika.* Retrieved August 27, 2021, from https://www.anandabazar.com/editorial/coronavirus-epidemics-and-pandemics-in-bengali-literature-dgtlx-1.1133067.

Mukhopadhyay, A. (Ed.) (2022). *Coronar Korcha: Mahamarir Aloandharite Banglar Mukhochhobi.* Rupali Publication.

Mukhopadhyay, D. (1971). *Tarasankar Samakal o Uttarkaler Drishtite.* Sahitya Prakash.

Mukhopadhyay, K. (2022). Picnic. *Desh, 89*(7), 32–35.

Mukhopadhyay, S. (2007). *Bharater Communist Party O Amra.* National Book Agency.

Multilateral Leaders Task Force. (2021, July 30). *Joint statement of the multilateral leaders task force on COVID-19 vaccines, therapeutics, and diagnostics for developing countries following its second meeting.* Retrieved January 10, 2023, from https://www.worldbank.org/en/news/statement/2021/07/30/joint-statement-on-second-meeting-of-task-force-on-COVID-vaccines-therapeutics-and-diagnostics-for-developing-countries

Multilateral Leaders Task Force. (2022, March 7). *Eighth Meeting of the Multilateral Leaders Task Force on COVID-19, 1 March 2022: "Third Consultation with the CEOs of leading vaccine manufacturers" Joint Statement*. Retrieved January 10, 2023, from https://www.worldbank.org/en/news/statement/2022/03/07/eighth-meeting-of-the-multilateral-leaders-task-force-on-covid-19-1-march-2022-third-consultation-with-the-ceos-of-leadi

Munshi, S. (2020, April 22). Starvation, police beatings and covid-19: For migrant workers stuck in Delhi, the choices are stark. *News18*. https://www.news18.com/news/india/starvation-police-beatings-and-covid-19-for-migrant-workers-stuck-in-delhi-the-choices-are-stark-2588163.html.

Nail, T. (2021). *Theory of the Earth*. Stanford University Press.

Narayana, D., & Venkiteswwaran, C. S. (2013). *Domestic migrant labour in Kerala*. http://www.lc.kerala.gov.in/images/Current/ismstudy.pdf

Nathanael, M. P. (2020, May 18). Licensed to beat, abuse and kill. *The Hindu*. https://www.thehindu.com/opinion/op-ed/licensed-to-beat-abuse-and-kill/article31609626.ece.

Nichols, R. W. (1981). The Goddess Sitala and epidemic small pox in Bengal. *The Journal of Asian Studies, 41*(1), 21–44.

Niller, E. (2020, January 25). *An AI epidemiologist sent the first warnings of the Wuhan virus*. Retrieved January 10, 2023, from https://www.wired.com/story/ai-epidemiologist-wuhan-public-health-warnings.

Niyazov, S. (2019, November 10). How A.I. will redefine economics. Retrieved January 10, 2023, from https://towardsdatascience.com/how-ai-will-redefine-economics-ec305e3cb687.

Ogle, V. (2019). Time, temporality and the history of capitalism. *Past and Present, 243*, 312–327.

Outlook. (2020, March 23). Curfew passes to be necessary for travel between Delhi, neighbouring areas. *Outlook*. https://www.outlookindia.com/website/story/india-news-curfew-passes-to-be-necessary-for-travel-between-delhi-neighboring-areas/349309.

OxCGRT. (2020). *Oxford COVID-19 government response tracker*. https://www.bsg.ox.ac.uk/research/research-projects/coronavirus-government-response-racker.

Oxford COVID Vaccine Trial Group. (2021). Safety and efficacy of the ChAdOx1 nCoV-19 vaccine (AZD1222) against SARS-CoV-2: An interim analysis of four randomised controlled trials in Brazil, South Africa, and the UK. *The Lancet, 397*(10269), 99–111.

Pandey, G. (2016). The woman who discovered India's first HIV cases. *BBC News*, August 30, 2016, https://www.bbc.com/news/magazine-37183012. Accessed on September 16, 2021.

Pandey, G. (2020, April 21). Coronavirus in India: Desperate migrant workers trapped in lockdown. *BBC News*. https://www.bbc.com/news/world-asia-india-52360757.

Pandhi, N. (2021). Ebola, COVID-19 and the moral injury of dignity. *The Wire*, 31 May 2021, https://thewire.in/health/ebola-covid-19-moral-injury-dignity. Accessed on October 10, 2021.

Parkins, K. (2021, April 27). Covaxin: India's homegrown Covid-19 vaccine brings hope and controversy. *Clinical Trials Arena*. https://www.clinicaltrialsarena.com/analysis/covaxin-indias-homegrown-covid-19-vaccine-brings-hope-and-controversy/.

Patel, C. (2020, July 13). COVID-19: The hidden majority in India's migration crisis. *Chatham House*. https://www.chathamhouse.org/expert/comment/covid-19-hidden-majority-indias-migration-crisis.

Pepin, J. (2011). *The origins of AIDS*. Cambridge University Press.

Pepys, S. (1825). *Memoirs of Samuel Pepys*. British Library. Retrieved May 1, 2021, from https://www.bl.uk/collection-items/memoirs-of-samuel-pepys.

Pernick, M. S. (2002). Contagion and culture. *American Literary History, 14*(4).

Peter, B., & Narendran, V. (2017). *God's own workforce: Unravelling labour migration to Kerala*.

Prakash, A. (2021). Shadow of the pandemic and the beleaguered liberal-democratic script in India. *India Review, 20*(2), 104–120.

Prakash, B. A. (1998). Gulf migration and its economic impacts: The Kerala experience. *Economic and Political Weekly*, *33*(50).

Prasad-Aleyamma, M. (2011). A market place for migrants: Mobility, settlement and social protection in Kerala. In R. Sabates Wheeler, & R. Feldman (Eds.), *Social protection and migration: Claiming social rights beyond borders* (pp. 164–182). Palgrave Macmillan.

Press Information Bureau. (2020, March 24). *Prime Minister's Office, Government of India*. Retrieved January 21, 2022, from https://pib.gov.in/newsite/PrintRelease.aspx?relid=200658.

Press Information Bureau. (2021, January 3). *Press statement by the Drugs Controller General of India (DCGI) on restricted emergency approval of COVID-19 virus vaccine*. https://www.icmr.gov.in/pdf/press_realease_files/HFW_DCGI_energency_use_authorisation_03012021_2.pdf.

Press Information Bureau. (2021, May 13). *Press briefing on the actions taken, preparedness and updates on COVID-19*. https://www.youtube.com/watch?v=ijLcZ8G84FI.

Prins, A. (2014). The plight of dwelling: East-Bengali refugees and the struggle for land in Kolkata. *Refugee Watch, 43 & 44*.

Prior, S. (2006). *Preparing for a pandemic influenza: A primer for governors and senior state officials*. National Governors Association.

PTI (2020, May 22). Quarantine centres in Uttar Pradesh are so bad they have become torture camps: Samajwadi Party. *The Economic Times*. https://economictimes.indiatimes.com/news/politics-and-nation/quarantine-centres-in-uttar-pradesh-are-so-bad-they-have-become-torture-camps-samajwadi-party/articleshow/75894700.cms.

PTI (2021, April 20). Serum hails financial aid from govt to ramp up Covid-19 vaccine production. *The Hindu*. https://www.thehindu.com/business/Industry/serum-hails-financial-aid-from-govt-to-ramp-up-covid-19-vaccine-production/article34367000.ece.

PTI. (2021, May 8). *War against COVID to be fought collectively, with public participation: Jitendra Singh*. Retrieved January 20, 2023, from https://economictimes.indiatimes.com/news/india/war-against-covid-to-be-fought-collectively-with-public-participation-jitendra-singh/articleshow/82481160.cms?from=mdr

Qadeer, I. (2005). Continuties and discontinuties in public health: The Indian experience. In A. K. Bagchi, & K. Soman (Eds.), *Maladies, preventives and curatives: Debates in public health in India*. Tulika Books.

Rajan, S. I., & Zackaria, K. C. (2016). Kerala migration survey 2014. *Economic and Political Weekly, 51*(6).

Raman, K. R. (2012). Currents and eddies': Indian-Middle East migration processes. *Cambridge Journal of Regions, Economy and Society, 5*, 189–205.

Raman, R. (2021, April 21). *India's war against Covid-19*. Retrieved January 10, 2023, from https://www.hindustantimes.com/opinion/indias-war-against-covid19-101618913917918.html.

Rao, K. S. (2016). *Do we care? India's health system*. Oxford University Press.

Rashid, O. (2020, March 30). Coronavirus: In Bareilly, migrants returning home sprayed with disinfectant. *The Hindu*. https://www.thehindu.com/news/national/other-states/coronavirus-in-bareilly-migrants-forced-to-take-bath-in-the-open-with-sanitiser/article31204430.ece.

Rawat, M. (2021, May 3). Just before 2nd covid wave hit India, ICU beds decreased by 46%, oxygen ones by 36%. *India Today*. https://www.indiatoday.in/coronavirus-outbreak/story/just-before-2nd-covid-wave-hit-india-icu-beds-decreased-by-46-oxygen-ones-by-36-1796830-2021-05-03.

Ray, A. (2009). *Kalantarer Kathakar: Tarasankar*. Akshar Prakashani.

Reed, C. (2007). The Rev Jerry Falwell: Rabid evangelical leader of America's 'moral majority'. *The Guardian*, May 17, 2007, https://www.theguardian.com/media/2007/may/17/broadcasting.guardianobituaries. Accessed on October 5, 2021.

Remesh, B. P. (2003). Changing consciousness and image of Kerala labour in the 20th century. *Labour and Development, 9*(1).

Resnick, S. A., & Wolff, R. D. (1987). *Knowledge and class—A Marxian critique of political economy*. The University of Chicago Press.

Reuters, Jadhav, R., & Kalra, A. (2021, April 17). India's capital Delhi faces hospital beds shortage as coronavirus cases surge. *Reuters*. https://www.reuters.com/world/india/india-reports-another-record-daily-rise-covid-19-infections-2021-04-17/.

Rose, N. (2001). The politics of life itself. *Theory, Society & Culture, 18*(6), 1.

Roy, S. N. et al. (2017). *Migrants in construction work: Evaluating their welfare framework*. Centre for Policy Research.

Rude, G. (1981). Review: The 'poverty of theory' debate. *Saothar, 7*, 62–68.
Rude, G. (1995). *Ideology and popular protest*. University of North Carolina Press.
Saha, M. (2020). *Labour train*. Boiwala Bookcafe.
Samaddar, R. (2020). *The postcolonial age of migration*. Routledge.
Samaddar, R. (2021a). *A pandemic and the politics of life*. Women Unlimited.
Samaddar, R. (2021b). *A pandemic and the politics of life*. Women Unlimited.
Samaddar, R. (2021c). *A pandemic and the politics of life*. Women Unlimited.
Samanta, A. (2012). Small pox in nineteenth century Bengal. *Indian Journal of History of Science, 47*(2), 211–240.
Sarasin, P. (2020, March 31). Understanding the coronavirus pandemic with Foucault? *Genealogy+Critique*. Retrieved September 28, 2021, from https://www.fsw.uzh.ch/foucaultblog/essays/254/understanding-corona-with-foucault.
Satia, P. (2020). *Time's monsters: How history makes history*. Harvard University Press.
Scheppele, K. L. (2018). Autocratic legalism. *The University of Chicago Law Review, 85*(2), 545–583.
Scroll Staff. (2021, January 4). Insider predictions: What does the future of publishing look like after the pandemic? *Scroll*. Retrieved January 4, 2021, from https://scroll.in/article/983020/insider-predictions-what-does-the-future-of-publishing-look-like-after-the-pandemic.
Sen, M. (2011). *Jonojagorone Narijagorone*. Thema.
Senga, M., et al. (2017). Contact tracing performance during the Ebola virus disease outbreak in Kenema district, Sierra Leone. *Philosophical Transactions: Biological Sciences, 372*(1721).
Sengupta, S., & Banerjee, P. (2016). Refugee movement: Another aspect of popular movements in West Bengal in the 1950s and 1960s. In S. Sengupta, P. Banerjee, & A. Sengupta (Eds.), *People, politics and protests I: Calcutta & West Bengal, 1950s–1960s*. Calcutta Research Group.
Sewell, W., Jr. (2005). Logics of history: Social theory and social transformation. University of Chicago Press.
Shaju, P. (2020, March 30). Kerala: Migrant workers say they want food, ask to be taken back home. *The Indian Express*. https://indianexpress.com/article/india/coronavirus-india-lockdown-kerala-migrant-workers-say-they-want-food-ask-to-be-taken-back-home-6337850/.
Sharma, A. L., Singh, T. R., & Singh, L. S. (2019). Understanding of HIV/AIDS in the international border area, Manipur: Northeast India. *Epidemiology and Infection, 147*, e113, https://www.ncbi.nlm.nih.gov/pmc/articles/PMC6518467/pdf/S0950268818003564a.pdf. Accessed on November 6, 2021.
Sharma, D. C. (2015). India still struggles with rural doctor shortages. *The Lancet, 386*(10011), 2381–2382.
Sharma, S. (2020, April 13). 2020. India cannot fight a pandemic with police Lathis. It must ensure people have food—and dignity. *Scroll.in*. https://scroll.in/article/958993/india-cannot-fight-a-pandemic-with-police-lathis-it-must-ensure-people-have-food-and-dignity.
Sharma, S. N. (2020, September 6). How the recent decision by GST council has further deepened states' financial woes. *The Economic Times*. https://economictimes.indiatimes.com/news/economy/policy/how-the-recent-decision-by-gst-council-has-further-deepened-states-financial-woes/articleshow/77951570.cms.
Siddiqi, D. (2020, April 22). In pictures: The long road home for India's migrant workers. *Aljazeera*. Retrieved December 24, 2021, from https://www.aljazeera.com/gallery/2020/4/22/in-pictures-the-long-road-home-for-indias-migrant-workers.
Singh, P., Ravi, S., & Chakraborty, S. (2020, March 24). COVID-19: Is India's health infrastructure equipped to handle an epidemic? *Brookings*. https://www.brookings.edu/blog/up-front/2020/03/24/is-indias-health-infrastructure-equipped-to-handle-an-epidemic/.
Singha, T. (1999). *Maranjoyi Songrame Bastuhara*. Dasgupta's.
Sinha, D., & Sengupta, S. (2019). *How maternity benefits can be extended to informal women workers*. https://thewire.in/women/how-maternity-benefits-can-be-extended-to-informal-women-workers.

Sivasundaram, S. (2020). The human, the animal, and the prehistory of COVID-19. *Past and Present, 249.*

Slack, P. (1988). Responses to plague in early Modern Europe: The implications of public health. *Social Research, 55*(3).

Som, V., & Pullanoor, H. (2021, September 27). WHO's Covaxin clearance delayed further over technical queries: Sources. *NDTV*. https://www.ndtv.com/india-news/covaxin-faces-more-delay-for-who-clearance-technical-queries-need-to-be-answered-by-bharat-biotech-sources-2555676.

Sreerekha, M. S. (2017). *State without honour: Women Workers in India's Anganwadis*. Oxford University Press.

Stanway, D. (2020). The shadow of SARS: China learned the hard way how to handle an epidemic. *Reuters*, January 22, 2020, https://www.reuters.com/article/us-china-health-sars-idUSKBN1Z L12B. Accessed on November 10, 2021.

Stone, L. (2001). The revival of narrative: Reflections on a new old history. In G. Roberts (Ed.), *The history and narrative reader*. Routledge.

Sugrue, T. J. (2022). Introduction: Preexisting conditions. In T.J. Sugrue, & C. Zaloom (Eds.), *The long year: A 2020 reader*. Columbia University Press.

Swaminathan, P. (2015). The formal creation of informality, and therefore, gender injustice: Illustrations from India's social sector. *Indian Journal of Labour Economics, 58*(1), 23–42.

SWAN. (2020a). *21 Days and counting: COVID-19 lockdown, migrant workers, and the inadequacy of welfare measures in India*. http://publications.azimpremjifoundation.org/2272/1/lockdown_and_distress_report_by_stranded_workers_action_network-2.pdf.

SWAN. (2020b). *32 Days and counting: COVID-19 lockdown, migrant workers, and the inadequacy of welfare measures in India*. https://covid19socialsecurity.files.wordpress.com/2020/05/32-days-and-counting_swan.pdf?fbclid=IwAR0-kuFz9pV9drrshn7NLnOUOuVbkv7NbrGzc qMLBMwyel0isEsaoLO-dw0.

Tagore, R. (1905). *Rabindra Rachanabali* (Vol. 7). Visvabharati.

Tagore, R. (1940). *Rabindra Rachanabali* (vol. 6). Kolkata: Visvabharati.

Tagore, R. (1991). *Galpaguchho: Visvabratai Akhando*. Visvabharati.

Taher, A. (2021, June 27). *Porijayi*. Sillypoint. Retrieved December 8, 2021, from https://www.sillypoint.co.in/post/%E0%A6%AA%E0%A6%B0%E0%A6%BF%E0%A6%AF%E0%A6%BE%E0%A7%9F%E0%A7%80/id/ud3z6OsM8eSDmJoIa8xQ.

Tapper, M. (1995). Interrogating bodies: Medico-racial knowledge, politics, and the study of a disease. *Comparative Studies in Society and History, 37*(1).

Tarafdar Majumdar, S. (2020). *Basundharar Nabojagaran*. Pandulipi.

The Calcutta Municipal Gazette. (1947, November 1–29). Vol. XLVI & XLVII, No. 24 & 1–11.

The Calcutta Municipal Gazette. (1957, January 23). *Refugees at Sealdah* (Vol. LXV, No. 21).

The Calcutta Municipal Gazette. (1957, November 2). (Vol. LXV).

The Calcutta Municipal Gazette. (1958, January 18). (Vol. LXVII, No. 12).

The Hindu. (7 Nov, 2021). *Poor living conditions at migrant worker camps*. https://www.thehindu.com/news/national/kerala/poor-living-conditions-at-migrant-worker-camps/article37367787.ece

The Ministry of Rehabilitation. (1955–56). Assistance to displaced TB patients (Report on the Working). Government of India.

The New York Times. (17 March 2021). *8 Dead in Atlanta spa shootings, with fears of Anti-Asian bias*. https://www.nytimes.com/live/2021/03/17/us/shooting-atlanta-acworth. Accessed on March 19, 2021.

The U.S. Department of Homeland Security Contributors. (2006). *Pandemic influenza preparedness, response, and recovery guide for critical infrastructure and key resources*. U.S. Department of Homeland Security.

Thompson, E. P. (1978). *The poverty of theory and other essays*. Monthly Review Press.

TNN. (2021, August 2). Covid-19: To meet its vaccination target, India needs to give 92 lakh shots per day. *Times of India*. https://timesofindia.indiatimes.com/india/covid-19-to-meet-its-vaccination-target-india-needs-to-give-92-lakh-shots-per-day/articleshow/84959504.cms#:~:text=Covid%2D19%3A%20To%20meet%20its,92%20lakh%20shots%20per%20day&text=India%20will%20need%20to%20administer,those%20aged%2018%20or%20more.

Tomich, D. (2011). The order of historical time: The *Longue Duree* and micro-history. *Almanac. Guarulhos, 2*, 52–65.

Tumbe, C. (2021). *The age of pandemics, 1817–1920. How they shaped India and the World*. Harper Collins.

UNDP. (2020). *COVID-19 and health system vulnerabilities in the poorest developing countries*. Transition Series, UNDP Global Policy Network Brief—HEALTH. Available at https://www.undp.org/sites/g/files/zskgke326/files/publications/undp-gpn-transitions-series-health-COVID-19_and_Health_System_Vulnerabilities_EN.pdf. Last accessed August 23, 2021.

University of Oxford. (2020, July 20). *New study reveals Oxford coronavirus vaccine produces strong immune response*. https://www.research.ox.ac.uk/article/2020-07-20-new-study-reveals-oxford-coronavirus-vaccine-produces-strong-immune-response.

Vyas, M. (2020, August 18). An unhealthy recovery. *CMIE*. https://www.cmie.com/kommon/bin/sr.php?kall=warticle&dt=2020-08-18%2011:02:19&msec=596.

Walker, J. (2016). Civil society's role in a public health crisis. *Issues in Science and Technology, 32*(4).

Wallace, R. (2020). *Dead epidemiologists: On the origins of COVID-19*. Monthly Review Press.

Wallerstein, I. (1974). *The modern world system* (Vol. 1).

Weber, R. (1995). Re(creating) the home: Women's role in the development of the refugee colonies in south Calcutta. *Indian Journal of Gender Studies, 2*(2), 202.

WEIGO, UNICEF and ILO. (2021). *Family-friendly policies for workers in the informal economy: Protecting and ensuring social protection and care systems for all children and families in the context of COVID-19 and beyond*. Available at https://www.unicef.org/media/102821/file/Family-Friendly%20Policies%20for%20Workers%20in%20the%20Informal%20Economy%20.pdf. Last accessed July 23, 2021.

West Bengal State Assembly. (1949, March 4). (Vol. 22, No. II).

West Bengal State Assembly. (1955, September 9).

West Bengal State Assembly. (1957, June–July). *Assembly proceedings official report* (Vol. 17, No. 3, pp. 9–10).

Wiechmann, I., et al. (2012). History of Plague. *RCC Perspectives*, (3).

Wolff Richard, D. (2020). *The sickness is the system—when capitalism fails to save us from pandemic or itself*. Democracy at Work.

Wright, L. (2021). Lawrence Wright traces the parallels between the black death and the COVID-19 pandemic. *Lit Hub*. https://lithub.com/lawrence-wright-traces-the-parallels-between-the-black-death-and-the-covid-19-pandemic/.

Xu, R., et al. (2004). Epidemiologic Clues to SARS Origin in China. *Emerging Infectious Diseases, 10*(6). https://www.ncbi.nlm.nih.gov/pmc/articles/PMC3323155/pdf/03-0852.pdf. Accessed on November 6, 2021.

Zachariah, K. C., Mathew, E. T., & Rajan, I. S. (2000). *Dynamics of migration in Kerala: Dimensions, differentials and consequences*. CDS.

Zee Media Bureau. (2021, October 3). Retrieved January 10, 2023, from https://zeenews.india.com/india/war-against-covid-19-not-over-it-can-return-with-vengeance-aiims-task-force-chief-2399261.html

Zhang, Y., et al. (2012). The characteristics of imported cases and the effectiveness of outbreak control strategies of pandemic influenza A (H1N1) in China. *Asia Pacific Journal of Public Health, 24*(6).

Zubașcu, F. (2021). Do not blame South Africa for the Omicron variant. *Science Business*, December 2, 2021, https://sciencebusiness.net/news/do-not-blame-south-africa-omicron-variant. Accessed on December 12, 2021.

www.ingramcontent.com/pod-product-compliance
Ingram Content Group UK Ltd.
Pitfield, Milton Keynes, MK11 3LW, UK
UKHW022211051026
15624UKWH00001B/114
9789819948147